Industrial Studies Series

MARKETING AND PRODUCT DEVELOPMENT

Dale Littler

University of Manchester Institute of Science and Technology

Philip Allan

First published 1984 by

PHILIP ALLAN PUBLISHERS LIMITED
MARKET PLACE
DEDDINGTON
OXFORD OX5 4SE

British Library Cataloguing in Publication Data

Littler, Dale
  Marketing and product development. –
  (Industrial studies series)
  1. Marketing
  I. Title   II. Series
  658.8   HF5415

  ISBN 0-86003-531-X
  ISBN 0-86003-633-2 Pbk

Typeset by MHL Typesetting Ltd, Coventry
Printed and bound in Great Britain by T J Press Ltd, Padstow

Contents

In memory of my mother who passed on her wisdom

Preface

Marketing has been effectively practised for many centuries, but its rise to formal acceptance as a function of business has been relatively recent. Frequently it is regarded as an activity mainly concerned with advertising and selling, rather than as an activity devoted to seeking out what individuals and organisations want and to developing products and services tailored to satisfying those wants. In general, contemporary customers have now become more subtle and demanding in what they require: it is increasingly likely that they will seek quality, service, guaranteed delivery, good design, and reliability. Given the increased competitiveness from foreign companies in both domestic and overseas markets, and the significance of overseas trade to the UK economy, it is critical that UK firms pay heed to these modern requirements if they are to survive and grow.

Marketing itself embraces a set of activities, including product development, pricing, advertising, personal selling, and distribution. In order to perform its tasks effectively it needs to work with other functions in the firm, such as Research and Development, and Production.

The aim of this book is to provide an introduction to why marketing is important and to what it involves in the context of the firm. The book begins by explaining the role that the marketing function plays in enabling the company to meet its objectives. The nature of markets, the many influences affecting demand, and the way in which companies organise themselves to meet these different market demands (with, of course, particular emphasis on the part that marketing has to play) are then described. The many means of obtaining information in order to improve the effectiveness of marketing decisions are outlined. The remainder of the book then concentrates on the development of the product offering, including its pricing, advertising, and distribution. Decisions on the way a product can be modified during its life are examined. Finally, consideration is given to how a company can market its products overseas. Overall, this book provides an indication of the vital importance of marketing and the scope of its activities, using examples to illustrate some of the issues raised.

Various people have helped in the preparation of this final version. Thanks are due in particular to Christine Theobald who typed the original drafts, Professor John Pickering and Dr Alan Williams who provided helpful comments, James Lethem who collected some of the data, and the teachers who tested the first version. I am deeply indebted to them all. Obviously, I take full responsibility for all errors and omissions.

Acknowledgements

The photographs used in this book are reproduced by kind permission of Austin Rover Limited, Camera Press, Keystone Press Agency, Fine Lady Bakeries, Lever Brothers Limited, A.C. Nielsen Company Limited, Oxford and County Newspapers, Rowntree Mackintosh plc., J. Sainsbury plc.

Oxford's busy shopping centre: consumers are the focus of marketing strategy

1

The Nature of Marketing: An Introduction

Consumption is the sole end and purpose of production.
(*Adam Smith,* The Wealth of Nations)

The difference between marketing and selling is more than semantic. Selling focuses on the needs of the seller, marketing on the needs of the buyer. Selling is preoccupied with the seller's need to convert his product into cash; marketing with the idea of satisfying the needs of the customer by means of the product and the whole cluster of things associated with creating, delivering and finally consuming it.
(*Levitt,* Marketing Myopia)

In contemporary Western Societies, marketing is a commonly-accepted and widespread activity that has an established role in most medium and large business corporations. Its rise to formalised respectability is, however, a fairly recent phenomenon, even though the philosophy and rudiments of marketing have been practised by entrepreneurs for many centuries. In this chapter, it will be shown that successful marketing is founded on careful attention to what purchasers and users require. This is termed the **demand philosophy** and it should permeate the whole of the organisation. Effective marketing necessitates more than the renaming of the traditional sales department and the recruitment of one or two marketing personnel. The fact that, in the past, many UK firms may not have accorded such a 'demand-oriented' approach the importance it merits, may be partly responsible for their poor performance in combating foreign competition in both domestic and overseas markets. The consequent increase in import penetration and reduction in share of world trade has been a marked feature of the UK economy in recent years.

In the second section of this chapter, attention shifts to the *role of marketing within the firm*, where it will be seen that it has a special responsibility for implementing the 'demand philosophy' by ensuring the formulation and development of product offerings which are acceptable to the ultimate consumer. In this role, marketing performs a variety of tasks including pricing, advertising, promotion and distribution.

This chapter, then, is concerned with answering three basic questions:

(a) What is marketing?
(b) Why is it important?
(c) What are the major aspects of marketing?

The Philosophy of Marketing

In the following two cases, the marketing philosophy was not followed – with expensive consequences.

A New Approach to Retailing

Monsieur Dumas had worked for many years as the manager of the food department for one of the top French departmental stores, AUX. Although he had been successful in increasing the profitability of the operation – through careful stock control and selection of the product range – the senior management of AUX believed that the space allocated to food could be more profitably employed as a Boutique. Monsieur Dumas was asked to leave.

M. Dumas, committed to improving the efficiency of retailing, decided to invest his savings in a 'new type of store' which would aim to increase turnover per square metre, eliminate shoplifting, reduce labour and offer distinct benefits to the customer.

His idea was simple: instead of having real products on display, as in a normal supermarket, he would only put a dummy of the product on the shelf. Underneath each sample would be a punch card containing details of the product. The customer would take the punch cards for each of the products required, and place them in a small plastic basket which had been picked up at the entrance.

The cards would be fed into a computer at the exit and the information passed directly to a warehouse at the back, where a team of packers would assemble the goods and deliver them to the customer at the exit. The customer would obtain an itemised list of all the products purchased together with their prices.

M. Dumas's store contained approximately 2,000 product lines (a normal supermarket contained around 5,000) ranging from liquor to canned products and breakfast cereals. It opened in the Rue Lyons, an up-market commercial area near the centre of Paris. Nearby were branches of two of the main supermarket chains in France.

At the launch of his store M. Dumas expounded on the benefits of his approach that would 'revolutionise retailing in France'. He argued that his store was more efficient because:

- it needed less *selling* space than the traditional supermarket for equivalent turnover (75 square metres as opposed to 600 square metres);
- it eliminated pilfering, since customers only received the goods after they had paid for them — although the opportunity for stealing by the staff still remained;
- it enabled more effective stock control since the computer gave a daily and weekly print-out of sales for each product stocked;
- it reduced manpower costs because staff were no longer required to place the stock on the shelves.

He suggested that this was an innovative means of shopping that was in tune with the mood of the 1970s: 'Shoppers will no longer be jostled by supermarket baskets in crowded aisles; they will be able to shop in a relaxed, impersonal atmosphere. Queuing will become a thing of the past. This efficient way of shopping is just what the customer wants.'

In the first month, he achieved a turnover lower than that needed to cover the costs of the rent of the premises, the hire of the computer, staff wages and other running costs. Unfortunately, sales fell in the second month, and continued to decline in subsequent months, despite a heavy advertising campaign in the locality of the store.

It may be that the customer liked the atmosphere of the traditional supermarkets, with their special promotions and colourful displays. Perhaps customers preferred being able to see, touch and mentally weigh products. Perhaps his approach was too revolutionary anyway. He became so convinced of the merits of his method that he overlooked the facts that:

- His store needed much the same *total* area as a traditional supermarket for the same turnover. Whereas most of a traditional supermarket is made up of selling space, his store needed a large stock room (of 535 square metres as opposed to 40 square metres for one of his nearest supermarket rivals). Consequently, Dumas's concept achieved very little saving in total amount of space required (possibly of the order of 30 square metres).
- The computer involved a high rental.
- He had a limited stock of products; he did not, for example, sell fresh foods. This meant that customers had to shop elsewhere for certain goods and undoubtedly in many cases they bought the products that Dumas sold from these other outlets at the same time.
- The manpower savings were not as real as he imagined — he needed no shelves, but he needed more stockroom employees.
- Customers perhaps did not have to wait as long in the queue at the cash register, but they still had to wait for their orders to be prepared.

A New 'Resin-Based' Concrete

Jonah Wilson was the Managing Director of a small but highly successful family-owned construction company which concentrated on building specially-designed houses, offices and factories. It had received national recognition for the quality of its buildings. On a trip abroad to a Construction Machinery and Materials Exhibition, Wilson came across a machine for manufacturing a resin-based, or polyester, concrete. The machine, developed and marketed by a Finnish firm, Concretax, mixed resin with quartz sand and various additives (such as a catalyst) in carefully controlled proportions on a continuous basis. The resulting polyester concrete was emitted through a nozzle into moulds. Within a short time the moulded products could be removed from the moulds and left to harden. They were ready for use in 24 hours.

The polyester concrete seemed to Wilson to have distinct advantages: higher strength; finer texture; greater resistance to chemical attack; and it was lighter in weight than traditional concrete. Moreover, it cured and set faster (24 hours after setting, the polyester concrete reached a higher strength than normal concrete in a 28 days setting period). This meant fewer moulds were required, a faster response to customers' orders, and less stocks and, thereby, less storage space. However, the resin was extremely expensive, so that the polyester product was more costly to produce. Wilson believed that its 'unique' properties far outweighed any price disadvantages. He therefore purchased a Concretax machine at a cost of £100,000, hired factory space and employed two operators.

He decided to manufacture two products: a drainage channel in a variety of widths, and concrete 'decorative' tiles in several colours. The drainage channel had a smooth inner surface and it would, so Wilson argued, enable maximum flow. It was considerably lighter than its competitors and therefore should be cheaper to lay. Its removable lightweight cover meant that cleaning was easy. Moreover, its high chemical resistance suggested applications in chemical plants. Originally, though, local authorities were regarded as the major purchasers of the product for use in pedestrian precincts, car parks, highways and so on. For such applications, borough engineers would specify the product. It was found, though, that there was already a wide range of competitive products manufactured from traditional concrete and that engineers found these perfectly acceptable. The engineers argued that Wilson's product would have to offer a considerable price advantage in order to persuade them to recommend its use. They were, in any case, highly critical of the polyester concrete product: they disliked its design, particularly the removable covers which could easily be stolen; they found the finish rough and unhomogeneous; whilst they felt that the heels of women's shoes could lodge in the holes in the cover. Moreover, they wanted evidence of its technical performance, specifically on its porosity and durability. They noted that it would have to satisfy British Standards Specifications before it could be accepted.

The decorative tile product could be manufactured in many different sizes and was approximately half the weight of a normal concrete tile. Wilson believed that the product had many applications: for example, it could be used as a facia material for shop fronts and counters and as a wall and floor tile in kitchens and bathrooms. Its competitors included Terrazzo, quarry tiling, concrete tiles and slabs, vinyl, mosaic, and marble. The high cost of the resin effectively meant that it was priced much higher than many of these rival products, such as Terrazzo.

Wilson knew that the use of such materials depended on the recommendation of architects who specified the materials to be employed in buildings. In general, architects criticised the high price of the product and its appearance, many finding it extremely ugly. They said it scratched too easily to be even considered as a floor product. They also wanted more information on its performance − all building materials have to satisfy stringent criteria; in particular, they were extremely concerned about its resin base, and whether or not this could constitute a significant fire risk. One architect placed the end of the tile in a gas fire, and the tile immediately burst into flames, emitting toxic fumes.

Both Dumas and Wilson firmly believed that they had products which offered substantial benefits and had therefore proceeded to invest heavily. Neither undertook any research to ascertain whether or not potential purchasers considered these products as having any benefits. Yet it is the advantages and disadvantages as perceived by potential purchasers that is important, *not* how the seller views the products. Indeed, it appears that many of the features which Dumas and Wilson regarded as benefits were in fact viewed as disbenefits by possible purchasers! Often, individuals committed to the 'rightness' of their products will spend a considerable amount on advertising and promoting their products to persuade people likewise. But if the intrinsic features of the product are seen as unsatisfactory, then such an approach is likely to be a very costly failure. There are many examples in the history of business ventures of products which initially appeared to be extremely attractive to their developers, but because they did not meet the wants of a large enough proportion of the market they turned out to be commercially unsuccessful.

The supersonic aircraft Concorde was seen as satisfying a latent demand for high speed air travel. Sales of the supersonic airliner were predicted at many hundreds. But the costs of travelling at such high speeds are prohibitive; and there were not enough customers wanting faster journeys and able to pay the inevitably higher fares required in order to cover the huge development costs of the aircraft and yield a profit.

As will be seen, a strict attention to the wants of purchasers and users of products is the outstanding hallmark of successful products. Indeed, various studies of new products have suggested that one of the major factors differentiating commercially successful innovations from those that have been failures is a careful attention to the requirements of the potential purchasers.

The Demand Orientation

The focus of marketing, then, is the potential purchaser and user of the products and services, and ideally it is the identification of needs and wants in the marketplace that is the initiating force to corporate development of both existing and new products (see Figure 1.1(*a*)).

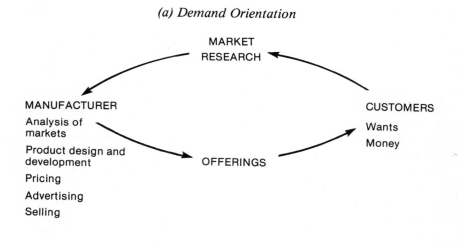

(a) Demand Orientation

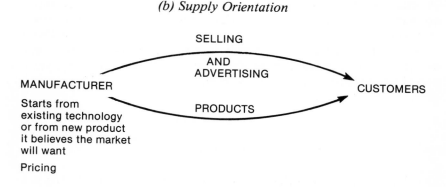

(b) Supply Orientation

Figure 1.1

The organisation should allocate its resources so as to optimise the possibility of selling its output and it can most appropriately ensure this by focusing on demand: marketing then as a discipline is primarily concerned with demand; supply is seen as a response to demand.

In attempting to satisfy demand, it is obvious that the organisation should only engage in those activities that enable it to attain predetermined objectives. Objectives of organisations may be varied and can include one or more of the following: the overall maximisation of the return on the resources it employs (that is the attainment of maximum profit); the maximisation of sales; the long-term survival of the company (involving the trade-off of short-term gains against long-term profitability); or the maximum satisfaction of, say, certain classes of employees (e.g. managers).

The Supply Orientation

The mirror image of the demand orientation is where the organisation decides what it will produce and sell with scant, if any, systematic examination of the requirements of the market. Such a decision may be founded on what is administratively convenient, the whims of a 'top man' who considers it a 'good idea', the existing manufacturing technology, and so on. Both Wilson and Dumas adopted such an approach. Under such conditions, whether or not the product is successful is very much a matter of chance. In vain attempts to make the product successful, the organisation will very often resort to aggressive selling and advertising in order to 'persuade' or 'convince' the market of the merits of the new product. Of course, a heavy expenditure on selling may well be successful in getting some people to try out the product once. Indeed, the initial response may produce a steep rise in the sales curve, suggesting a highly successful product development. Unless the product, when used effectively, satisfied the requirements of the consumers, repeat sales may not materialise. Moreover, first adoptors may well be active in communicating adverse comments to those who have yet to purchase. The result is predictable: a decline, and sometimes a dramatic collapse in sales, with the company compelled to withdraw the product from the market, often after substantial expenditures have been incurred. We will term this approach 'the supply orientation' (see Figure 1.1(*b*)).

Reasons for the Importance of Marketing

It has already been noted that the formal interest in and emphasis on marketing has been a fairly recent phenomenon. But why has marketing become regarded as increasingly important? Several possible underlying explanations can be identified:

(1)   the increasing affluence of modern Western societies, leading to a significant increase in discretionary income;

(2)   a consequent tendency for consumers to seek out intangible, psychologically-based features in the products and services they buy;

(3)   the intensification of competition;

(4)   the substantial costs incurred in the development of new products.

Increase in Discretionary Income

Discretionary income can be defined as the amount of income remaining to the consumer after tax and national insurance contributions and after he has satisfied his basic need for food, shelter, clothing and heating. It is distinct from **disposable income** which is the amount of income after tax and national insurance contributions.

Manifestly, what is meant by discretionary is not only extremely subjective (because what is interpreted as 'basic' needs will nowadays vary significantly from person to person) but it is also a function of changing societal tastes and attitudes over time. There is thus no reliable quantitative measure of average discretionary income, although in developed economies it may account for upwards of 50 per cent of total income.

It can generally be assumed that as the general level of wages and salaries has risen, the amount of discretionary income has also increased. There is considerable competition for this portion of consumers' income since it can be fairly freely allocated among an extremely wide and diverse variety of possibilities.

Mr Smith is married with two young children. The total household disposable income is approximately £9,000. The net amount remaining after mortgage, personal and household insurance, rates, gas and electricity amounts to almost £6,000. Given that the average annual food bill amounts to approximately £2,600 and that an allowance has to be made for clothes, he is still left with a substantial sum which he can allocate with considerable freedom. He can of course save some—perhaps with a view to some major purchase in the future, for example a more substantial or luxurious house, a new car, a more sophisticated hi-fi set, an extra holiday, and so on. The extent to which he saves (if at all) will be affected by, *inter alia*, his preferences between the longer-term wants and the immediate wants for greater variety and richness of food, alcohol, clothes, eating-out, hobbies, general leisure activities ...

Each individual will have a different pattern of demands. Given the widespread affluence in most industrialised countries, many consumers have discretion over a significant proportion of their income. There is competition between all sellers for this share of consumers' income. For example, a food manufacturer can be competing not only with other food manufacturers and with restauranteurs but also with the manufacturers of records, beer, soft drinks, furniture, tennis rackets, golf clubs ... the list is endless.

This widespread mass consumer choice is a relatively recent phenomenon, one that has arisen particularly during the post-war period as general real *per capita* income has increased. Agrarian and craft-based societies were marked by general deprivation; they were subsistence economies in which the majority barely earned enough to sustain, clothe and house themselves. With the onset of industrialisation, average consumer income increased and with it the demand for basic products. In this rapidly growing stage, demand far outstripped supply, and the ordinary consumer was faced with little true choice: the decision for him was not whether he should purchase one particular brand or another; rather, whether he could obtain the product at all.

The decision on what to produce was comparatively simple: for the most part, manufacturers knew that there was a high unsatisfied demand for basic products and that they would generally be able to sell all that they could produce. This was manifestly a supply-oriented economy, with *production* being the major concern.

With continued economic development, the rate of increase in demand for these essentials declined as these basic needs were satisfied. At best, demand for these necessities became dependent mainly on the need for replacements and on increase in population. During the rapid growth phase, many firms would have been attracted by the high sales and profits obtainable and would have established manufacturing facilities as a result. When demand slackened, there was a surplus of capacity for these types of goods. The natural reaction was, of course, for firms to engage in aggressive selling in order to increase the demand for their own particular products. Those firms which were less efficient at production and selling were ultimately driven out of business until eventually a new equilibrium of demand with supply was reached.

As there is a limit to which sales tactics can stimulate demand for basic products, those firms striving for sales and/or profits growth were eventually compelled to consider other means of capturing a share of this rising discretionary income. Some firms recognised that the more closely they tailored their products and services to these newly-emerging consumer wants, the greater the likelihood that consumers would exercise a preference for their goods.

With the increase in *total* income, the emphasis has been less on necessities and more on goods with a higher 'added value'. Customers have generally become more selective and perhaps fickle. The President of a major American producer of baking products and cake mixes noted in 1960 that his company must pay increasing attention to the specific wants of the American housewife: 'whether or not she will buy lemon pudding cake in preference to orange angel food' (Keith (1960) pp. 35–38). This change in the nature of demand, in turn, affects the suppliers of the materials, components and services used by companies making the products purchased by consumers: they may have to develop and produce different flavourings, a wider variety of fabrics, better designed components, and more technically sophisticated machinery.

Increase in Intangible Wants

A second major feature of Western economies has been an increasing tendency among the mass of the population for 'psychological' or 'intangible' wants to affect purchasing behaviour. This has persisted despite increasing unemployment. Maslow (1954) viewed needs as a hierarchy, ordered in descending importance (see Figure 1.2). He suggested that basic physiological needs, such as hunger and thirst, have to be satisfied before others in the hierarchy, such as the desire for status, become important. It is clear that in modern Western economies, the income of the majority of consumers permits them to satisfy amply their essential needs, whilst, at the same time, leaving a surplus which permits the satisfaction of 'higher-order needs'. For instance, consumers may strive to express their individuality through the products they purchase. In response, marketers are increasingly striving to build up appropriate images for their products, as well as devising products and services which cater for these higher-order values.

Demand for Cosmetics

There is an extensive range of women's cosmetics on the market. Even though it has been well publicised that most cosmetics tend to have the same basic ingredients, the demand for expensively packaged and highly priced brands continues to increase. Why? Is it because the purchasers of these more costly products are behaving irrationally? More likely, the consumer is deriving some inner satisfaction; for example, consumers may perceive themselves as sophisticated and wish to reinforce this self-image, as well as to project it to others, through the products they buy. On the other hand, they may wish to heighten their status by demonstrating that they can afford to purchase these products. Alternatively, they may

Figure 1.2 *Maslow's Hierarchy of Needs*

genuinely believe that the higher price and the glossy package are outward indicators of higher quality. If bought as presents, they may be regarded as tokens of appreciation, in which case the price paid may be viewed as an indicator of the regard of the donor. There is obviously a rich variety of explanations.

The fact that the wants of the consumer are no longer immediately apparent emphasises the need for manufacturers to direct effort to researching into the hidden 'needs' and 'motives' of consumers; that is, to adopt a 'demand approach'.

Increasing Technological Competition

A third trend of modern industrialised societies is that of growing competition, resulting mainly from the development of new technologies. The view that competition has increased and intensified is not, however, accepted by all. Indeed, some commentators argue that the growth of large firms, and the attendant concentration of British industry, has resulted in a marked reduction in choice, a failure to compete effectively on price, and a poor performance in the introduction of new products. One of the chief protagonists in the debate is J.K. Galbraith (1967), who argues that large industrial corporations exercise formidable market power which they will often deploy to hoist goods onto a compliant consumer. In his view, for a significant proportion of the market, consumer sovereignty has been replaced by producer sovereignty. In this sense, large manufacturers can successfully impose products on the market through the sheer force of their selling and advertising.

However, to argue that the intensity of competition is dependent on the number *and* size of firms in an industry is to adopt a very restricted perspective. First, as we have seen, in today's environment *all* firms are competing for a share of increasing consumer discretionary income; competition in this sense should not be viewed from a narrow industry perspective.

Secondly, this century has witnessed a tremendous rise in expenditure on research and development, resulting in numerous scientific and technological advances that, in turn, have spawned a stream of new products. It could justifiably be argued that the development of a wide range of technologies is one of the hallmarks of the twentieth century. The net result is that there are now often several means of satisfying a particular end-use requirement. Consider, for example, packaging for food products: a food manufacturer can select from the tin can, glass container, plastic pouches, treated cardboard or paper. Whatever he chooses will depend on his particular criteria, such as cost, ease and speed of filling, consumer convenience, the effect on the quality of the product, durability, and attitudes of distributors such as retailers. For many end uses, Metal Box, which holds a major share of the UK tin can market, is not just competing with other tin can manufacturers; rather, it is competing with the manufacturers of all forms of packaging. Indeed, to ensure its continued growth, Metal Box has diversified into these rival technologies. Such technological competition augments traditional intra-industry firm rivalry.

Thirdly, the substantial investment in the development of new technology means that a firm is under a constant threat from innovative technologies, which could, at the extreme, make obsolete its traditional technology—with disastrous consequences on sales and profits. New technologies may be superior because they are more effective in satisfying consumer wants; in addition, they will usually be more efficient in their use of resources. This, of course, can mean that they will often be cheaper and of higher quality. In addition, new technologies will tend to have great potential for further improvement, thereby giving them an even greater advantage.

Case of Matchbox Toys[1]

Lesney Products, the manufacturer of 'Matchbox' diecast model cars, saw its profits zoom from £8,302 in 1954 to £5.6 million in 1969, when its sales were £19.3 million. It consistently made a return of over 25 per cent of sales. The demand for its range of cars was international—over 80 per cent of its cars were exported—and it won several Queen's Awards for Export Services. Faced with such a high demand for its products, greater emphasis was placed on increasing output, with the ultimate aim being to produce one million toys each working day.

However, in the late 1960s, Mattel Inc.—the world's largest toy manufacturers, with sales of over $250 million—introduced 'Hot Wheels': 'Mattel's gimmick was to give its little cars thin axles and fast wheels and twenty yards of track on which to cavort'. The launch of its range was backed by a heavy advertising budget; Mattel's budget in the UK alone was £250,000. Consumers opted for 'Hot Wheels' at the expense of Lesney's products, which became outdated virtually overnight. Lesney's machinery became worth little more than its scrap value.

Fortunately, Lesney's high engineering skills, and the entrepreneurial drive of its founders, enabled it to produce its own rival product, called 'Superfast' cars, in a short time. It could therefore make a quick recovery: in 1972–1973, pre-tax profits of £1.9 million were made on sales of £20.2 million. Nevertheless, the company had passed through an undoubted traumatic period.

In hindsight, it is easy to point out Lesney's mistakes. Yet, even though it was working desperately to meet the rising demand for its products, was it justified in doing nothing to counteract the impending Mattel threat which, by its own admission, it knew was forthcoming? After its comeback, one commentator remarked: 'It (Lesney) has had to appreciate the changing values of the toy world in a very rude way—the fact that toys have become a fashion industry and that it is now no longer enough to float to the surface on the strength of one product ..., that now there has to be real continuity of management, there has to be product planning and corporate planning and all the paraphernalia of good corporate administration'.

The American economist Schumpeter argued that the environment in which firms operate is dynamic, and that sooner or later companies will be exposed to competition:

1. Based on Mansell, (1973) pp. 85 *et. seq.*

> from the new commodity, the new technology, the new source of supply, the new type of organisation ... competition which commands a decisive cost or quality advantage and which strikes not at the margins of the profits and the outputs of the existing firms but at their foundations and their very lives. (Schumpeter (1950) p. 84)

The implication is, of course, that firms need to be continuously alert to the possibility of such external challenges: no matter how dominant the company regards itself in the markets it serves, or how technically advanced it considers its product, it may find its market position eroded by a new technology. In this sense then, there are

> ... no invulnerable standard product lines, no natural monopolies whose position cannot be eroded by a new product, a new technique, a shift in consumer preference. (Shanks 1967)

In a famous article, Levitt (1960) argued that firms should define their business in terms of the basic needs they are striving to satisfy, and not in terms of technologies or products. The reason is evident: consumers' needs for food, drink, transport, shelter, clothing, and so on, remain immutable; but the *means* of satisfying them can change dramatically over time, as can consumer preferences. For instance, Levitt suggested that the demise of the US railways stemmed from their failure to adapt to the emergence of the automobile and later the aircraft. The railway firms saw themselves as satisfying the demand for travel by rail, rather than defining their objectives as satisfying the need for transport. Similarly, the oil companies should not consider themselves as merely involved in exploration, mining, refining and marketing activities related to oil; rather they are in the 'energy business'. However, a number of criticisms can be levelled at Levitt's prescription:

(1) There is the problem of semantics in defining the 'basic needs' as the focus of the business. For example, are the producers of cinema films trying to satisfy 'communication needs' or 'entertainment needs'?

(2) It is obviously simplistic to suggest that, say, firms concerned with the mass transportation of people can become manufacturers of automobiles 'virtually overnight'. Not only would railroad companies need considerable resources to establish these new businesses − whilst at the same time maintaining their existing businesses − but also they would tend to require different types of skills: for example, the management tasks associated with the provision of a railway service will be very different from those demanded by a continuous production line in an automobile plant.

(3) During the embryonic stage of new technological development there may be several competing designs; considerable ability

and luck will be required in identifying the design that will be dominant in the future. A failure to back the accepted design can be expensive.

The way in which the demand for a company's product can rise and decline has been conceptually represented in the **product life cycle**. As can be seen from Figure 1.3, this consists of four stages: introduction, growth, maturity and decline.

During the introduction of the new product, sales tend to be low and demand increases slowly, since few people are aware of the new product. Sales begin to 'take-off' as more people learn of it from advertising and promotion and from those who have already purchased the product. This is the growth stage. Eventually, sales stabilise because the product has been purchased by the majority of those willing and able to do so. A high proportion of sales, then, consists of repeat purchases. Finally, sales of the product begin to decline as a result of the introduction of new improved products and/or changes in consumer tastes.

It should be noted, however, that this is an *ideal* representation of changing demand for a product over time; in practice, many products will have life cycle patterns that will vary significantly from that depicted in Figure 1.3. For example, some may have a prolonged mature stage (Figure 1.4(*a*)), whilst others may be 'rejuvenated' (Figure 1.4(*b*)) as a result of product reformulation, alterations in package design, renewed advertising and promotion, and so on. The product life cycle of any product may be extended through

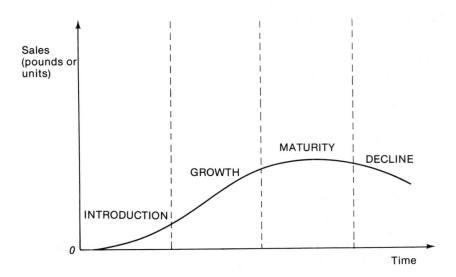

Figure 1.3 *An 'Idealised' Product Life Cycle*

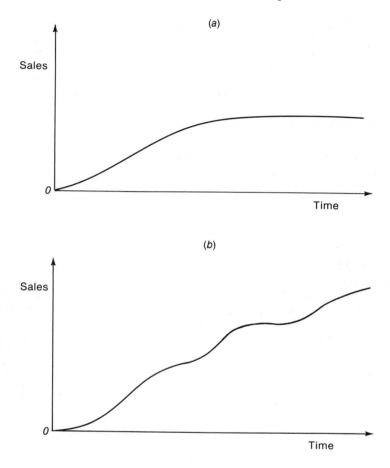

Figure 1.4   *Alternative Product Life Cycles*

appropriate managerial action. Furthermore, the duration of the product life cycle will differ significantly depending on the product. For example, the life cycle of a proprietary pharmaceutical product can be as little as eighteen months, whereas that for a car may be several years. It is often argued that the product life cycle is shortening and although this thesis may well agree with everyday observation, there is little supportive systematic evidence.

Given this background of intensifying competition, it is increasingly important to have an effective approach to the identification of future wants, to forecasting the possible nature of competition, and to developing products that have visible competitive advantages. As we shall see later, marketing has an extremely valuable role to play in this process.

The High Cost of Product Development

A fourth contemporary phenomenon is the high cost generally incurred in the development of new products.

A high technology product, such as a new computer system or aeroplane can involve the expenditure of hundreds of millions of pounds. Even a less technologically sophisticated product, such as an automobile, may require considerable engineering development and capital investment, and therefore cost similar amounts – the BL Metro, for example, took several years and many millions of pounds to develop.

The Case of Video Discs

The high demand for home entertainment has generated a plethora of new products – radios, televisions, audio systems, video games, and video recorders – that are the basis of a vast growth industry. A battle is currently being fought between three giants of the consumer electronics industry; each is marketing a different and incompatible video disc player. These use discs, as opposed to tapes, to play back pre-recorded films, etc. The most expensive is the Philips system, which is based on laser technology, whilst the American RCA unit is the simplest and cheapest. Sandwiched between the two, in terms of technical sophistication, is the Japanese JVC system. Since the discs made for one system will not play on another system, each manufacturer has to build up its own catalogue of pre-recorded discs. The stakes are high: both the Philips and RCA systems have involved expenditures of £75 million; both have recently spent large amounts on advertising their products. Not only is it a question of which system will ultimately secure majority market approval, but also whether or not there is a market demand for a video disc player: 'Sony, one of the most respected names in electronics, have for some time been saying that they will wait and see before entering the field themselves ... they do not think there is any hope at all for the disc. Their reason is that the video cassette is already gaining great popularity, and as the technical quality rises and the price falls, they can see little advantage in the video disc. After all, you cannot record on a disc; you are restricted to what you can buy or rent from the local shops'. (Huff (1981) p. 622)

Advanced technology can realistically be assumed to require substantial expenditures. Yet even the development of more mundane products, involving no radical technological breakthroughs, can be costly. A new grocery product, for instance, can cost from half a million pounds upwards, even where no new manufacturing plant and equipment is necessary. General expenses in advertising, promoting and distributing to mass markets can account for a large proportion of this.

The Marketing Function in the Firm

So far, it has been argued that companies need to pay careful attention to the factors likely to influence the demand for their products and to act in the light of this information. This 'demand philosophy', as it has been termed, should infiltrate the whole of the firm and not reside solely in the marketing function. Marketing, though, does have a special responsibilty for applying this philosophy: it can do this by gathering data on the market; devising appropriate product propositions; and formulating and implementing plans for launching these products. In performing these requisite tasks, it obviously has to work in concert with the other functions of the firm — these usually being finance, manufacturing, and research and development, with possibly distribution and sales (see Figure 1.5).

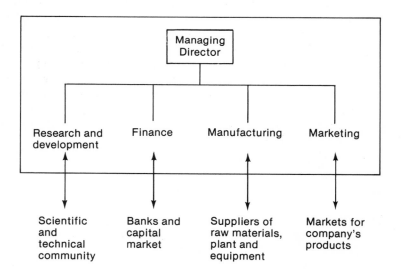

Figure 1.5 *Marketing Function in the Firm*

It has been argued that because of its unique role at the interface between the firm and the purchasers of its product, marketing should have a paramount position in the firm. In practice, whether or not marketing has a pre-eminent position will be a function of several factors, of which the nature of the business will be an important one.

For instance, in companies engaged in fast-moving consumer goods markets — such as confectionery, soaps and detergents, cigarettes and food — marketing will often provide the impetus for the total organisation. In firms in areas where technology is advancing rapidly, in many cases ahead of manifest demand (such as in microelectronics and biotechnology), much greater emphasis will be placed on research and development, which generally will not be merely responding to the initiatives of the marketing departments. In companies where there are considerable economies of scale in production, much stress will be placed on ensuring optimum efficiency of manufacturing operations.

There are, of course, considerable potential problems in those instances where one function is supreme. For example, as discussed above, a production-oriented company, preoccupied with optimising manufacturing efficiency, may pay scant regard to what the market requires. In other cases, a tendency to concentrate on technological innovation may lead to the development of advanced technological products, often for prestigious reasons; unfortunately, these may often be too expensive and sophisticated for the market. Indeed, it has been convincingly argued by several commentators that this has tended to be a feature of much of the UK's technological development in the post-war period. A far more commercially successful policy is likely to be based on the development of products, incorporating incremental changes in technology, that not only have the characteristics desired by the market but which also can consequently be sold at a price which consumers are willing and able to pay. Finally, too much concentration on marketing may lead to a short time horizon and the consequent failure to appreciate fully the significance of longer-term technological developments. Such myopia could seriously hazard the future survival of the company.

The commercially-successful company is more likely to have developed a harmonious balance between the different functions, based on an appreciation of the necessity of:

(a) financial planning and control to ensure that, at worst, costs do not exceed revenues, and that finance is available to fund desired investment programmes;

(b) efficient manufacturing; since, for example, a successful marketing strategy will depend on, among other things, reliability and quality;

(c) effective research and development to provide its products with superior competitive advantages, and to enable the company to keep abreast of technological advances, so that it can initiate, as well as quickly respond to, technological developments;

(d) good design, to ensure not only that products can be manufactured cost effectively, but also that they meet the aesthetic requirements of customers.

Specific Role of Marketing

In essence, marketing is broadly concerned with developing new products to satisfy emerging needs or to capitalise on newly-identified market opportunities, and with reappraising and modifying existing products in the light of changing marketing requirements — particularly important given the dynamic nature of modern society. In the case of new product development, it ascertains — through market information — the attributes which its target consumers seek in their products; it develops product concepts or broad statements summarising the essentials of the product, aimed at meeting these market requirements; it liaises, where necessary, with research and development and manufacturing, in the translation of this intangible statement into a physical product that can be manufactured efficiently at a price acceptable to its target market; and it undertakes the communication and distribution of the developed offering.

A number of aspects of the role of marketing merit further discussion. First, it has often been accused of adding costs, particularly through heavy advertising, selling and packaging. However, some have argued that marketing can be viewed as adding value, through giving the product what have been termed place, time and form utilities: it ensures that the company markets the products the customer wants, where he wants them, and at a price he is willing and able to pay. Furthermore, given the state of development of present-day society, advertising can be viewed as a means not only of effectively informing mass markets of the attributes of its products but also — through the creation of product associations and images — of supplying intangible values, such as those of prestige and image, sought by some of today's consumers. Careful attention to packaging is necessary to ensure adequate protection of the product and, for perishable produce, a possible longer life. Nevertheless, it would also be true to say that a high, and sometimes unnecessary, proportion of marketing effort is geared to giving the firm some competitive advantage (however ephemeral), with little, if any, substantial benefit to the consumer. In this respect, marketing may well have to reassess its role in relation to a more educated consumer.

A second point of note is that marketing should consider itself as being involved in making 'integrated offerings' to its target consumers. In practice, this means that the firm is concerned to ensure that all the elements of the product — its price, its packaging, the outlets where it is sold, the image of the product, where it is advertised, even its brand name — are all compatible with each other, and that the final total product meets the expectations of the market.

> Estée Lauder has developed a high-priced product range aimed at the more affluent segments of the market. This means that its products are given a superior image, are expensively packaged, are advertised in 'quality' women's magazines and Sunday newspapers and are distributed through the better department stores using Estée Lauder-employed sales representatives.

It would obviously be inappropriate for a company such as Estée Lauder, given its established marketing strategy, to price its products cheaply and sell through exclusive stores; or conversely, to retail its products through chain stores such as Woolworth, which has a reputation for cheapness.

Where organisations are selling to other organisations (such as manufacturers) as opposed to consumers, the notion of an 'integrated offering' assumes a broader meaning. These organisations will often be involved in assembling a 'package', embracing a range of products and services, which is aimed at solving a customer's problem. For example, a firm may not just buy a computer; rather, it may require a management information system, of which the computer is only a part. Other ingredients of the system would probably be the programmes used to ensure storage and, where necessary, processing of the data; printers; floppy disc units; and visual display units. The marketing of systems is becoming increasingly important.

> Developments in micro-electronics are having a significant impact on the suppliers of office equipment. The sellers of typewriters and photocopiers will be increasingly involved in selling 'office systems' that 'word-process', reproduce, store data, and provide access to external information sources.

Thirdly, it can be seen that the marketer has several variables at his command. These are collectively referred to as the *marketing mix* and simplistically embrace: price; the product, promotion (including sales and advertising); and place (or distribution). With the addition of market analysis and marketing research, these are in essence the major tasks of marketing (see Table 1.1).

Given a limited expenditure, the marketing practitioner has to allocate his resources so as to achieve his objectives, which can range from long-run market share to maximum profits in the short term. As will be seen throughout the remainder of the book, the marketer is

Table 1.1 *Major Tasks of Marketing*

Marketing task	Possible activities
Market analysis	Examination of structure of markets. Identification of market opportunities. Estimation of total possible sales and company's market share.
Marketing research	Evaluation of effectiveness of marketing policies. Concept testing. Test marketing.
Product development	Development of appropriate products for particular market targets. Deciding on packaging. Branding decisions. Determining service back-up.
Pricing	Setting total price. Determining role of price in promotion. Establishing retailers' margins. Assessing demand – price relationships. Researching value of product as perceived by market.
Sales	Sales force management. Establishing sales territories and sales targets. Monitoring sales performance.
Distribution	Determining optimum level of distribution. Merchandising. Establishing distribution network.
Advertising and promotion	Liaison with advertising agency. Devising advertising theme. Copy writing. Decision on media to be used (newspapers, magazines, radio, television, etc).

basically concerned with attaining the *optimum*. He may, for example, have to assess the gains from increased expenditure on market research against the risk of immediate launch with little, if any, information on the market. Or, given an objective of maximising revenue in a specific period, he may have to consider whether or not it would be more beneficial to develop a 'quality' product and sell it at a high price, or aim the product more at the mass market, set a low price, and hope to secure high revenue through rapid turnover. Again, the marketing manager, faced with declining sales of one of his major products as a result of the introduction of a similar product by a competitor, is faced with an array of possible alternatives: he may decide to allocate more to promotion; he may decrease price; or alternatively, he may improve the quality of the product to give it a perceived competitive advantage. However, his options are not, in reality, either so simple or so clear cut, for, of course, he may increase expenditure on promotion *as well as* changing the price, and he can do both by various amounts. In turn, these can be combined with alterations in one or more of the many other variables under his control.

Assessing the impact of each of these alternatives together with the possible reactions of competitors would indeed be a formidable task, even given the assistance of a computer. Furthermore, it has to be recognised that much of the data employed in such an analysis would be highly subjective and speculative — and this has led to some questioning of the utility of such exercises. At this juncture, let it suffice to note that the marketer is concerned with making decisions that involve trade-offs between changes in several variables; that the effectiveness of such decision making can be considerably improved by adopting an analytical approach, the sophistication of which will be dependent on the data and time available; and that, in the end, he will have to use his judgement in making what he hopes is the optimum decision, in the light of the best available evidence.

Summary

In this chapter, a distinction has been drawn between a demand and a supply orientation. Modern marketing practice is founded on meeting the requirements of consumers, and such a philosophy must pervade the total enterprise, from marketing through to research and development. This focuses attention on understanding consumer and industrial buying behaviour. The rationale for adopting such an orientation was discussed in terms of rising discretionary income, an increase in intangible wants, greater competition, and the high costs of new product development and therefore the need to minimise the risks of failure.

The marketing function in the firm is specifically concerned with implementing this philosophy: it does this by researching markets and by formulating and developing 'integrated offerings'. The marketer has several main variables which he can manipulate: for simplicity these can be termed the 'marketing mix'. His major purpose is to obtain the optimum mix.

Further Reading

Galbraith, J.K. (1967) *The New Industrial State,* Hamish Hamilton.
Huff, C. (1981) 'Risky disc', *The Listener,* 7th May.
Keith, R.J. (1960) 'The marketing revolution', *Journal of Marketing,* June.
Levitt, T. (1960) 'Marketing myopia', *Harvard Business Review,* Vol. 38.
Mansell, C. (1973) 'Lesney's model comeback', *Management Today,* June.
Maslow, A.H. (1954) *Motivation and Personality,* Harper and Row.
Schumpeter, J.A. (1950) *Capitalism, Socialism and Democracy,* George Allen and Unwin.
Shanks, M. (1967) *The Innovators,* Penguin Books.

Review Questions

(1) 'Marketing is solely concerned with meeting purchasers' and users' needs'. Is this strictly true?

(2) Do you consider that there are any problems in the implementation of the 'demand philosophy' in the case of advanced-technology products?

(3) Summarise the reasons why you consider that a firm manufacturing consumer goods needs to pay attention to 'marketing'.

(4) Discuss how the trend towards 'higher-order needs' could affect the future demand for goods.

(5) Explain what is meant by the 'marketing of systems'. Describe how it might apply to a manufacturer of machinery for the textile industry.

(6) Describe the main marketing tasks in the case of:
  (a) the producer of specialised chemicals for use in the manufacture of dyestuffs;
  (b) the manufacturer of soft drinks.

The market place: direct interaction between buyers and sellers

2

The Nature of Markets

In contemporary Western economies, 'markets' are somewhat far removed from the bazaars of the Middle East or the simple village fairs where pedlars sold their wares. Rather, they tend to be sophisticated, complex and extensive. Indeed, the nature of modern markets has been shaped by several major trends in the twentieth century, of which the growth in the amount of discretionary income, the development of mass production with its high economies of scale, and the considerable innovations in transport and forms of distribution are of particular importance. It is essential, as has already been emphasised, for marketers to understand the nature of the markets in which they sell their goods and also the way in which these markets are likely to change in the future.

Traditionally, markets were places where buyers and sellers exchanged goods and services, often for money, although bartering was, and still is, employed in some countries. Today, the term 'market' is used to signify groups of potential purchasers (whether these be consumers or organisations) to which, often specific, goods are sold. Thus, one refers to the 'consumer market' or 'industrial market' as well as the market for new houses, pet foods, machine tools, and so on.

In this chapter, a simple means of classifying markets is adopted; five types of market are identified, namely: consumer; industrial; institutional; distribution; and government. Consumer and industrial markets are analysed in some detail. It is seen that these markets are not homogeneous, but can, in fact, be subdivided according to certain criteria. This is termed market segmentation. Segmentation is important in practical marketing, since it enhances the effectiveness of the marketing effort, as well as assisting in the identification of market targets. Some means of segmenting, particularly consumer markets, are examined.

Markets: A Classification

A market was historically a place where buyers and sellers met to barter or to exchange money for goods. 'Street' markets are still a feature of many cities, towns and villages, and they, perhaps, best exemplify the notion of a market as it is traditionally conceived. At another level, one can refer to regional markets for particular products, such as the market for beer in the North East; whilst at a national level, the housing market embraces the actual or potential demand for houses, flats, apartments, and holiday homes, both for purchase or rent, throughout the UK. From cursory examination, it is obvious that there is a diverse range of markets. For our purposes, we are going to adopt a simple topology that divides markets into five main classes:

(1) *Consumer markets* where goods and services are purchased for final consumption without undergoing any further transactions.
(2) *Industrial markets* where goods and services are purchased by companies involved in the production of other goods which are subsequently sold either to other manufacturers or to final consumers. Examples of such products would include machine tools, car parts, steel, bulk chemicals.
(3) *Distribution markets* where goods are purchased by those involved in distribution, such as retailers and wholesalers. The changing nature of these markets can have profound repercussions for manufacturers. The discussion of the nature of these markets is postponed until Chapter 10.
(4) *Government markets* where goods or services are sold to central and local government. The total expenditure involved can be substantial, amounting to a significant proportion of gross domestic product. Among the sectors involved would be defence, government expenditure on its own administration, motorways ...
(5) *Institutional markets* embrace those areas involving organisational purchasing (excluding industrial, distribution and governmental markets). These markets have grown rapidly over recent decades. They would include universities, hospitals, charitable institutions ...

The distinction between categories of goods based on this classification is not clear-cut in certain cases. For example, it is obvious that car parts can be both industrial and consumer goods since they are sold to car manufacturers and to consumers. However, the processes involved in their marketing will be very different in the two cases. The former involves the sale of bulk quantities to a handful of technically-knowledgeable organisations. The buyers may well devise the specifications of the products they wish to purchase. In the latter case, the market consists of millions of potential customers, many of whom lack any detailed technical knowledge, making only small purchases. Distribution is more complex, requiring the use of a widespread retailing network with depots to service them. Successful marketers in the consumer market are more likely to have recognised the importance of branding and packaging.

Consumer Markets

The UK consumer market consists of approximately 56 million consumers and its total value amounted to £135,000 million in 1980. Table 2.1 indicates, in broad terms, how consumers allocated their expenditure in 1979 and the way in which the pattern has changed from 1961. As would be expected with rising income, the proportion spent on food has declined significantly (from 24.5 per cent to 17.9 per cent), and there have also been decreases in the amounts spent on tobacco (6.8 per cent to 3.7 per cent) − perhaps not surprising in the light of the well-publicised anti-smoking campaigns − and clothing and footwear (9.7 per cent to 7.7 per cent). Consumers are spending more on housing (an increase from 9.9 per cent to 14.4 per cent), transport and vehicles (9.1 per cent to 13.5 per cent) and alcohol (6.0 per cent to 7.7 per cent).

Table 2.1 *Percentage of Total Consumers' Expenditure at Current Prices (1961 and 1979)*

Item	1961	1979
Food	24.5	17.9
Housing	9.9	14.4
Fuel and light	4.5	4.6
Alcohol	6.0	7.7
Tobacco	6.8	3.7
Clothing and footwear	9.7	7.7
Durable and household goods	4.8	4.9
Transport and vehicles	9.1	13.5
Other goods, services and miscellaneous	24.7	25.6
Total	100	100

Source: National Income and Expenditure, Central Statistical Office

Classification of Consumer Goods

Consumer goods can be divided into three main categories:

(1) Fast-moving consumer goods, which are purchased frequently, are relatively inexpensive, and often involve little, if any, pre-purchase conscious consideration. Many household and grocery products fit into this category; examples include detergents, confectionery, and soft drinks.

(2) Durable goods, which are purchased relatively infrequently, are often expensive, and may involve detailed conscious pre-purchase consideration. Several different brands may be assessed before a decision to purchase is made. Many electrical products, such as washing machines, refrigerators, televisions and radios are of this nature.

(3) Speciality goods tend to be infrequently purchased items which may not be stocked widely. They are often expensive, branded items which consumers will actively seek out. Examples might include champagne, smoked salmon, records by specific artists, Cartier watches.

Distinction between Customer and Consumer

Many purchases are, of course, made for or on behalf of others. For example, some goods are bought as presents whilst even more purchases are made for collective consumption − an instance of the latter being the housewife buying for the family. There is, therefore, an important distinction to be made between the customer − the actual purchasing unit − and the consumer, or the individual who actually uses or consumes the goods. The attitudes, views and reactions of consumers will undoubtedly be taken into account by customers, and for marketers to focus only on the buyers of their products, thereby ignoring the fact that their behaviour is influenced by others, can lead to inappropriate marketing policies.

Categorisation of Consumer Markets

In general, the consumer market can be divided into three categories of purchasing units. These are: households; families; and individuals. *Households* can be defined as groups of people who live and eat together, although households can also consist of one individual. Members of a household may or may not be related. *Families* consist of a married couple, with or without children or a lone parent with children. In practice, most households consist of a single family or of someone living alone. But some households do include more than one family, the members of a family plus one or more other persons such as a lodger, or two or more unrelated persons living together. Where individuals make purchases for themselves, they can be regarded as separate decision-making units even though they may be members of a household or part of a family.

A teenager living at home will still be dependent on the family unit, and many purchases, including much food, will be made for the family unit of which he is a part. However, he may also have his own 'discretionary income' from full-time or part-time employment. He may use this to spend on his own clothes, on a variety of leisure activities, on records, a motor bike or automobile. The youth market has been an important growth market in the last three decades.

Since only approximately 1 per cent of households consist of more than two families, the two terms can, for the most part, be used interchangeably. In any case, most government statistics refer to households rather than families.

A marked trend is the significant increase in the number of one-person households (from 12 per cent of the total households to 23 per cent) during the period 1961 to 1979 (see Table 2.2). This is a consequence of both the rise in the number of single old people in the population, and of the greater tendency for young people to seek independence at an earlier age by leaving home and setting up their own households. Moreover, the fact that households are tending to be

Table 2.2 *Households by Size: Great Britain, 1961 and 1979*

Size of household	% of total households	
	1961	*1979*
1 person	12	23
2 people	30	32
3 people	23	17
4 people	19	17
5 people	9	7
6 or more people	7	4
Total households	100	100
Average household size (no. of people)	3.09	2.67

Source: Office of Population Censuses and Surveys

Table 2.3 *Distribution of Final Household Income among Households, 1978*

	Top 20%	21 – 40%	41 – 60%	61 – 80%	Bottom 20%	Total
	Quintile groups of households					
Proportion of final income	36	24	18	13	9	100

Source: Family Expenditure Survey, Central Statistical Office

smaller (for example, the average household size has declined from 3.09 people in 1961 to 2.67 people in 1979) can have significant implications for marketers. It may affect the demand for large pack sizes, whilst there may be more household discretionary income available for the purchase of durable goods.

A second way of analysing households is in terms of their income. For example, from Table 2.3 it can be seen that there are significant differences in income between the top 20 per cent of households which in 1978 accounted for 36 per cent of final income, and the bottom 20 per cent which had only 9 per cent.

Household income has, of course, been affected significantly by the rise in the number of working housewives. The proportion of married women in paid work has grown from 29 per cent in 1961 to 48 per cent in 1979. Even in recession, there are around a million more women in employment than there were fifteen years ago. Not only does it mean that families have, as a result, far greater spending power, but it also means that there have been far-reaching changes in lifestyle. Working housewives not only become more independent, they also have far less time (and indeed energy) to direct to household chores. The increase in demand for many types of products, such as quick-prepared foods, deep freezers, automatic washing machines, dishwashers, and many other types of kitchen appliances, has paralleled this increase in women having remunerated employment.

Life Cycle

It has been suggested that a further way of examining the market is by dividing it into groups according to people's stage in, what has been termed, the 'family life cycle'. According to this view, there are nine life cycle stages (see Table 2.4), ranging from the batchelor stage through the married stages to the solitary survivor stage, each of which is characterised by a different demand pattern as a result of varying needs and discretionary incomes. For example, the retired solitary survivor with very little income is likely to require medical aids of one form or another and nutritional, convenient-to-prepare, single-portion foods. The lifestyle of this group contrasts vividly with that of the batchelor stage, where discretionary income will tend to be high and commitments few. Such 'batchelors' will tend to seek experience of life, and therefore be experimental and innovative. It is argued that by obtaining a more 'rounded' picture of market subgroups in this way, the marketer can gain greater insights into possible wants and, therefore, can be in a more advantageous position to recognise possible opportunities and formulate appropriate 'offerings' to fill them.

Structure of Population

The population of a country, of course, gives the gross market size, and generally there have been massive increases in population in most countries throughout the twentieth century. The number of UK citizens has, for example, grown from 38.2 million in 1901 to 56 million today; it is expected to rise to 58.4 million in 2001 (Office of Population Censuses and Surveys; see Figure 2.1). In recent years, though, the birth rate has shown a tendency to decline (see Table 2.5), probably as a result of the widespread availability of improved and

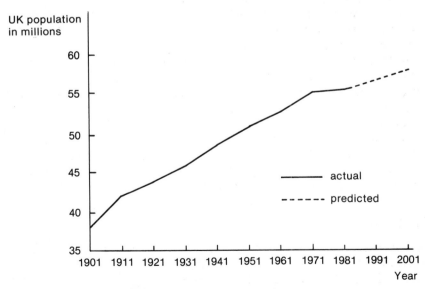

Source: Office of Population Censuses and Surveys

Figure 2.1 *UK Population 1901–2001*

Table 2.4 *Family Life Cycle*

Life cycle stage	Features of group	Demand characteristics
Bachelor	Young, single people	Earnings are generally low since they are at the start of their career. They have few financial commitments so that their discretionary income is quite high. Interested in leisure activities, fashion, and 'pop' culture. They are also interested in the purchase of vacations, cars, clothing, records. The establishment of their own residence away from the family means that they will purchase basic household furniture and equipment.
Newly marrieds	Young, no children	This group is affluent since both parties are working. They are establishing a home, and so they will tend to require basic housing, furniture, durable goods, cars. Leisure activities are likely to be important. Overall, they have a high rate of expenditure with little saving.
Full nest 1	Young married couples with youngest child under 6	The first child is born and the wife usually stops working resulting in a significant fall in household income. They purchase baby goods, and tend to become more 'economical' minded. Do-it-yourself is likely to become more important.
Full nest 2	Young married couples with youngest child 6 or over	Total income tends to increase because of husband's advancement and often the wife's return to work. The products that tend to be purchased in large amounts include many foods, cleaning materials, bicycles. Holidays are considered important as are various recreational activities.

Full nest 3	Older married couples with dependent children	Family income continues to increase. More wives return to work, and even one or more of the children may have some employment part-time. This group has a high average expenditure on durable goods, primarily because of the need to replace older items. Consequently, there will be demand for new furniture, luxury appliances, automobiles.
Empty nest 1	Older married couples with no children living with them and the household head in the labour force	Both savings and home ownership will be high. This group has an interest in travel, recreation and self-education. Often spend heavily on grandchildren
Empty nest 2	Older married couples with no children living with them and the household head retired	Income is drastically reduced. This group tends to stay at home more, and spend more on medical appliances, and products that aid sleep, health and digestion
Solitary survivor 1	Older single people in labour force	High income with high discretionary income
Solitary survivor 2	Older retired single people	Low income with a demand for economical, single portion packs

Source: Adapted from Wells and Gubar (1966) pp. 355 – 363

Table 2.5 *Birth Rate: Great Britain, 1951 – 1979*

Year	Crude birth rate
1951	15.7
1956	16.0
1961	17.8
1966	17.8
1971	16.1
1972	14.8
1973	13.8
1974	13.1
1975	12.4
1976	11.9
1977	11.6
1978	12.2
1979	13.0

Source: Office of Population Censuses and Surveys
Note: Birth rate is measured by live births per 1000 persons, all ages

accepted means of contraception, the greater career orientation of many women and the influence of women's liberation movements of one sort or another, and more emphasis on materialism. The marketer, however, is less likely to be concerned with the size of the total population than with its structure, particularly as this pertains to the target groups to which the products are to be sold. Companies, then, need to analyse changes in market structure, assess the impact on their existing product ranges, and appraise new opportunities that such changes could present in the future.

There has been a significant decline in the number of live births throughout the 1970s. Companies catering for the 'baby market' such as Gerber, Johnson and Johnson, and Heinz were faced with a significant fall in their sales. One of the responses was to widen the appeal of their products: thus, Johnson and Johnson developed an advertising theme depicting adults pampering themselves with its talc, suggesting that people treat themselves as a Johnson's baby. Other firms, such as Mothercare, extended their product ranges to embrace the pre-teenage child.

This fall in the birthrate is, however, being attended by an increase in the number of people aged over 65, and this is likely to generate a substantial demand for other types of products.

As can be seen from Figure 2.2, which gives the proportion of people

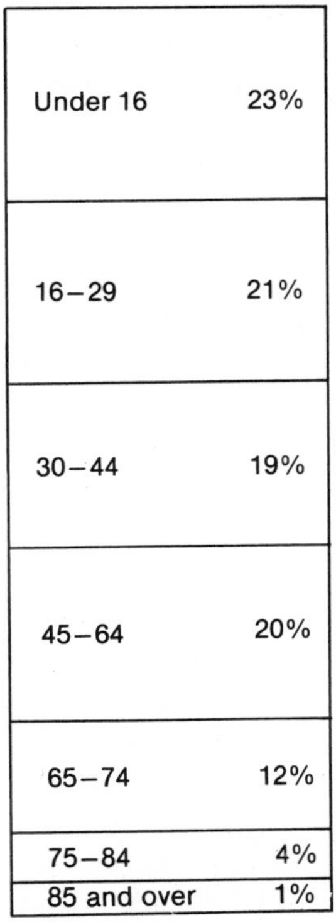

Under 16	23%
16–29	21%
30–44	19%
45–64	20%
65–74	12%
75–84	4%
85 and over	1%

Figure 2.2   *Age Structure of UK Population (1979)*

in various age groups for 1979, 17 per cent of the population is 65 or over, representing 9.5 million people. Since approximately six per cent more boys than girls are born each year, there are obviously more young men than young women. However, more men than women die each year, so that from about age 50 the number of women exceeds the number of men.

Regional Markets

A further point worthy of note is that the UK population is not spread uniformly. Rather, there are appreciable differences in density: the South East has 619 people per square kilometre; other regions, like East Anglia, are comparatively sparsely populated (148 people per square kilometre). In addition, there are areas of very high concentration. Thus the metropolitan counties of Merseyside and Greater Manchester have population densities in excess of 2000 people per square kilometre.

In recent years, there has been an exodus from the inner city areas, with people moving to the outer suburbs and to the new towns. Regions can differ in average incomes, attitudes and tastes, and patterns of expenditure, and it can be highly profitable for a company to develop products uniquely geared to satisfying the special requirements of a region.

Differences in Income

It was seen earlier (see Table 2.3) that there are considerable differences in household income, and it is not surprising to find that there are significant variations in individuals' income. For example, the top 10 per cent of the population receive 23 per cent of the total personal income, as compared with only 3 per cent for the bottom 10 per cent of the population.

Social Class

A further, and extremely popular and useful means of subdividing markets is in terms of social class (or socio-economic grouping), where occupation is the key indicator. The two principal approaches of categorising social class are the Registrar General's classification which contains five classes (one of which contains two subgroups) as shown in Table 2.6 and his classification of socio-economic groups which contains seventeen groups and is used as the basis of the 'social class' analysis employed in the General Household Survey (see Appendix 2.1). In general, because of its greater simplicity, the former tends to be used more often in practice.

The underlying rationale of the use of social class is that each class can be viewed as homogeneous, having its own subculture with a common set of beliefs and attitudes. Each, therefore, exhibits a uniform behaviour pattern. It might be expected that people from higher social classes will tend to have had better schooling, receive higher incomes, live in their own homes (as opposed to council-owned property), and so on, than those from lower social classes. Consequently, it could be deduced that they will have the same interests, and allocate their expenditure according to a broadly similar pattern. It must be accepted that there is a degree of circularity in the argument: for example, people in social class one are professional people who will generally have undergone some form of higher education, with perhaps some additional training; it is therefore inevitable that members of this class will have achieved a higher standard of income. A further comment is that traditional social class barriers may become indistinct as the general level of education of the population improves, and as the differences in income between classes diminishes. A further

Table 2.6 *Social Class of Economically Active and Retired Population, 1971*

	Social class	Percentage of economically active and retired population	
		(M)	(F)
I	Professional occupations, (including doctors, lawyers, chemists and clergymen)	4.7	0.8
II	Intermediate occupations (including most managerial and senior administrative occupations, e.g. sales managers, authors, MPs, colliery managers, personnel managers, senior government officials, school teachers, farmers, physiotherapists, and nurses)	17.1	13.6
III	Skilled occupations (N) Non-manual (including typists, clerical workers, sales representatives and shop assistants)	11.3	29.5
	(M) Manual (including cooks, railway guards, plasterers, bricklayers, foremen packers, and foremen in the engineering and allied trades)	36.5	8.0
IV	Partly-skilled occupations (including barmen, bus conductors, canteen assistants, and telephone operators (but not supervisors who are 111N))	17.2	20.3
V	Unskilled occupations (including office cleaners and stevedores (but not foremen who are 111M), lorry drivers' mates, and labourers)	8.1	6.0
	Not classified	5.0	21.8
	Total (millions)	18.18	12.18

Source: Census of Population 1971

factor that needs to be taken into account is the impact of the large numbers of working wives.

For instance, many lower social class households could have significantly higher incomes than professional class households where the wife is not employed. It is likely that increasingly there are considerable differences in income among members of a social class, and that perhaps classes can be analysed in terms of privileged, average and underprivileged members; there may be interesting and significant variations in purchasing behaviour between the three. These criticisms aside, for the present purposes social class can be accepted for what it is: a widely employed and useful practical tool that can aid the marketer in formulating his marketing strategy and tactics.

Contemporary Features of the UK Consumer Market

The UK consumer market, then, can be seen to be experiencing a number of contemporary trends. The declining birth rate and the greater average longevity of the population mean that there will be fewer children and a large number of retired people in the population, whilst the 'baby boom' of the 1960s has resulted in a higher proportion of young people. The average size of households has been decreasing, and there are more one-person households. The greater number of working women, particularly housewives, has raised the total income of many households, whilst the tendency for women to be more independent has affected social attitudes and broken down traditional roles. People tend to be better educated, and more aware of their rights; they travel more, and as a result of this widening of experience, tend to become more experimental at home. Within the UK, people tend, on average, to be more mobile, because of the increased ownership of cars; moreover, they tend to change jobs and move house more frequently. The sense of community in many areas is no longer prevalent. Increasing mobility has been a factor, but so have the ambitious urban renewal programmes of the post-war years that have destroyed large areas of older properties, and resulted in the transfer of masses of people to new towns or anonymous housing estates on the outskirts of existing cities and towns. Such factors have many effects on people's attitudes, aspirations and behaviour and it is obvious that a sound appreciation of such aspects of the market is necessary if marketers are to be able to anticipate and meet consumer demands.

Industrial Markets

Industrial markets are those where raw materials, plant, equipment, semi-finished goods (such as synthetic yarns, steel), components and other products are sold to companies which then use them in some way in the production of other goods and services.

> A large bakery has to purchase mixers, ovens, moulds, trays and vans (for the delivery of its products) before it can even begin to make bread. It will purchase large quantities of flour, yeast and the necessary additives on a regular basis, deliveries of some of its materials being made several times per week. In addition, the administration of the bakery will require filing cabinets, typewriters, and other similar office equipment.

> British Petroleum (BP) is primarily concerned with the exploration, drilling and refining of petroleum products. It purchases complex rigs for drilling (its North Sea platforms cost hundreds of millions of pounds), thousands of miles of pipes for oil refineries and for distributing its products, large storage tanks and large oil tankers. For many of its purchases BP will lay down the technical specifications and invite companies to tender for the order.

Types of Industrial Goods

It is obvious that there are several types of industrial goods: they can range from large items of capital equipment such as storage tanks to items such as flour, tinplate and chemicals. Table 2.7 categorises the main types of industrial goods.

Differences between Industrial Goods and Consumer Goods

In general, several features distinguish industrial goods from consumer goods. First, many industrial purchases involve complex decision making by several people. For example, the decision to invest in a major piece of production equipment could involve production engineers, accountants, and the purchasing department as well as outside consultants. Many consumer decisions are made singularly or by husband and wife.

Secondly, the individuals involved in industrial purchasing tend to be more technically proficient, having detailed understanding of the technology and the specifications they require. Many consumers, on the other hand, lack any appreciation of the technology of the products purchased. Thirdly, not only will many industrial purchasers define the technical specifications of the products sought but they will also invite quotations from selected companies. Contracts tend to be widely employed. Fourthly, many industrial purchases involve the buying of substantial capital items or bulk quantities of material.

Table 2.7   *Classification of Industrial Goods*

	Type of goods	Examples
I	Raw materials	Agricultural produce, e.g. hops, vegetables, tea Natural materials, e.g. coal, unprocessed oil, aluminium ore
II	Processed materials	ethylene, steel, vegetable oil
III	Manufactured parts	transistors, compressors, tyres
IV	Accommodation	factory buildings, land
V	Fixed plant	oil storage tanks, packaging equipment, generators
VI	Movable equipment	fork lift trucks, hand-power tools, typewriters
VII	Maintenance and repair items	paint, adhesives, hammers
VIII	Operating supplies	electricity, lubricating oils
IX	General services	office cleaning, equipment maintenance
X	Professional services	marketing research, auditing

Quantity discounts are common. Fifthly, industrial markets have fewer buying units.

These aspects also tend to apply to institutional, government and, to some extent, distributors' markets. In particular, the fact that purchases outside consumer markets are made by several people (who are usually technically proficient) is general in organisations. The group of decision makers involved in some way with organisational purchases has been termed the *buying centre*, defined as

> ... all those individuals and groups who participate in the purchasing decision-making process, who share some common goals and the risks arising from the decisions. (Webster and Wind (1972) p. 6)

The buying centre consists of people who may have one of five roles identified as important in organisational purchases (Webster and Wind (1972) pp. 78–80):

(1) Users: those who actually use the product or service. They often

Table 2.8   *Some Data Given in the Business Monitor Series for Three Industrial Sectors*

	Brewing and malting (1978)	Bread and flour confectionery (1978)	Footwear (1979)
Enterprises (no.)	123	1,113	514
Establishments (no.)	203	1,344	591
Total sales and work done(£000)	3,093,833	1,423,781	898,296
Gross output (£000)	3,113,524	1,425,319	915,532
Total employment (£000)	61.3	129.6	71.3
Total net capital expenditure (£000)	175,646	48,658	13,397

initiate the original purchase request and may be important in defining the specifications of the goods required.

(2) Influencers: are usually technical personnel who assist in defining specifications and in evaluating alternatives.

(3) Buyers: are those who have formal authority for selecting suppliers and arranging the terms of the purchase. In more complex purchases, high-level officers may be involved in the negotiations.

(4) Deciders: these have either formal or informal power to select the suppliers. In the routine buying of standard items, the buyers are often the deciders. In more complex buying, the officers of the company are often the deciders.

(5) Gatekeepers: they are individuals who effect the flow of information to others.

Structure of Industrial Markets

The industrial market is not, of course, a homogeneous collection of corporate purchasers. In reality, it embraces large numbers of industries, and products and services. An accepted way of categorising the industrial market is the standard industrial classification (SIC). This contains six broad groups (or orders) within which there are further subdivisions (or minimum list headings). Statistics are gathered by the government on the industrial sectors, given in the SIC and published separately each quarter in the Business Monitor series. Data are published on *inter alia* the number of employees, turnover, number of firms operating (or 'enterprises') and the number of separate manufacturing units (or 'establishments') − see Table 2.8.

Size of Firms

Not surprisingly, the composition of industries in terms of the number and size of firms can vary considerably: from monopolies, where one firm dominates output, to those industries where a major proportion of the output is accounted for by a large number of relatively small firms. However, a contemporary phenomenon (at least in the UK) is the rise of oligopolies where the output of many industries is produced by just a few large companies. Examples of such industries are brewing, cigarette manufacture, synthetic fibres, and bulk chemicals.

Government, Institutional and Distribution Markets

All three markets involve organisational decision making and, therefore, will have many similarities with industrial markets in that:

(a) purchasing decisions tend to involve several people;
(b) technical criteria tend to be relatively, if not primarily, important;
(c) the 'technical awareness' of at least some of those involved with the decision is generally higher than is the case for consumer markets;
(d) the purchase is large in terms of the quantity involved (e.g. mass quantities of paper, chemicals etc.) or the size of the good (e.g. machine tools, oil refinery storage tanks and power generators);
(e) quotations and contracts are common.

Government Market

Total government expenditure (including local authority spending) has risen steadily over the post-war period until the 1970s when there was an explosion in real expenditure. Central and local government expenditure on goods and services amounts to 23 per cent of GDP. A high proportion of this is in the form of pay for their employees.

Central government gives grants to local authorities and finances other services which involve a degree of local discretion (e.g. expenditure on education, Health Service, prison service), although central government will, of course, often be responsible for major decisions (such as the building of new prisons) as well as setting the overall level of expenditure. Decisions on the allocation of the remaining lump of government expenditure tend to be more centralised. They might include the spending on its own administration, defence, and motorways.

Institutional Markets

Institutions are not involved in manufacturing; generally, they buy-in goods and services in order to provide a service. They may be in either the public (i.e. financed by government or local authorities) or private sector of the economy. In the case of the former, institutions will have a degree of discretion over their own purchases, even though the level of expenditure and in some cases various technical criteria will be specified by government. Universities, for example, are centrally funded, yet each will purchase its supplies separately. Decisions in the private sector tend to be less constrained. Examples of institutions include: schools, prisons, hospitals, universities, charities, and government laboratories.

Distribution Markets

It is evident that many goods are not sold directly by the manufacturers to their final purchasers, but involve a distributor of one sort or another. Examples are retailers and wholesalers. In some sectors of the consumer market, retailers have considerable market power and therefore constitute important and indeed powerful purchasers who can in many cases virtually dictate terms. In such instances, manufacturers have found themselves faced with threats to their profitability; only those adept and far-sighted will survive in the long term under such circumstances. Various facets of distributors are discussed in more detail in Chapter 10.

Market Segmentation

It is clear from the discussion of the consumer market that it is not a homogeneous mass of consumers; it can at least be divided up into broad subgroups on the basis of a number of criteria such as age, class, income, geographical location and so on. It may be that such subgroups exhibit broad similarities in purchasing behaviour. For example, as we have seen in Table 2.6, members of social class (I) can be expected to have different 'lifestyles', and therefore have different desires and purchasing priorities from those of social class (V). This principle, that the market consists of groups of customers with broadly similar wants, is the basis of **market segmentation**.

The early marketers concentrated on particular groups of customers, generally those situated near to the producing unit. This was inevitable in medieval societies where transport over distance was inadequate and risky and where 'production', because it was based on individual skills, was inevitably limited. As societies developed, income was increasingly used as a basis for segmenting markets. The 'industrial revolution' dramatically changed the nature of production and distribution and resulted in the rise of mass marketing, a trend accentuated in the twentieth century by the development of mass communications. Increasingly, with the rise in the amount of discretionary income, marketers realised that more and more consumers sought products which more closely satisfied their individual wants than did the standardised, mass-produced articles. Manufacturers saw that it was possible to divide the market, according to various criteria, into groups of consumers exhibiting similar preferences.

In practice, market segmentation involves classifying markets into homogeneous groups and developing offerings tailored to meet the specific wants of these subgroups. It can be regarded as a compromise between producing as many offerings as there are customers, based on the premise that each has specific wants, and producing one offering which leaves large groups of customers incompletely satisfied.

> The market for soup used to be dominated by one type — canned soup, produced in a standardised form. Today, several different types and forms are produced. The demand for dietary products has given rise to a lucrative dietary segment; the need for quick snacks, particularly during office hours, has generated the dehydrated 'instant' soup range; whilst a segment of the market wanted wholesome, more substantial soups which could act as a quick, nutritious and 'filling' meal, and hence the introduction of the 'chunky' canned soup ranges.

> Henry Ford is alleged to have centred his business strategy on the principle that consumers could have any car they wanted, provided it was a black model T. Certainly, the Ford Motor Company was compelled to alter its business philosophy when it saw competitors, which developed ranges of automobiles more suited to the requirements of particular segments, making significant inroads into Ford's market share. Today, the consumer is faced with a plethora of model types and some manufacturers, in particular Ford, produce accessories enabling purchasers to 'customise' their cars.
> There are now mini cars aimed at the 'economy'-minded segment; family cars aimed at those with children; sporty cars; and cars aimed at the executive segment.

> The market for newspapers is generally segmented in terms of social class and political opinion. Age is increasingly important since, as was seen from the life cycle, purchasing patterns are a function of age. The *Guardian*, for example, has a 'liberal' editorial line

which is reflected in many of its features; it is very much a 'young' paper with almost 70 per cent of its readership under 44 and 23 per cent of these under 24. It is also 'upper' class. The *Daily Express*, on the other hand, has a 'conservative' political line, and very much a readership profile that is older − 54 per cent are over 45 − and lower class − 54 per cent are in the C₂ D E social classes (*National Readership Survey* 1979).

It is obvious that a clearly-defined market target is vitally important for a newspaper, since advertisers concerned about the effectiveness of their media expenditure will want to ensure that they communicate with the segment(s) at which they are aiming their products. Figure 2.3 suggests an approach to segmenting the newspaper market.

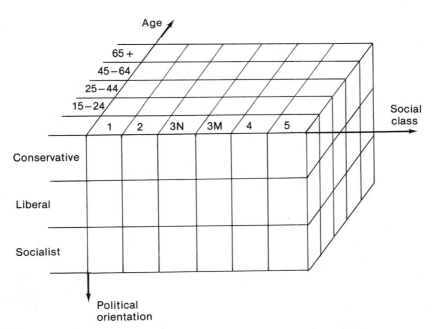

Figure 2.3 *Three Dimensional Matrix for Segmentation of Newspaper Market*

Advantages of Segmentation

Market segmentation offers a number of distinct benefits.

(1) Companies can obtain real competitive advantages among certain group(s) of consumers.
(2) Segmentation can improve the effectiveness of marketing operations since marketing efforts are focused specifically on those groups of consumers who are most likely to want the

48 *Marketing and Product Development*

products offered; there is a lower risk of waste of effort on those groups which are less likely to purchase.

(3) Segmentation can facilitate the identification of market opportunities: for instance, by segmenting a market which previously has been offered only standardised products, the marketer may be able to identify dissatisfied segments for which it would be highly profitable to develop specific offerings.

Disadvantages of Segmentation

It is only to be expected that market segmentation may, particularly for companies which previously manufactured standard items for the mass market, prove to be more expensive.

(1) There may be higher R and D costs in order to develop different versions of the basic product.
(2) There will be shorter production runs and 'changeover' production costs since expensive plant and equipment may be idle as labour adapts machinery to produce different versions of the product.
(3) There may be higher inventory costs, since adequate stocks of a range of products will have to be held, whilst media costs may be higher through the loss of quantity discounts, as the advertising budget will have to be divided amongst several product types instead of one or two.
(4) The amount of management time and effort involved may be higher.

All this suggests that the costs of market segmentation can be greater than those associated with a standardised marketing approach. It is important, then, that the company ensures that the benefits of segmentation — such as greater competitive advantage and effectiveness of marketing operations — outweigh the possible costs, as outlined above.

Criteria for Market Segmentation

There are four criteria that, in theory, need to be satisfied in order for market segmentation to be worthwhile:

(1) it should be possible to identify clearly the individual members of segments;
(2) it should be possible to quantify the potential size of the market segment(s) in terms of possible sales revenues, costs and profits;
(3) the size of these markets should be *substantial* enough to make segmentation worthwhile;

(4) it should be possible to target the marketing effort specifically at the aimed-for segments. It is unlikely to be useful, for example, if a company, in order to communicate with its target audience, has to advertise in mass-circulation journals and newspapers.

Means of Segmenting the Consumer Market

The consumer market can be segmented using several variables, ranging from the more objective, such as demographic or economic factors, to the more subjective or inferred, like attitudes, personality and benefits sought. The variables employed can also be classified according to whether or not they are general or specific to particular situations. *General descriptors* are independent of the product and the circumstances faced by the customer when making buying or consumption decisions. *Specific descriptors* are based on situation-specific events such as the nature of the purchasers and users of particular products (heavy versus light users, brand-loyal versus non-brand-loyal users).

A matrix of the bases of segmentation can be drawn using the general or situation-specific nature of the variable, and the nature of the measurement procedure i.e. whether or not it is objective or inferred. Figure 2.4 depicts such a matrix and gives some of the bases that might be used.

	CUSTOMER CHARACTERISTICS	
	General	Situation specific
OBJECTIVE	Demographic Socio-economic	Usage patterns
INFERRED	Personality Life style	Attitudes Perceptions and preferences

Source: Adapted from Frank, Massey and Wind (1972).

Figure 2.4 *Bases for Segmenting the Consumer Market*

Objective Variables   The demographic variables which embrace age, sex, race and geographical location are the easiest to observe and measure and consequently tend to be frequently employed. Although some commentators are sceptical about their usefulness, it can be assumed that they give at least broad indications of preferences that, in the absence of anything more specific, can form a useful basis for the formulation of marketing strategy.

The socio-economic variables include social class and income. With regard to social class, it has been argued that it is most applicable in assisting in the identification of broad patterns of consumer behaviour, e.g. store choice, types of publications read. However,

> Mass marketers of consumer goods ... will probably find social class of little value in identifying market segments for their individual brands. As in demographic analysis, social class structure generally offers little insight into the factors that are associated with preference among brands in a product category. (Barnett (1969) p. 154)

It may be that there are appreciably different quantities of a product consumed by different groups. One popular theory assumes that half of the consumers account for around 80 per cent of sales. By identifying the characteristics of the 'heavy half' and the features they seek in the products they purchase, the manufacturer would be in a more favourable position with these consumers (Twedt 1964). However, focusing on the 'heavy half' may not necessarily be the most effective strategy: first, several manufacturers may be doing the same, in which case competition for this segment of the market may be intense. It might be more profitable, then, to concentrate on the 'light half'; or it may even be appropriate to assess what benefits non-users are seeking. Secondly, there is no reason to suppose that the 'heavy half' is uniform in its preference

> ... not all heavy consumers are usually available to the same brand — because they are not all seeking the same kinds of benefits from a product. For example, heavy coffee drinkers consist of two types of consumers — those who drink chain store brands and those who drink premium brands. The chain store customers feel that all coffees are basically alike and because they drink so much coffee they feel it is sensible to buy a relatively inexpensive brand. The premium brand buyers on the other hand, feel that the few added pennies (which the premium brands cost) are more than justified by their fuller taste. Obviously, these two groups of people, although they are both members of the 'heavy half' segment, are not equally good prospects for any one brand, nor can they be expected to respond to the same advertising claims. (Haley (1968) p. 31)

Inferred Variables   There is also a set of directly-unobservable variables which may affect consumers' purchasing actions and which,

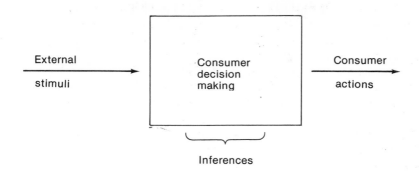

Figure 2.5 *The 'Black Box' of Consumer Decision Making*

therefore, can possibly be employed as a basis for segmentation. Since these are difficult to measure they have to be inferred, and consequently there is considerable scope for inaccuracy (see Figure 2.5). Included under this heading are personality, lifestyle, attitudes and perceptions. Considerable difficulties are being encountered in the application of these concepts, and therefore, of course, in satisfying the criteria for segmentation as outlined. Some have argued, though, that it may be possible to identify market targets using personality or life-style variables. For example, Kotler (1972) suggests that 'there are the *swingers*, who seek up-to-date goods and fast-paced, hedonistic living; *status seekers*, who try to buy goods that will reflect a high status in society; and *plain Joes*, who seek ordinary, unfrilled goods that do their job.' Such suggestions may be useful working hypotheses, and little more. It is difficult enough to classify individuals according to personality traits, and these problems are compounded when attempting to discern a relationship between extroverts, say, and their wants. It is not surprising, then, that attempts to classify consumers according to personality variables have met with little practical success.

An alternative approach to these traditional methods has been advanced. Termed **benefit segmentation**, it involves differentiating buyers not according to *a priori* notions of demographic or psychographic groups but more in relation to various benefits which buyers are seeking from particular products. Haley (1968, pp. 30–35) suggests that it might be possible to identify four segments in the toothpaste market — one particularly concerned with decay prevention, one with brightness of teeth, one with the flavour and appearance of the product, and one with price. He suggests that:

> *The decay prevention segment* contains a disproportionately large number of families with children. They are seriously concerned about the possibility of developing cavities and show a definite

preference for fluoride toothpaste. These individuals tend to be hypochondriacs. They are the worriers.

Brightness of teeth segment includes a relatively large group of young marrieds. They smoke more than average, and lead active lives. These are the sociables.

Flavour and appearance segment is one where a large proportion of the decisions regarding the brand is made by children. The use of spearmint toothpaste is well above average. They are more ego-centred than other segments. This is the sensory segment.

Price-oriented segment has a high proportion of men. It tends to be above average in terms of toothpaste usage. Brand loyalty is not a feature. In terms of personality, these people are more individualistic. This is the independent segment.

The identification of these segments could have significant implications for advertising copy and the choice of media. For example, one could expect to focus on the product for the sensory group, on socially-oriented situations for the sociable group, and perhaps on competitive comparisons for the independent group.

Further examples of benefit segmentation are given by Yankelovich (1964, pp. 83–90). For example, he suggests that it is possible to segment the market for watches along the following lines:

(1) people who want to pay the lowest possible price for any watch that works reasonably well;
(2) people who value watches for their long life, good workmanship, and superior styling;
(3) people who look not only for useful product features but also for meaningful emotional connotations (e.g. gift).

Research performed by Yankelovich suggested that the market for watches was distributed among the segments in the following way: segment (1), 23 per cent; segment (2), 46 per cent; and segment (3), 31 per cent. Socio-economic data would not have highlighted these segments since it was found that high-priced watches were purchased by both high- and low-income groups. High-income groups would often buy cheap watches which they would throw away when servicing was necessary. Timex noted that all the major watch companies were focusing on segment three, so it decided to aim its marketing at segment one, but in the process it also managed to capture segment two. The producers of the higher-priced watches had associated product quality with water resistance and shock resistance, but Timex was able to offer these features at a much lower price. Moreover, Timex advertised all the year round, and since the other watch companies focused on the Christmas period, Timex obtained exclusive attention for ten months of the year. The company quickly grew to become the dominant force in the United States watch market.

One final comment: it may be that the plethora of brands seen on the market may not be a consequence of planned segmentation strategies; rather, it may be manufacturers' response to the increasing consumer propensity for novelty. Indeed, one commentator (Reynolds (1965) pp. 107–111) has argued that in order to capitalise on the desire for novelty, manufacturers should aim at a 'variety strategy' – that is, at marketing a number of brands with a broad general appeal so that the probability of the consumer purchasing the company's own products is increased, given the assumed high state of flux in the market.

Industrial Market Segmentation

It is also possible to segment the industrial market. Among the more commonly used methods of segmentation might be: end users of the product; size of purchaser; and geographical location.

Summary

Markets are where marketers sell their products, and in this chapter five types of markets have been identified and examined. It is obvious that effective marketing is founded on having a good appreciation of the markets in which companies sell their products.

Both the consumer and industrial markets were examined. It was noted that both can be analysed according to a variety of criteria. For example, the consumer market can be considered in terms of households, distribution of income, and social class; whereas the industrial market can be viewed in terms of the nature of the industry and size of firms.

It has been shown that markets can be segmented, that is, divided into groups of organisations or individuals who have common set(s) of preferences. Market segmentation should enable the practical marketer to improve the effectiveness of his marketing operations. He should gain a greater understanding of particular groups of consumers, devise market offerings that cater specifically for their wants, and target his marketing specifically at these groups. Market segmentation can also assist in identifying untapped market opportunities.

Further Reading

Barnett, N. L. (1969) 'Beyond market segmentation', *Harvard Business Review,* January – February.

Frank, R. E., Massey, W. F. and Wind, Y. (1972) *Market Segmentation,* Prentice-Hall.

Haley, R. (1968) 'Benefit segmentation: a decision-oriented research tool', *Journal of Marketing,* July.

Joint Industry Committee for National Readership Surveys (1979) *National Readership Survey.*

Kotler, P. (1972) *Marketing Management: Analysis, Planning and Control,* Prentice-Hall.

Reynolds, W. H. (1965) 'More sense about market segmentation', *Harvard Business Review,* September/October.

Twedt, D. W. (1964) 'How important to marketing stratgegy is the 'heavy user'?' *Journal of Marketing,* January.

Webster, F. E. (Jnr.) and Wind. Y. (1972) *Organisational Buying Behaviour,* Prentice-Hall.

Wells, W. D. and Gubar, G. (1966) 'Life cycle concept in marketing research', *Journal of Marketing Research,* 3, November.

Yankelovich, D. (1964) 'New criteria for market segmentation', *Harvard Business Review,* March/April.

Review Questions

(1) List some institutional markets.

(2) What do you consider are the main differences between marketing to the industrial market and to the government market?

(3) What are some of the major trends in the consumer market? What new product opportunities are they likely to generate?

(4) What criteria would you employ for segmenting the market in the following cases:

    (a) a new newspaper
    (b) lorries
    (c) soaps for the consumer market
    (d) photocopiers

Appendix

Appendix 2.1(a) *Registrar General's Socio-Economic Groups*

---

1 Employers and managers in central and local government industry, commerce, etc − large establishments
2 Employers and managers in industry, commerce, etc − small establishments
3 Professional workers − self-employed
4 Professional workers − employees
5 Intermediate non-manual workers
6 Junior non-manual workers
7 Personal service workers
8 Foremen and supervisors − manual
9 Skilled manual workers
10 Semi-skilled manual workers
11 Unskilled manual workers
12 Own account workers (other than professional)
13 Farmers − employers and managers
14 Farmers − own account
15 Agricultural workers
16 Members of Armed Forces
17 Occupations inadequately described

Appendix 2.1(b)   *Corresponding Socio-Economic Groups*

General Household Survey socio-economic groupings		Groups	Examples
Number	Name		
1	Professional	3, 4	Doctors, lawyers, chemists, and clergymen
2	Employers and managers	1, 2, 13	Sales managers, MPs, colliery managers, personnel managers, senior government officials, and farmers
3N	Intermediate and junior non-manual	5, 6	Nurses, physiotherapists, sales representatives, clerical workers, typists, telephone operators, and shop assistants
3M	Skilled manual (including foremen and supervisors) including own account, non-professionals	8, 9, 12, 14	Railway guards, foremen packers, foremen in engineering and allied trades, and bricklayers
5	Semi-skilled manual and personal service	7, 10, 15	Cooks, canteen assistants, barmen, and bus conductors
6	Unskilled manual	11	Lorry drivers' mates, labourers, stevedores, and office cleaners

Shoppers depart: the impact of wintry weather on demand

3

Demand

*As if a woman of education bought things because
she wanted 'em*

(*Sir John Vanbrugh*, The Confederacy)

*Consumer wants can have bizarre, frivolous or
even immoral origins*

(*J. K. Galbraith*, The Affluent Society)

The marketer will be interested in understanding the factors underlying demand for at least three main reasons:

(1) One of his aims will be to at least maintain his company's position in the market place, and generally to increase its profits.
(2) He will be interested in identifying opportunities for new products, and some grasp of the trend in factors influencing demand will aid him in this.
(3) He will be interested in forecasting demand.

Demand and sales forecasting is important in its own right for making a range of strategic and operational decisions.

This chapter commences with discussion of the differences between potential, latent, and realisable demand, and continues with an examination of the major factors influencing demand. These, it will be seen, can be divided into two major types: those over which the firm has no control, such as government policy, the level of income, and an important group of influences on consumer behaviour which will be collectively termed the psycho-social factors; and those which the firm controls directly, these being, in essence, the 'marketing mix' variables.

Potential, Latent and Existing Demand

Synfibre, a large manufacturer of a range of synthetic yarns for the textile industry, was faced with a decline in the rate of increase of sales in its traditional markets as the maximum demand or *market potential* was reached. In considering other outlets for its fibres, it eventually focused on the carpet market since it concluded that the potential market, £X over the next ten years, was likely to be substantial. Its *forecast* indicated that total sales over the next five years would amount to £0.3X. There would thus be a considerable *latent demand*. Given the price and technical qualities of its products, together with the company's excellent reputation, it was concluded that by year 5 its *market share* would equal 25 per cent. Whilst undertaking these detailed market investigations, Synfibre identified a possible new market opportunity for a stain-resistant carpet, and it consequently initiated a development programme aimed at producing a treatment that would give its existing fibres liquid-repellent properties.

It can be seen that there are significant differences between the commonly employed terms 'market potential', 'latent demand', 'market forecast' and 'market share'.

Market Demand

Market demand for a product is the amount that could be purchased per year in a defined geographical area, for a specified environment and for specified marketing effort. Two terms used in this definition demand some explanation. First, **the environment** refers to the economic, social, technological and legal influences which can be expected to affect demand. As we shall see in Chapter 4, a company will make assumptions about the general conditions under which it will be operating in the future. Second, **marketing effort** embraces all those stimuli which a company may employ to increase total demand for the product(s) and, in particular, demand for its own product(s). It embraces the marketing policies it adopts on, for instance, pricing levels, advertising expenditures and distribution levels. Marketing effort can be said to have several dimensions including:

(a) the expenditure on marketing;
(b) the way this is allocated between the different elements of the marketing mix (for example, the emphasis given to advertising as against price) and
(c) the effectiveness of these allocations.

As the marketing effort increases, the market demand will generally increase. Eventually, there will be a limit to the number of customers

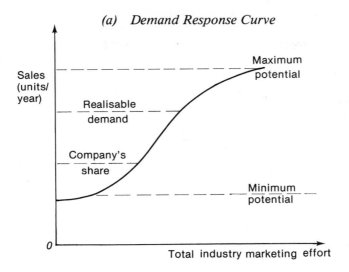

(a)   Demand Response Curve

(b)   Realisable Demand, Market Potential and Company Share

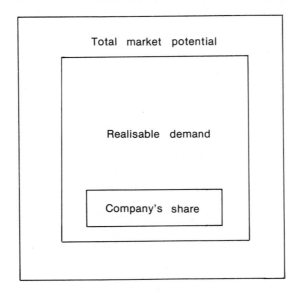

Figure 3.1

willing and able to purchase, and to the amount each wishes to purchase. This is termed the **market potential**. Figure 3.1(a) gives a total demand response curve showing sales for various levels of industry marketing effort.

This then is the maximum amount that could be purchased. In the case of the preceding example, the market potential for synthetic fibres in the textile industry would have been reached if all the textile manufacturers equipped to use Synfibre's fibres had employed them in the manufacture of all those products for which synthetic fibres were feasible. In practice, market potential will rarely, if ever, be achieved. But the assessment of market potential can be a useful starting point when considering the 'worthwhileness' of a new venture. It is important to recognise that market potential is a dynamic concept: it can change with time and with economic conditions. For example, the potential in a recession may be significantly different from the potential in a boom (see Figure 3.2).

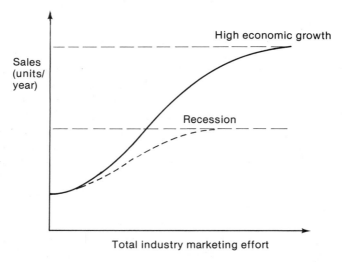

Figure 3.2 *Market Potential in High Economic Growth and Recession*

The demand that is actually realised in total will depend not only on the total marketing effort of the industry, but also on consumers' willingness and ability to buy. In addition, there will often be a considerable residual of potential customers who, for various reasons, do not purchase; the most potent explanation is that they lack the necessary income, although dissatisfaction with the nature of the existing products on the market is a further possible cause. Marketers may be able to 'mobilise' this latent demand: Synfibre, for instance, found that there was a considerable potential latent demand for a stain-resistant carpet fibre.

Where there are several firms competing, a company's share of the market will be a function of its own particular marketing effort (see

Figure 3.1(*b*)). Synfibre, for example, believed that it would obtain a significant proportion of the market, based on not only the superior qualities of its product, but also its reputation for service and delivery.

As will be shown, many companies strive to predict the level of future demand. Such a market forecast will be based on various assumptions about its own and competitors' marketing programmes.

'Apparent' Demand

The fact that there is a forecasted, large, potential demand does not inevitably lead to the conclusion that the market is highly attractive for a particular firm. First, only a small proportion of the total potential may be converted into realisable demand. Secondly, for various reasons, the company's eventual market share may be too small to make its entry into that market commercially viable. For instance, the prospect of a large potential market may act as a magnet for other companies: competition may be intense, with the result that the market share available to any one company will be much smaller than originally anticipated. A more likely outcome, though, is that large companies will drive out smaller companies, often by employing severe price-cutting and aggressive-selling tactics. Thirdly, the market may be subject to 'in-feeding' and 'reciprocal trading', both of which can mean that the available market is smaller than it first appeared.

In-feeding exists when companies satisfy their own requirements for raw materials, components, and so on. Such 'in-fed' markets are, understandably, particularly resilient to attack from outside suppliers. The market available to 'outsider' companies may be significantly circumscribed. For example, in the case of the market for hydraulic cylinders in the UK, the total market value was £25.7 million but of this, £19.7 million was provided by the same companies which used them, leaving an 'open' market value of only £6.0 million (Wilson and Atkin (1976) pp. 117–127).

In the case of reciprocal trading, companies enter into agreements to purchase goods and services from each other and this can similarly result in a more restricted market opportunity than was at first apparent.

Industrial Demand

An important feature of industrial demand is that it ultimately depends on consumer demand, and in that sense it is said to be 'derived'. Therefore, when assessing the demand for their products, manufacturers need to trace the chain of demand. Thus, the manufacturers of integrated circuits will, in many cases, sell these to manufacturers of

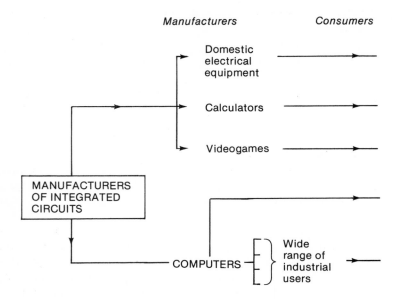

Figure 3.3   *Derived Demand*

electronic goods, many of which will then be sold directly to consumers (see Figure 3.3). In the case of other products, such as computers, the relationship with consumer demand is more subtle. In the case of computers used by banks, it can be seen that the size and quantity required will be a function of such variables as the number of bank accounts and the number of financial transactions.

It is also worth noting that certain classes of capital goods are bulky and expensive and are purchased infrequently. They are often manufactured as batch items. Bulk tankers and electrical generating plant are extreme examples. These types of goods raise special problems, a particular example is the problem of ensuring a steady stream of orders to prevent peaks of demand followed by significant lags that can only generate production difficulties.

Factors Affecting Demand

From what has been noted so far, it is apparent that there are many factors stimulating and moulding demand. For simplicity, these can be divided into two broad categories:

Exogenous factors: those which are external to the firm and over which the manufacturer has little, if any, control;
Endogenous factors: those which the manufacturer can manipulate

and which will directly influence the manufacturer's share of the total demand.

Exogenous Factors

Many of these external influences on demand have already been described. They embrace demographics; macro-economic variables; income; legislation; competition; and the social and psychological factors affecting consumer purchasing behaviour.

The aggregate demand for all goods is clearly dependent on the total population, but as was clear from Chapter 2, the pattern of demand is a function of the structure of the population in terms of age, culture, and geographical distribution. For instance, the presence of sizeable ethnic minorities in certain parts of the country constitutes an important market for certain classes of products. In any case, tastes and preferences can vary quite significantly from one region of the country to another. The picture of the Northener as a lover of black puddings, tripe and strong ale may be a wide generalisation, but such stereotype depictions have usually a strong basis in fact. Manufacturers who ignore regional differences and treat the UK market as uniform in some instances do so at their peril.

The Case of Walker's Warrington Ale[1]

In autumn 1979, Tetley Walker launched Walker's Warrington Ale in the Merseyside and Warrington areas. This was a new high gravity beer (which at 1,043° was well above the average specific gravity of beers sold in the North West). It was sold at a premium price in 200 Tetley Walker pubs as well as in some other outlets, and it was marketed as a beer that would 'recapture the days of dancing, gaslight, the rattle of horses' hooves and carriage wheels over cobbled streets . . .' Tetley seemed to have believed that it would be an inevitable success and the beer was not test marketed to ascertain consumers' reactions before its launch. Perhaps the company was persuaded by the knowledge that beers of similar strengths and prices had been accepted well in the South. By the summer of 1981, the beer had been withdrawn from many of its original outlets, and its sale was restricted to some largely business and tourist Liverpool City Centre pubs, some Wirral commuter belt pubs, and to a few pubs in Southport and Blackpool. In November 1981, the beer was withdrawn completely. A Director of the Campaign for Real Ale suggested that it was: 'The wrong beer, in the wrong area at the wrong time; too strong and too expensive for Merseyside in a time of depression.' The lesson is that what might be acceptable in the relatively affluent South East, may not necessarily go down well in the North West.

1. Adapted from '*Mersey Drinker*' (1981).

> In a recent study, Nielsen found that there were interesting regional differences in the consumption of selected product classes. In general, it concluded that 'Southerners have a penchant for cream, natural cheese, mustard and sausages, whereas Northerners use more stock cubes, packaged processed cheese, canned soups and canned mince and soya.' (Nielsen 1981)

A second major influence on demand is the state of the economy. It has already been seen that the market potential for products will be different in a recession than in a boom (see Figure 3.2); products such as automobiles, clothing, furniture, and electrical equipment can be expected to be purchased less, whilst there will be a general trading down from expensive merchandise when there is a downturn in the economy. A further interesting phenomenon is the tendency for people to save more during a period of economic uncertainty. This unwillingness to spend can have a traumatic impact on demand.

On a micro-level, a further important determinant of demand is income: consumers must be willing *and* able to purchase. It would appear reasonable to assume that as consumers' disposable income increases, a smaller proportion will be spent on basic necessities, such as food, housing, and clothing. In fact, this is not invariable; for example, if inflation in the cost of building construction is higher than the increase in the Retail Price Index as such, consumers may be compelled to increase the share of their income to housing just to maintain the *status quo*. The general trend is increasingly supplemented by credit, which is more easily available. Actual purchasing power can, then, be considerably more than suggested by income. The widespread adoption of credit cards, has, to quote the Access advertising slogan, taken the 'waiting out of wanting'. Figure 3.4 shows a tenfold increase in the number of transactions using a credit card between 1971 and 1979. It is estimated that credit cards are currently used in over 250 million transactions a year with a total value of approximately £9,000 million.

Legislation can also have a significant impact on demand, both directly and indirectly. For example, changes in the way in which tax was levied on cigarettes made larger cigarettes relatively cheaper and stimulated the demand for king-size brands, much to the chagrin of Imperial Tobacco which had previously had a dominant share of the market through its sale of small cigarettes. Another illustration is where government specifications for anti-pollution control have stimulated research and development by the automobile manufacturers and their suppliers, and generated a new market for pollution control equipment. A further example is government information campaigns, such as that devised and financed by the Department of Energy focusing on means of saving energy, and hence money, in the wake of the substantial increases in the price of oil. This campaign

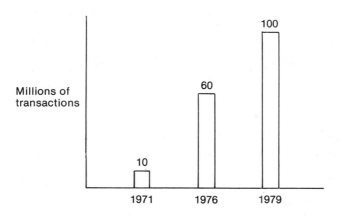

Source: Inter-Bank Research Organisation

Figure 3.4 *Number of Transactions by Credit Card in Great Britain*

has, undoubtedly, heightened consumer awareness and aided in stimulating demand for various means of domestic and industrial insulation.

An obvious and often adverse effect on the sales of an individual manufacturer stems from the actions of competitors, and unfortunately these are often unpredictable. A company can invest substantial sums in the development of a new product which it forecasts will attain a high level of profitability rapidly, only to see its prospects undermined by the launch of a superior innovation, developed clandestinely by a major competitor. Apart from the secret development of new products, competitors may, and often do, adopt a variety of quite legitimate tactics to prevent companies making inroads into what they traditionally regard as *their* markets: for example, they may initiate a price war in the belief that the new rival will not be able to sustain losses for more than a short period; they may embark on a widespread advertising campaign or commence an aggressive promotional programme, offering dealers significant discounts. Even when competitors have lived alongside one another for many years in established markets, one company may suddenly change its policy with regard to its existing product lines. Certainly, when considering future policies, manufacturers should direct careful attention to the prediction of the possible range of actions of their competitors (something which experience suggests not enough do sufficiently).

It is now widely accepted that the consumer's demand for goods is also affected by a myriad of, what might be termed, behavioural and social factors. These include:

(a) personality; for example, an introvert might have different tastes and preferences to an extrovert;
(b) culture; for example, someone from West Africa can be expected to have different priorities and some different wants to someone from Australia;
(c) motivation; these are the so-called, often unconscious, internal drives that underlie much of our behaviour;
(d) perception; for example, people with different beliefs and attitudes can interpret the same phenomena differently;
(e) social influences, such as friends, work colleagues, and family; for example, there are strong pressures to conform to a standard behaviour pattern set by family, friends and acquaintances.

The above are just some of the 'behavioural' influences that collectively are included under the umbrella of 'consumer behaviour'. This has become one of the major areas of study in marketing in recent years.

Endogenous Factors

Those factors which are under the direct control of the firm are, in essence, the **marketing mix** variables or the four Ps of price, promotion, place and product.

Price has, of course, been traditionally regarded as the paramount factor influencing demand, although later advertising was also accorded an important role. However, there is considerable evidence that, for certain markets, what have been termed the 'non-price' factors — design, technical performance, delivery, reliability, durability and service support — can have a significant impact on demand. Through the 1970s, the average value per tonne of our engineering exports fell below that for Germany and France. NEDO noted that:

> Since their (France and Germany) export shares have tended to rise whereas ours have fallen over the period covered, this suggests that our products are not as good as theirs in some or all of the following ways — range and design, quality, product reliability, technical specification, delivery dates, back-up service. In other words, the 'non-price' factors and not price are the prime consideration in many markets. Where these factors are given insufficient attention companies will lose business to overseas competitors. (National Economic Development Office 1977)

To rely on price at the expense of these other variables, as many UK manufacturers have tended to do, may not lead to the anticipated favourable results. The dramatic decline of the UK's share of the world market for manufactured goods may be caused, in no small part, by the failure to be sufficiently innovative and meet the expectations of potential customers on delivery dates, technical service, and so on.

To be effective in the market, manufacturers are likely to deploy the full range of these non-price factors to differentiate their products in some way from those of their competitors. They provide a personal service, or, at the other extreme, aim to be at the forefront of technology and offer customers innovative products. Thus, a company such as Philips have tried to establish a reputation for being 'simply light-years ahead' and have supported their claims by spending heavily on research and development and producing a stream of advanced electronic products.

Companies producing basically similar products have to be even more astute in the use of the marketing mix variables to differentiate their products.

> The marketer of petrol is faced with formidable problems in trying to maintain and even increase its share of a declining market. To many customers 'petrol is petrol', even though some petroleum companies have tried to claim otherwise. Other approaches have been to build a strong corporate image (as was the case with ESSO with its tiger campaign). Most of the major companies, however, have now adopted a strategy of extending the role of traditional petrol stations to that of motorists' shops, offering a wide range of attractive merchandise in an attempt to counteract the threats from the small maverick companies.

Sensitivity of Demand

Companies will strive to focus on those factors most sensitive to demand in their target market segments. They would thus like to know the elasticity of demand to various influences.

The notion of **price elasticity of demand** is likely to be the most familiar. This is defined as:

$$PE_d = - \frac{\% \text{ change in quantity demanded}}{\% \text{ change in price}}$$

at some defined point in time. When PE_d is less than one, then demand is said to be *inelastic*. In this case, if price is increased, the volume of sales will fall, but total revenue will increase. If the PE_d is greater than one, demand is said to be *elastic*; this means that if price is increased, sales volume will fall and will result in a reduction in revenue. Some products may be regarded as basic necessities and will be relatively unresponsive to changes in prices; but where a product has close substitutes, then there is a tendency for the PE_d to be highly elastic. The demand for butter and margarine would fall into this category.

By employing the marketing mix variables to differentiate the product, marketers are obviously striving not only to shift the demand curve outwards, but also to steepen the demand curve and make PE_d relatively inelastic. They will need to adopt policies which are most effective not only in reducing the price elasticity of demand, but also in generating high demand responsiveness in their own right. For example, marketers considering, say, the increase of expenditure on advertising, can be expected to want to know the likely impact on sales. Figure 3.5 depicts a possible advertising–sales response curve.

$$\text{Elasticity of advertising expenditure} = \frac{\% \text{ change in demand at time (T + N)}}{\% \text{ change in advertising expenditure at time T}}$$

where (T + N) is some time after T.

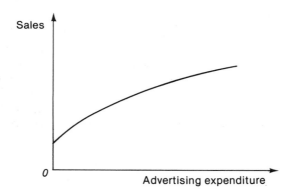

Figure 3.5   *Sales to Advertising Response Curve*

Some classes of products may have a high advertising elasticity, particularly fast-moving, consumer products. But in many cases, there will be some delay in the sales response, as consumers, for a variety of reasons, may take some time to react to the change in expenditure on advertising. For example, a reduction in advertising expenditure will not necessarily lead to immediate changes in sales volume, for there may well be a considerable 'carry-over' effect from previous expenditures.

The manufacturer will be similarly interested in the responsiveness of sales to the other endogenous variables. There may, however, be some degree of interaction between the variables, in which case the marketer will need to ascertain the demand elasticity of different marketing mix 'sets'.

Since demand is also vulnerable to a wide range of exogenous factors, the marketer would also, ideally, be interested in:

(a) the income elasticity of demand;
(b) the cross elasticity of demand for various products, since this is an indication of the degree of complementarity and substitutability of products.

For example:

$$\text{Cross elasticity of demand for margarine and butter} = \frac{\%\text{ change in demand for butter}}{\%\text{ change in price for margarine}}$$

In summary, then, the company's sales are dependent on an array of factors, and those within its direct control are not necessarily the primary determinants of demand. Competitors' responses and other external influences can have a dramatic impact. In making assessments about future sales, marketers may have to anticipate possible competitors' reactions, make certain assumptions about the degree of responsiveness of demand to the various possible marketing mixes, and so on. The estimation of demand resulting from various marketing mixes in each set of environmental conditions would indeed be a formidable task. It would not be surprising, then, if many managers were to adopt a form of decision-making behaviour that is a judicious mix of intuition and experience, founded on the principle: 'concentrate on what one can quantify, and ignore what one cannot'.

Demand Assessment

A large food manufacturer is considering whether or not it should proceed with the development of a new convenience food product. In order to make its decision, it would like to have some information on the probable future sales of the product, given various assumptions about price and the degree of marketing effort.

The manufacturer of televisions for the domestic market makes annual forecasts of the sales of sets so that it can plan its production between colour and black and white television.

The sales manager of a producer of kitchen equipment makes estimates of the likely pattern of sales for the range, for different geographical regions, so that he can set appropriate sales targets for each member of his salesforce.

In the early 1960s, the brewery companies were concerned with assessing the way in which lager sales would develop, the ultimate stable share of the market they would reach, and the impact this would have on the sales of other beers. Such information had obvious implications for the extent and timing of investment in plant and equipment and was necessary if companies wanted to take advantage of this new opportunity (as well as maintaining their share of the total beer market), particularly as it takes some years before new brewing capacity comes 'on stream'.

From the above examples, it is clear that the assessment of future demand is important for a wide range of decisions, both long- and short-term, involving *strategic* issues such as whether or not to invest in new business areas, and *operational* issues on the management of existing businesses. Perhaps the most important reason why forecasting of future sales is important is that, in the short term, it determines the future level of activity of the company (for example, level of production), whilst in the longer term it affects the total allocation of resources of the company between different business areas.

Most companies make annual sales forecasts which are then monitored on a regular basis to see if predictions meet actual sales. If not, remedial action may have to be taken. These forecasts act as a basis for deciding on the level of production and stocks, manpower requirements, the level of marketing expenditure, and so on. Longer-term forecasts, made for several years ahead, can be used to identify the trends in demand for the company's products and will assist in making capital investment decisions and the shifting of effort from, for instance, low-growing or declining products to new, or higher-growth products.

Forecasting, then, can assist in minimising the possibility of two costly errors: the *outlay* error, where the company incurs costs as a result of a production level which is too high because of optimistic predictions of demand; and *opportunity* costs because an over-pessimistic evaluation of future sales prospects led to a failure to invest in sufficient capacity to enable demand to be satisfied (perhaps giving competitors an opportunity to take up some, if not all, the additional demand), or even to a failure to develop a new product, which was then successfully developed by another company.

To summarise the discussion on the applications of demand assessment, it can be seen that it is important for three main reasons:

(1) The analysis of market opportunities. Thus, when evaluating whether or not it will be sufficiently remunerative for the company to invest in a particular product, it will be necessary to have some indication of the potential sales, the realisable demand, and the firm's market share.

(2) The planning of marketing effort. Forecasts of sales for each of the company's products will be invaluable in the allocation of its resources.

(3) Control of marketing performance. Sales attainable can be monitored and compared with forecasted targets. Significant shortfalls may indicate a need for urgent managerial action.

Assumptions Underlying Forecasting

In general, forecasts of future sales rest on three assumptions: an interrelationship between the variables; stability; and manageability.

The first major assumption is that there exists a relationship between the variable that is being forecasted, usually sales, and another variable, called the independent variable. This second variable is usually 'time'. Typical examples of such relationships are the variation of population, or gross national product or energy consumption with time. The fact that a relationship between variables may be discerned does not imply causation; in many cases, the independent variable simply varies consistently with the dependent variable. There may be no understanding of why it appears to do so.

A further basis for forecasting is the assumption that the relationship between the variables either remains constant over time, or that it changes in a way that can be anticipated. In practice, this may be rather naive; as we shall see, uncertainty about the future is prevalent and experience indicates that circumstances can change dramatically from year to year.

Finally, it is assumed that the relationship between the variables can be summarised in easily comprehensible and manipulative mathematical formulae and that data for feeding into such models are available at reasonable cost.

Some Difficulties

There are problems in sales forecasting: the major difficulty stems from the uncertainty that inevitably clouds the future. Events can arise unexpectedly, and circumstances change in unpredicted ways. A traumatic example was the substantial increase in oil prices in the wake of the 1973 Arab−Israeli War. This had a significant impact on all those businesses that had grown accustomed to large supplies of cheap oil. It also, of course, created new business opportunities. The assumption of stability is, therefore, somewhat dubious.

It is not surprising, then, that there is some considerable inaccuracy in forecasting. For example, one study of the sales forecasts for 63 new products, and of the earnings for 53 of them, found that only approximately one in four of the sales forecasts and one in six of the earnings forecasts for the first year were within 10 per cent of those actually obtained. The results for the full planning period — an average of three years — were little better. The median error for sales forecasts was 26 per cent and for earnings forecasts was 46 per cent (Tull (1967) p. 249).

Forecasts are very much dependent on the individuals making them and this introduces a major source of error. Estimates made internally by the company's analysts are subjected to the biases of the forecasters; but, given experience of their performance in the past, it may be possible to make appropriate allowance for these (by, for example, reducing the forecasts of consistently optimistic forecasters by some factor). It is also important to have an appreciation of the political context of the decision for which the forecast is made. For example, those seeking approval for a new product development programme may overestimate its sales in order to cast the project in a more favourable light. Salesmen may also be tempted to make optimistic forecasts of sales, in order to ensure that there will be plentiful supplies for their customers.

Sales do not, of course, proceed independently of any stimulus or impediment; rather, they are a consequence of many extraneous and endogenous factors. In particular, as has already been noted, a company's actual sales are affected by marketing effort and forecasters should, at least, take into account the projected marketing expenditure when estimating future sales.

Forecasting Techniques

In selecting the appropriate forecasting method, the analyst needs to take into account:

(a) the form of the forecast: a trend; a range of sales forecasts giving various degrees of likelihood; a forecast for a particular year, etc;
(b) the accuracy specified;
(c) the accessibility of the data required by the techniques;
(d) the time he has available to make the forecast.

A variety of methods are available, ranging from simple subjective estimates of future demand to those involving the formulation and manipulation of complex mathematical models. Given the uncertainty, it is possible to improve estimates by employing several forecasting techniques, comparing and contrasting the results obtained and carefully analysing the possible reasons for any wide discrepancies. Figure 3.6 depicts the various stages that might be involved in making a forecast.

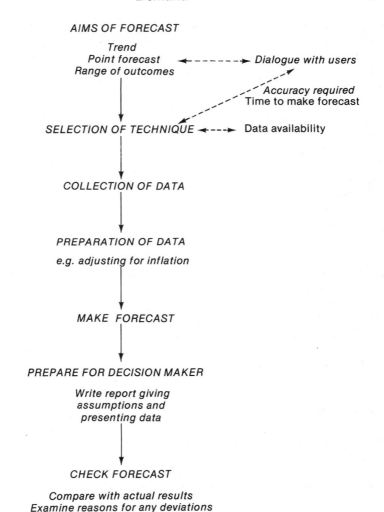

Figure 3.6   *Forecasting Methodology*

At least four main forecasting techniques can be identified:

(1) Judgement
(2) Time series
(3) Surveys
(4) Correlations

Judgement Forecasts

These are based on an assessment by one or more individuals, who usually work within the company. They tend to involve little if any systematic analysis, and are highly subjective. Often, they are made by a senior employee of the company (such as the chairman or managing director) who becomes enthusiastic about a particular project.

> The vice-president of the Cessna-Aircraft company believed that there was a significant, but unexploited, demand for a twin-engined plane 'with US power plants mounted in tandem instead of laterally as in conventional designs. (This would prevent asymmetrical thrust, thereby reducing the hazards of flying with one engine out.)' However, market assessments, made using rigorous forecasting techniques, did not support his judgement. Nevertheless, the company developed the plane, but sales did not achieve the predicted level. The executive argued that the responsibility for this shortfall was the design of the aircraft. This was accepted by the company, suitable design modifications were made − 'the incorporation of retractable landing gear' − and sales subsequently increased to the level forecasted. 'The model became − for a time − the most successful product in the firm's line.' (Wentz 1972)

It is argued that assessments based on judgement are the best that can be achieved in the case of radically new products where there is no previous experience on which to make a forecast. But it is probably as well to supplement in-company judgement forecasts with estimates made by outside experts, market research, and so on. The use of this multi-assessment approach will increase in value with the expected investment in the development of the new product. Moreover, there are always problems in autocratic organisations when expenditure plans are made on the basis of the opinion of the 'top man', who may be unwilling to concede that his 'pet' project is a failure. There will be no basis for questioning the original assumptions, and this can often lead to costly mistakes for the company.

Time Series Analysis

By plotting sales over time, generally a trend (one hopes, upwards) can often be detected. A forecast could be made by extrapolating past trends. This is often termed a 'naive' forecast, since it is based on the assumption that the future is a continuation of the past; but, as has already been noted, the socio-economic environment is highly dynamic, and significant changes, having dramatic impacts on demand, can occur from one period to the next. A second point worth noting is that there can often be considerable 'noise' surrounding the true trend line, and this 'noise' will have to be removed.

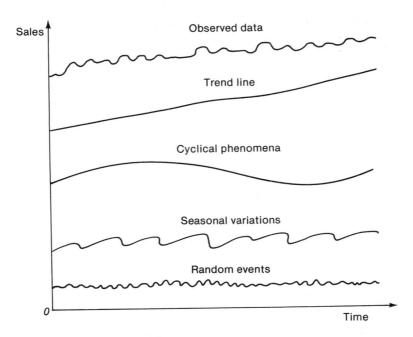

Sales

Observed data

Trend line

Cyclical phenomena

Seasonal variations

Random events

0

Time

Figure 3.7 *Time Series Analysis*

As can be seen from Figure 3.7, the observed data are composed of several phenomena:

trend is the pattern of sales over the long term;
cyclical (where cyclical phenomena are defined as being more than one year in duration) usually relates to the business cycle;
seasonal is the variation of sales over the year; for example, the sales of ice cream, soft drinks and lager will attain their peaks in the summer;
random covers the unpredictable, irregular events which can affect sales. These events include strikes, adverse weather, wars, etc.

Consequently, if the decision maker requires a long-term forecast, it is important to remove these other influences in order to obtain just the trend line, and a means of doing this has been devised. If short-term forecasts are required − such as the likely demand during the next three months − seasonal variations will have to be added back into the trend line, where these are an important influence.

Surveys

It is often possible to canvass groups of people either on their *opinions* of future sales or on whether or not they intend to purchase the particular product(s).

Three main sources of information are:

(1) the salesforce
(2) experts
(3) potential customers

The salesforce's opinions on future sales can be a valuable starting point, since they will tend to have good personal contact with purchasers, and therefore have a grasp of their future purchasing intentions. Salesmen, by their very nature, can tend to be optimistic, and may be too inexperienced about new products to be able to give a reliable forecast.

In certain cases, it may be appropriate to consult a body of experts – those who have a detached and comprehensive understanding of the industry. Consultations can range from unstructured discussions with a handful of experts, to a well-planned and structured 'Delphi' forecast. In essence, the latter involves an iterative procedure whereby selected experts are asked independently for the sales forecast for a particular time. The mean and median of all the estimates are then calculated, and the results fed back to the participants for their views. The process may be repeated (sometimes several times) until a general consensus emerges on these estimates (see Figure 3.8).

A final survey method involves simply asking, by personal interview or mail questionnaire, whether or not people will purchase the product(s) and in what quantities. Unfortunately, expressed intention to purchase is not necessarily a reliable guide to actual purchases for several reasons:

(1) circumstances may alter during the intervening period; for instance, rival products may be introduced, or discretionary income may change;
(2) in surveys, consumers may make a spontaneous response with little consideration. Upon reflection, their attitudes towards the product may change; they may be dissuaded after consultation with other members of the household, and so on;
(3) interviewees may give a response aimed at pleasing the interviewer. Such biases in surveys are now well acknowledged and are considered in more detail in Chapter 5.

Correlations

From a detailed examination of past data, it may be possible to discern a correlation between sales and one or other easily measurable variables. By statistically determining the nature of the relationship, this can be used as a basis for prediction, particularly if there is a time lapse between the independent variable(s) and sales.

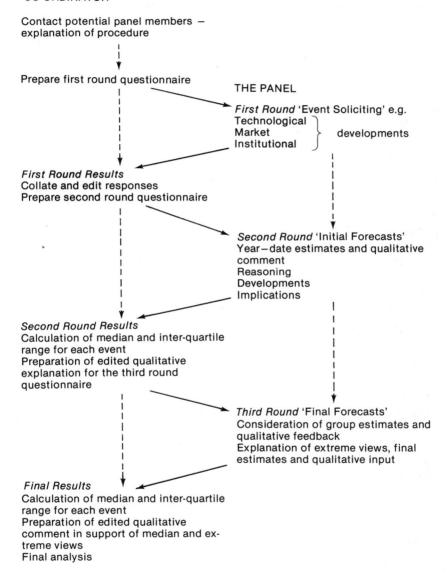

CO-ORDINATOR

Contact potential panel members —
explanation of procedure

Prepare first round questionnaire

THE PANEL

First Round 'Event Soliciting' e.g.
Technological
Market   } developments
Institutional

First Round Results
Collate and edit responses
Prepare second round questionnaire

Second Round 'Initial Forecasts'
Year–date estimates and qualitative
comment
Reasoning
Developments
Implications

Second Round Results
Calculation of median and inter-quartile
range for each event
Preparation of edited qualitative
explanation for the third round
questionnaire

Third Round 'Final Forecasts'
Consideration of group estimates and
qualitative feedback
Explanation of extreme views, final
estimates and qualitative input

Final Results
Calculation of median and inter-quartile
range for each event
Preparation of edited qualitative
comment in support of median and extreme views
Final analysis

Figure 3.8 *Flow Chart for the Delphi Forecast Using Three 'Rounds'*

Econometric Models

In the last few years, there have been considerable advances in the simulation of economic and market situations using mathematical models. Put simply, these models attempt to represent, in the form of a series of mathematical equations, the behaviour of the UK economy, or the housing market, or the demand for specific products, etc. The often complex mathematical formulae frequently hide a plethora of subjective assumptions about the relationships between the variables. Moreover, since many important influences are not directly measurable, surrogate factors are often employed; many of the variables substituted may be inappropriate.

Summary

A distinction has been drawn between potential and realisable demand. The factors influencing total demand and a company's share of the demand have been examined. These were divided into exogenous, (those beyond the direct influence of the company), and endogenous, (those which embrace the marketing mix variables). Various techniques for forecasting demand have been discussed, but it was noted that none guarantees a reliable forecast, mainly because of the high degree of uncertainty that surrounds the future.

Further Reading

National Economic Development Office (1977) *A Look at the Industrial Strategy: A Plan for Action.*
Nielsen Researcher (1981) No. 2, A.C. Nielsen Company Ltd.
'Mersey Drinker' (1981) Vol. 6, Nos. 2 and 5.
Tull, D.S. (1967) 'The relationship of predicted to actual sales and profits of new product introductions', *The Journal of Business*, Vol. 44.
Wentz, W.B. (1972) *Marketing Research: Management and Methods*, Harper and Row.
Wilson, A. and Atkin, B. (1976) *Harvard Business Review*, September – October.

Review Questions

(1) A manufacturer of consumer products reduces his advertising expenditure and notes that the sales of his products continue to rise.

He concludes that this reduction in advertising has had little effect on the demand for his products, and decides to reduce advertising further. Give your comments.

(2) What factors will affect the future market demand for:
(a) sewage-treatment plant?
(b) lead additive in petrol?

(3) What do you think will be the effect of:
(a) a reduction in the price of potatoes on the demand for (i) potato crisps and (ii) chocolate bars?
(b) an increase in the price of tea on the demand for coffee?
(c) a large reduction in income tax on the demand for frozen foods?

(4) How would you go about assessing the potential demand for:
(a) video-disc players
(b) micro-computers
(c) vegetable oils
(d) glass bottles

(5) The marketing manager of a manufacturer of consumer durables is proposing to undertake a survey of proposed intentions to purchase consumer durables as the foundation of its sales forecast. Give your comments.

Deciding corporate strategy: a meeting of the Board

4

Supply: Marketing Strategy and Organisation

"In case anything turned up",
which was his favourite expression.

(*Mr. Micawber in* David Copperfield)

Many of the companies found on the industrial landscape are complex systems, employing a diverse range of technologies and supplying a rich array of products for many different markets; they have generally evolved over many years, often by accretion and often haphazardly. Many others are small, producing a limited range of products for specific segments of the markets. Whatever the company's size, it is argued that it should make well-considered decisions on the markets it should be in and the specific offerings it should make, as part of a systematic regular process; this is generally referred to as *strategic planning*. It involves setting targets for the company as a whole and delineating the means of attaining these, based on a thorough analysis of the relative competitive attributes of the company and on various assumptions about the nature of the future environment. These details are generally included in a written document, called the corporate plan, which acts as a blueprint for corporate action. Marketing has an important part to play in the process, not only in supplying inputs to the analysis of the marketing environment of the company but also in defining the strategic options open to the company. The marketing plan describes the marketing objectives, strategies and specific tactics for the agreed products and markets. This chapter discusses both the process of formulating corporate strategy and the role of marketing in its implementation. The final section of this chapter considers means of organising the marketing department to ensure the effective co-ordination of the disparate marketing activities in order to meet the established corporate and market criteria.

The Concept of Corporate Strategy

It is widely acknowledged that successful companies generally have clearly-articulated goals and means of achieving these:

> Plessey is in the fast-moving area of electronics. It regards itself as being in 'integrated information technology', which is the 'convergence of communications and electronic data processing which has developed largely as a result of microelectronics'. Within this, it has defined its business as embracing 'a wide spectrum taking in telecommunications, military radio, radar, sonar, special processors, control and command systems especially for defence, avionics and modern office systems. (Plessey's) business is directed mainly towards the supply of high-technology equipment and systems to public purchasing authorities rather than consumer markets'. It has established high growth objectives (during the year 1980 to 1981 its pre-tax profits increased by 40.7 per cent), and it regards the continued development of new products as the means of satisfying these; this demands a high level of investment in research and development. (Plessey Annual Report 1981)

The essence of **corporate strategy** is in developing clear business philosophies, defining specific measurable objectives for future sales or profits, selecting markets, and finally deciding on the types of products that enable companies to compete most effectively within these markets.

Corporate Strategy: A Definition

The notion of corporate strategy has its origins in the military. In general, military strategy could be said to be:

> ... most simply the positioning of armed forces on the battlefield to accomplish the defeat of the enemy. Less simply, it is the deployment of resources against an enemy in pursuit of goals prescribed by the leaders of the state. (Learned *et al.* (1969) p. 15)

Military strategy is, then, concerned with the broad means of winning a war.

When applied to business, the notion of strategy is widened to encompass objectives, as well as the means of achieving these. Often, the strategy is embodied in a written plan. Chandler succinctly defined corporate strategy as:

> ... the determination of the basic long-term goals and objectives of an enterprise, and the adoption of courses of action and the allocation of resources necessary for carrying out these goals. (Chandler (1962) p. 13)

The analogy between military strategy and a company's competitive strategy has been drawn by Schon.

> The corporation is seen as a miniature nation: its weapons are products and processes, its battlefield is the market place, its enemies are the corporations with which it competes. Behind its walls it produces weapons and counterweapons, strategies and counter-strategies. (Schon (1967) p. XVI)

Corporate strategy can be said to be concerned with 'what', 'why', 'how' and 'when'.

First of all, strategy is involved with the question: 'what is the business of the company?' In the case of Plessey, for example, this was defined as being successful in the area of 'integrated information technology'.

Secondly, strategy embraces 'why the company is in business', that is, what specific targets it has set itself. For example, in the early 1970s British American Tobacco had an objective of achieving 10 per cent compound growth of profits per year.

Thirdly, the company needs to outline 'how it means to achieve its established objectives'. Just what markets is it operating in? What types of products will it need to offer in order to satisfy its established objectives?

Fourthly, the company needs to decide 'when it aims to achieve its goals and the period over which it will define its strategy'. Companies will generally only devise details of strategy for a specific future period; given the uncertainty, it is unlikely that they are concerned with detailing a corporate strategy for more than five years ahead. In fact, detailed projections will generally be limited to one or two years. Much long-term strategic planning is inevitably of a fairly probabilistic nature, and should involve significant allowance for contingencies.

Specifically, the company is concerned with defining the requirement(s) of group(s) of customers, or market segments, within its selected business(es), and making decisions on the products aimed at satisfying these customer requirements. For companies with an established set of products the process may involve a reappraisal and, in some cases, even a redefinition of the company's existing business. Companies that actively undertake strategic planning will generally produce a written plan embodying all these details; this then acts as the lodestar for the company as a whole. Such plans are periodically updated in the light of outcomes of decisions previously made and of changing environmental conditions.

But why are more and more companies involved in long-term strategy definition and in the obviously time-consuming task of planning corporate activities?

The Need for Planning

The reasons for the more widespread recognition of the importance of strategic planning can be traced to:

(a) the rapid pace of change;
(b) the emergence of large business corporations and the consequent need for effective co-ordination of activities;
(c) the need for means of evaluating corporate performance.

Environmental Change

The high rate of social, economic and technological change suggests the need for longer-term planning if firms are to be better placed to anticipate successfully future trends and events, and thereby more effectively respond to them. Moreover, through the distinct and intelligent formulation of strategy, companies may themselves be able to influence the environment; for instance, technological innovation can itself shape demand through the creation of new wants.

The importance of clear foresight and preparation for the future has been illustrated by a number of studies which suggest that external changes can, for the less alert company, result in its ultimate demise. Companies, then, need to monitor external changes and assess the possible implications for existing products, and for new product development.

The development of new products and the build-up of a manufacturing capability can take many years. Hence, there is a consequent need to think and plan ahead in order to be able to capitalise on market opportunities when they arise, as well as to obviate the unfelicitous occurrence of being caught unawares.

Unfortunately, within the company may prevail a reluctance to change because existing technologies and businesses have been successful in the past. Why should this not continue to be the case in the future? Consequently, activities may focus on short-term, fire-fighting activities. However, sooner or later, the organisation may be compelled to change. It is inadvisable that major decisions about future strategy should be panic responses to change. Often, this can mean that the company is not able to select those areas of growth which are most appropriate to itself (rather than to the competition) or that future development is not rationally considered. Companies, then, are advised to adopt a pro-active, as opposed to a reactive, strategy – that is, one which is founded on actively seeking out wants and devising appropriate innovative offerings to satisfy them, as opposed to one of responding to events or waiting (like Mr Micawber) for 'something to turn up'.

Co-ordination of Activities

A second major reason for planning is to ensure the effective integration of the many activities generally involved in meeting specific task objectives. For instance, as has been seen, firms are systems of often highly differentiable functions, yet the efficient attainment of customer satisfaction demands their close co-ordination. For example, 'manufacturing' needs to be fully informed of the possible pattern of demand throughout the year in order to plan its production schedules, not only to ensure that there is sufficient supply of the products when they are required, but also to minimise the required level of inventories which can be expensive to finance, particularly when interest rates are high. Similarly, there is no point in 'marketing' mounting expensive advertising and promotional campaigns if there are not sufficient quantities of goods to sell: not only will the firm incur unnecessary costs, but it may also build up considerable customer ill-will, as a result of frustrated expectations, through the failure to meet orders. In the same way, the development of new products embraces many different functional activities. Delays and ineffective task attainment caused through lack of communication and misunderstandings about total aims, can often lead to failure. Freeman and his colleagues, in a study of the chemical process plant industry, emphasise the need for good internal communications as a prerequisite of successful innovation:

> Lack of communication and excessive secrecy can be damaging (even) within one firm. There is empirical evidence as well as strong theoretical reasons to suggest that communication barriers between departments have often been the principal reason for failure to innovate. In one large British chemical firm, for example, the barrier between chemists and chemical engineers was so great that the chemical engineers were not consulted until the research work for a new process was completed. The work had taken several years but the chemical engineers were able to point out immediately that most of it had been wasted because it took no account of some elementary cost and engineering factors in full-scale plant design. An American contractor, whose internal communications were apparently better, launched the major new process innovation in this product field. (Freeman *et al.* 1968)

Evaluating Corporate Performance

Ideally, planning involves the unambiguous specification of targets, whether these be the dates when certain tasks should be completed, or the sales or profits of particular products for a specified period. These targets then act as useful means of monitoring performance: significant deviations between targets and results may point to the need to take appropriate remedial action. It may well be that the originally established objectives were unreasonable; but more likely, in the case of companies which have a reservoir of experience in strategic planning, there have been some significant unforeseen problems or some unpredicted external events, pointing to the urgent need for a reappraisal of the original plan. As has already been strongly emphasised, such uncertainties are a fact of life and companies should ensure that they have the means of identifying the impact of these − should they arise − and that they have in reserve appropriate contingency plans.

The Strategic Planning Process

From what has been said so far, it is apparent that corporate strategy embraces the company as a whole and is not concerned with just one part or function. It will tend to be a product of a co-ordinating and bargaining process between the main corporate areas of activity, namely: marketing; finance; manufacturing; and research and development. What, then, is the starting point of the strategic planning process? The company, unless it is newly formed, will already be operating in certain markets, with its own product ranges based on technologies in which it will have developed expertise. Its existing products and markets will often act as a launching pad for future strategy.

   This does not imply that a company should be tightly constrained within those technological and market areas in which it has traditionally been active; it may well be that considerable changes in its environment are fast making its products obsolescent, or that markets for its products are quickly disappearing. Severe surgery and revolutionary product innovation will, in such an instance, be imperative in order to ensure the company's future survival. In other cases, radical managerial actions will not be necessary; although, even where companies are currently enjoying high growth and profits, there is the need to be aware of the almost inevitable fact that this desirable state is unlikely to be maintained, and to make provisions for such eventualities, usually by investing in new businesses by one means or another. Burton is an interesting example of a company which thrived on a well-defined business strategy for several decades but which, in the light of significant changes in its markets, was compelled to define a new marketing philosophy.

Burton − From Manufacturer to Retailer

Burton has undergone a revolution in business philosophy since it was founded by Sir Montague Burton in 1900. For many years it was a retailer of made-to-measure and ready-to-wear men's suits that were made in its own factories. Much of the emphasis was on the efficiency of the manufacturing operations, its stores being viewed mainly as ordering points for the factories. It prospered on this formula and even took over its main rival, Jackson the Tailor, which had adopted a similar business approach.

By the 1970s, as profits plummetted it became apparent that a considerable reappraisal of its strategy was urgently required. The trend away from formal suits to casual clothing was having a traumatic effect on the company, and saddled with large factories and increasing stocks, it made a loss of £1.3 million in 1976, largely as a result of a steep decline in the sale of suits, aggravated by a prolonged and intense summer that year.

The reaction was to rationalise the business, curtailing or selling off peripheral activities, and cutting manufacturing capacity by one third. Its penetration of the women's market, which it had started some years earlier, was intensified using its successful Top Shop chain as the spearhead and by 1978 sales of women's wear accounted for 25 per cent of Group turnover. The Burton chain was revamped giving it a modern image and reformulating its retail mix so that it was more in tune with contemporary trends. However, perhaps the most innovative response was to establish a nationwide chain of Top Man stores with the stress on casual, modern clothes and accessories for the younger man. As a result of this reorientation, Burton returned to profitability in 1978, and by 1982 was making a pre-tax profit of £24.3 million.

When designing their strategies, companies will make assumptions about the socio-economic and technological climates within which they will be operating in the future. Such a scenario of the future is most appropriately a product of an iterative process between the corporate strategists and the various functions of the firm, as this is more likely to result in a comprehensive and better-informed view. The resulting consensus should be written-up and circulated around the different functions in the firm to ensure that all are working to the same set of assumptions. It will be within this framework that functions devise their own operating plans.

Figure 4.1 presents a much simplified outline of the strategic planning process; it is depicted as consisting of separate 'compartmentalised' stages which apparently follow some chronological sequence. It appears that the formulation of the functional plans, such as the marketing plan, is the last stage in the process. This is unlikely to be the case. As has already been noted, for the plan to be effective there needs to be a continuing dialogue between all parts of the organisation; furthermore, aspects of the plan will often be revised in the light of factors which emerge later in the process. For instance,

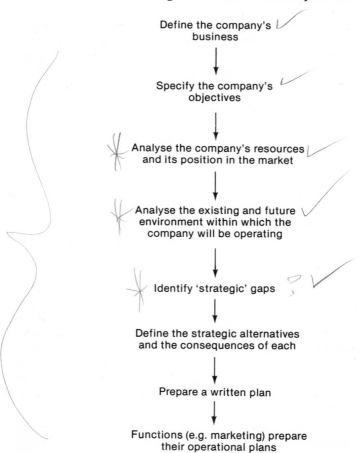

Figure 4.1   *The Strategic Planning Process*

the definition of overall 'business' of the company may be altered or refined as a result of analysing the corporate core strengths and weaknesses.

The Nature of the Company's Business

Commentators such as Levitt have argued that companies need to define the business they are in, and that this should be related to the basic market 'needs' they are striving to satisfy. But as has already been pointed out in Chapter 1, this can raise some semantic difficulties; also, companies may not find it easy to shift resources from one activity to another, particularly where the technological expertise involved in the new activity is dramatically different.

It has been argued that companies define their business in terms of the reserve of technological, manufacturing, financial, scientific and marketing skills which they possess (Simmonds 1968); this would certainly lead to a less restricted and more eclectic scope for new business exploration. The American company, Westinghouse, has in fact defined its business mission as 'being oriented to opportunities'; it is based on a willingness to invest in any area of suitable profit or growth potential in which Westinghouse has, or can acquire, capabilities.

Corporate Objectives

The company as a whole needs targets which are usually defined in specific quantitative terms such as 'a ten per cent increase in return on investment per annum'. Not only do these act as a unifying aim for the disparate parts of the company, but also as a criterion by which corporate performance can be assessed.

Internal Audit

The company should then undertake a detailed and thorough analysis of its past performance, and of its relative strengths and weaknesses. More particularly, the company performs a current market analysis of the sales and profit performance of its existing products. By this means, the company will be able to identify those areas where the company's performance has been weak and demands action because of, say, competitors' inroads through superior products.

The results of this market analysis will be an input into the evaluation of the total company; this will be an assessment of its competitive position with regard not only to particular products, but also to its research and development capabilities; its marketing expertise; its technology; its manufacturing capability; and its financial resources. The company's existing financial resources, or the ease with which it can raise capital, will obviously be an important determining factor of the company's ambitions for the future.

Environmental Analysis

The environmental analysis (which, as already mentioned, embraces the assumptions the company is making about the nature of the future external conditions under which it will be working) should contain a description of the nature of the likely social, economic, technological and political influences over a specified time span. It may also include an analysis of the possible future states and the assigning of probabilities to these. This 'environmental audit' in general acts as a basis for the definition of future strategy.

Identification of Strategic Gaps

The next stage of the process involves the extrapolation of the profits (or sales) obtainable from existing products, given the assumed future environment and the comparison with the levels of performance defined in the company's objectives. Any shortfall will point to the need for managerial action; and where there is a considerable deviation, more radical decisions will be required, including diversification into new areas of business (see Figure 4.2).

In Figure 4.2, the company is faced with a considerable gap (*AC*) between its stated aims (*C*) and projected profits (or sales) at time *T*. It may attempt to narrow this by intensifying marketing effort, reducing costs and so on; but these may only result in a partial closure of the

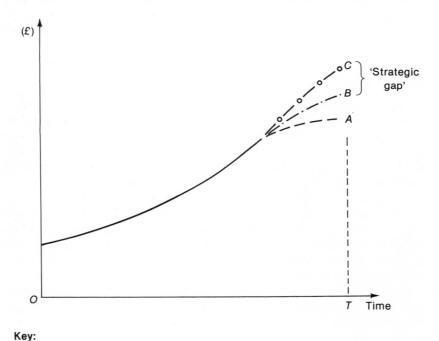

Key:

——— Represents sales (or profit) history of company's product range.

— — — Represents the forecast of profit (or sales) based on past trend and given that no action taken.

—·—·— Represents the projection of sales (or profit) of company's product range, given assumptions about the future environment, possible decisions (such as those regarding marketing) the company may make about its product range, etc.

—o—o Represents where the company would like to be at time *T*.

Figure 4.2   *Strategic Gap*

gap (to *B*). Other courses will be necessary, such as new product development and the acquisition of other companies in the same business (horizontal integration), in supplier or customer industries (vertical integration) or in different industries (diversification).

Strategic Alternatives

Against this detailed background, companies will have to decide how they are going to meet their objectives and in particular how they intend to fill the strategic gap. A firm is faced with a number of options, ranging from doing nothing to investing in new technologies. It may, for example, decide to withdraw from those areas which, although still profitable, will yield a lower return in the future than will investment in new products. Alternatively, it may be highly profitable to invest in the development of existing products − to extend the range, improve their quality, modernise the packaging, and so on. In other cases, it may conclude that, given the conditions facing its existing product range, profits are increasingly going to be squeezed. The opportunities for remedying the situation may be limited; in order to ensure long-term survival, the company may feel that it has little alternative but to seek radical new business openings that offer the prospect of being highly profitable. Indeed, many companies may feel obliged to invest in the fast-moving technologies such as microelectronics, biotechnology, robotics and optical fibres, for fear of being left behind.

Nowadays, many firms are involved in several different businesses, that is they produce diverse product ranges aimed at different markets. For example, a company such as Unilever markets soaps and detergents, ice cream, agricultural products, etc. BAT Industries produces cigarettes, paper products, and is involved in retailing. Companies need to define the strategic options for each of their businesses, the resources that each requires, and the possible consequences of each option. The selection of the appropriate option is not necessarily clear and nor is it, perhaps, as scientific as some would have us believe.

> This decision cannot be based solely on facts and analysis. It is also influenced by uncertain predictive judgements and qualitative trade-offs among a multiplicity of dimensions. The strategist will need the nerve and courage to make major and often irrevocable commitments in the face of uncertainty and imperfect analysis. Under these circumstances strategic choice becomes a highly personal decision. As such, it will be shaped by the personality of the strategist, particularly by what he sees as (1) his individual goals and ambitions and (2) his obligations to society. (Uyterhoeven *et al.* 1973)

Market Technology	Same	New
Same	No change or market penetration	Market development
New	Product development	Diversification

Figure 4.3   *Matrix of Strategic Options*

Figure 4.3 gives a simple matrix of options that the company may pursue. The options are:

(1) *Existing technology in existing markets*   The company either does not feel the need to change, or it strives to maintain (or more likely to increase) its share of its existing market by allocating resources to repackaging, redesign, advertising, promotion ... Many products have had their sales revitalised in this way.

(2) *Existing technology in new markets*   The company may strive to market its existing products in new markets. One obvious way of doing this is to extend the geographical range of its markets by exporting or by other forms of international marketing that are considered more fully in Chapter 11. The company may also extend the use of its existing products (through advertising, for example,) or it may modify its products slightly so that they appeal to different market segments.

(3) *New technology in existing markets*   The company may develop *new* products for those markets in which it already sells products.

(4) *New technology in new markets*   Finally, the company may decide to diversify away from its main business base. Technological innovation, and the acquisition of other firms are two of the main routes to diversification.

Technological innovation involves developing new products for new markets, although it is of course possible to invest in or take over companies that have already undertaken the development, or to license the technology. Often, the innovative strategy is highly risky and uncertain, but it can also be extremely profitable. There are several innovative strategies open to the company: it can be the *pioneer*, always aiming to be at the forefront of technology, being the first to launch new products. Such a strategy demands an extremely efficient and competent research and development department, and highly effective marketing. Alternatively, it may decide to be a *follower*, introducing new products in the wake of the pioneer. This may be a lower-risk strategy since the follower will have a better knowledge of the reaction of the market, as well as being able to benefit from the 'teething problems' and the often large advertising and promotional expenditures of those first in the field. The follower will often produce a different and superior product, but in order to do this effectively the company will have to have efficient R and D and marketing: it will have to have a short development time (to minimise the lead time of the pioneer) and it will need to be able to effectively differentiate its product from that of the forerunner.

A much lower-risk strategy is to *imitate* the products of those first in the field. In order to compete effectively the imitators will need to have some cost advantages from, say, efficient manufacturing or access to cheap raw materials.

Companies may adopt a *dependent strategy* whereby they innovate in response to the requests of their customers and through these requests the technical know-how may also be supplied. Or, of course, companies may follow a 'do nothing' policy as is the case with many small, craft-based firms. However, given the dynamic nature of the environment this can only result in their ultimate demise. Finally, companies may be opportunist and respond to immediate market fads or crazes. Such a strategy generally requires little, if any, research or development; it does, however, demand considerable entrepreneurial flair.

> Somportex is a small confectionery and delicatessen group which saw its profits rocket from £226,000 to £728,000 in the half year ending January 1981. Most of the half million pound gain is attributable to Slush Puppie, an iced drink sold through sweet shops and similar retail outlets. The product was noticed by Somportex's Managing Director on a trip to the USA; he liked it and secured the sole UK agency rights for the machine and the drink. It usually sells the machine outright and profits from supplying the ingredients — the cups, flavourings and a substance which helps to prolong the life of the ice crystals. In Europe, Somportex has sole distribution rights for the ingredients. Before long, it is estimated that the company will be making profits of over £1 million pre-tax (against less than £50,000 ten years ago) and the Chairman believes that 'saturation point for Slush Puppie is decades off' (Gilbert (1981) p.55). In fact, the company later suffered a loss due to a poor summer in 1982.

Companies may simply decide to buy into other areas by acquiring other firms. For example, BAT Industries, a major manufacturer of tobacco products, diversified into retailing in the UK by purchasing the Argos 'catalogue showroom' company, and various grocery store chains.

Selecting Business Opportunities

In considering new business opportunities, companies may start by asking:

(a) What businesses are likely to be important in the future?
(b) What are the demand prospects of each business opportunity?
(c) Will the company be able to enter the new business area at a cost and risk it considers reasonable?
(d) What are the prospects of the company attaining a high rate of growth in the new business?
(e) Does the company have the capability to maintain a profitable share of the market?

In Chapter 3, it is noted that high growth areas are often identified as such by other companies seeking new opportunities. The result is often intense competition and large losses before the shakeout of the weakest from the industry. Therefore, a company should exercise caution before leaping on the growth bandwaggon: it needs to be fairly certain of its ability to maintain a foothold in the market over a period when the market may need educating and when there may be a flood of entries, all fighting for a profitable share of the business. Only the largest, richest and most aggressive firms will survive. Therefore, when considering diversifying, firms might like to consider those options which offer some promise of competitive control through, for example, strong brand loyalty, a high capital cost of entry, or the requirement of highly specific management skills.

Marketing Strategy

Marketing has an important role in the corporate strategy process: first, it is responsible for providing data on the sales and profits performance of the existing products; secondly, it will supply information on the future conditions confronting the firm in each of its markets; and thirdly, it will have a vital part to play in the identification and evaluation of new opportunities for the company.

In addition, as with the other functions, it will also have responsibility for implementing the corporate strategy. Thus, marketing will work according to its own plan, as indeed should research and development, manufacturing, and so on. Each plan should be formulated after a consensus has been reached on the overall objectives and business orientation of the company. In fact, the importance of all parts of the organisation working to the same set of assumptions about the future environment has already been heavily stressed. In this sense, then, the corporate plan can be regarded, for the most part, as a composite of individual functional plans.

What then is the distinction between marketing strategy and corporate strategy? Marketing strategy is, of course, only concerned with marketing, whereas corporate strategy embraces the total organisation. Marketing strategy is devised within the framework of an established corporate strategy. It is concerned primarily with selecting market targets and with formulating marketing mix(es). The choice of targets will be based largely on criteria such as demand potential, company share, profitability, and so on; market segmentation is clearly of significance. The development of product 'offerings' should be based on a sound appreciation of the parameters influencing purchasing behaviour in the chosen segments.

It is also worthwhile noting that the total marketing strategy is itself composed of strategies for each of the main product groups or businesses. The 'marketing plan' embodies these marketing strategies.

The Marketing Plan

The **marketing plan** is a written document that contains details of the marketing programmes which will make a contribution to meeting corporate objectives. In a multi-product (or multi-business) company the final marketing plan may embrace a number of individual plans relating to each area of 'activity' (e.g. products).

For each product (or product group) the marketing plan should contain details of:

(a) profit objectives;
(b) sales forecasts;
(c) past performance (e.g. sales, profits);
(d) nature of competition;
(e) future market, technological trends likely to have an impact on the product(s), etc;
(f) product(s) strategy: target segments, broad description of marketing mix;
(g) pricing policy;
(h) anticipated costs and revenues;
(i) advertising and promotional campaigns;
(j) selling campaign;
(k) distribution strategy and policies;
(l) marketing research policy.

Such marketing plans may have a time horizon of several years ahead; the means of achieving these long-term aims will generally be described on a year-to-year basis, although details will obviously be much less defined for more than two years ahead. The annual targets can be employed as a control to assess the extent to which long-term strategy is being attained. Subsequent plans are not inflexible; they will often be reappraised and altered in the light of experience.

The main aims of the marketing plan are to spell out the sales and profit objectives, the budgets, and the policies with regard to pricing, advertising, selling, marketing research, and the product.

Marketing Organisation

It has been suggested that planning of the nature described above can act as a powerful cohesive force, bringing together the different functional actors in a co-operative effort to achieve established corporate objectives. But, of course, it is not sufficient merely to have such planning exercises to ensure that there is wholehearted integration; the effective implementation of strategy necessitates an organisational structure facilitating maximum co-operation and co-ordination.

The focus shifts to the marketing function. What forms of marketing organisation are appropriate to satisfy the dual aims of ensuring that offerings are devised in the full light of market requirements, and that there is full harmonious support from all the different marketing activities?

At this juncture, it is worth noting that even today many firms probably lack a formal marketing department: they may possess a sales function which is preoccupied with maximising sales; they may even have a marketing manager who, because he is pulled in many directions − communicating with advertising agencies, supplying research and market data to the Board, devising promotional material, liaising with sales force, and so on − has his effectiveness significantly diminished. If, in these firms, only lip service is paid to marketing, in others, marketing may still not be recognised as having a vital role to play in the long-term survival of the company. Increasingly, though, companies are establishing a fully-fledged marketing organisation with representation at board level. Such top-level support for marketing is essential: without it, companies can all too easily become embedded in the mire of their own conceit. Firms can become wedded to products because these have been successful in the past; they can develop products which they believe the market should want. Unfortunately, these introverted attitudes are only too frequently likely to lead to product failure and, without dramatic remedial action, to ultimate corporate demise.

Given, then, that the company recognises the significance of marketing, how can the marketing department best be organised to optimise the satisfaction of our criteria? Three main structures will be discussed: functional organisation; product manager system; and the market manager system.

Functional Marketing Organisation

Figure 4.4 represents a typical marketing organisation, although of course firms need not necessarily have all the activities mentioned. It recognises that within marketing, many of the activities are highly differentiated: marketing research is, for example, a highly specialised activity demanding considerable and often rare research skills. There are two main problems with this form of organisation: first, many companies nowadays market a wide range of often diverse products, yet it would appear that the day-to-day management of them all resides in just one man − the marketing manager − who is answerable to the marketing director. He in turn will be responsible for much of the definition of those products' strategies. Under these conditions, it would be difficult to ensure the requisite degree of support for individual products since effort will be too widely disseminated. One solution is, of course, to appoint assistants to the marketing manager, and these may in fact assume responsibility for particular groups of products. Secondly, this form of organisation raises the problem of obtaining effective integration; however, this is not a problem which is in any sense unique to this form of organisation.

Figure 4.4 *Functional Marketing Organisation*

Product Manager System

The product manager organisation (see Figure 4.5) has evolved from

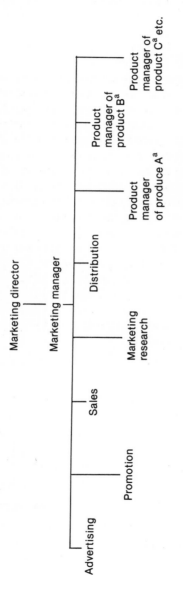

Marketing director

Marketing manager

Advertising | Promotion | Sales | Marketing research | Distribution | Product manager of produce A[a] | Product manager of product B[a] | Product manager of product C[a] etc.

(a) This may be a group of products and there may be individual brand managers in which case:

Product manager of product group A (B, C, etc.)

Brand manager of x | Brand manager of y etc.

Figure 4.5 *Product Manager Organisation*

the appointment of assistant marketing managers. Obviously, as the importance of individual products grew, companies considered that they merited their own individual managers; indeed, many products are multi-million pound businesses. In turn, many of these products spawned a spread of brands, and these may be allocated their own managers; hence the notion of brand management was born.

The responsibilities of product or brand management (the two will be employed synonymously) are many and can vary significantly from firm to firm. In all cases, though, the product manager is responsible for co-ordinating all those activities involved in the marketing of products. Thus, he will generally liaise with the advertising agency, the salesforce, marketing research and manufacturing. In companies where there has been a long history of product management, however, he may also be responsible for product development (and thus for commissioning research and development) and for the ultimate profitability of the product.

Overall, the main tasks of the product manager can embrace the following:

(1) developing a long-range strategy for the product;
(2) preparing an annual marketing plan;
(3) liaising with advertising and merchandising agencies to develop advetising copy, programmes and campaigns;
(4) stimulating interest in and support of the product among salesmen and distributors;
(5) gathering data on the product's performance, customer and dealer attitudes, and new opportunities;
(6) dealing with day-to-day problems concerned with the marketing of the product;
(7) initiating product improvements to meet changing dmarket needs.

In addition, where there is considerable experience of product management, these may be extended to:

(8) product profit and loss responsibility;
(9) direct control over the technical development of the product;
(10) new product responsibility for related products.

A number of criticisms have been levelled at the product manager approach, in particular that he is not awarded the authority commensurate with his responsibilities. For example, he generally has no superiority over Research and Development and yet he may require technical improvements in his product; he may be forced to seek the support of his marketing manager, who may be occupied with more pressing problems, or he may have to resort to exhortation and special pleading:

> Probably the biggest single problem most companies face in the use of a product manager is that they saddle him with great responsibility and yet refuse him the corresponding authority. Outside his own department, the product manager has no line authority in the classical organisational sense. He cannot, for example, order the salesmen or sales manager to do something. Even though advertising may be critical to the success of his plans, the product manager does not select the advertising agency. Perhaps the most burdensome aspect of the product manager's responsibility is that he is made accountable for the profitability of his brand and yet is often denied any control over production costs, setting of prices, or determination of advertising budgets. (Stanton (1967) p.181)

A second major criticism is that product management tends to be regarded as a lower peg on the promotion ladder. Product manager recruits, therefore, tend to be young and often inexperienced; those showing flair and dynamism will all too quickly be promoted, and those that do not will be moved euphemistically 'sideways'. Consequently, they are not given the opportunity to develop the necessary in-depth knowledge to be able to deal effectively with those parties, often from other functional areas, whose co-operation is so necessary for optimum success.

These criticisms aside, product management still tends to be widely employed, for, theoretically at least, it obviously makes sense to invest one individual (who, one hopes, has entrepreneurial flair) with the ultimate responsibility for a major product.

Market Manager System

An alternative approach is to organise the marketing department according to the customers or markets that it serves. For example, a railway system caters for the distribution needs of a range of major customers, all of whom may have significantly different requirements. Under such circumstances, it might be appropriate to appoint managers who are responsible for liaising with each of these customers, for obtaining a detailed knowledge of their requirements and for co-ordinating all the activities required to meet these effectively. Such an approach has been termed 'market centering' and it can obviously supply the company with a distinct advantage:

> When market leadership is threatened by a competitor who has achieved sufficient product parity to deprive the leader of price superiority, market centering can restore a competitive advantage with the more creative marketing techniques it develops from improved knowledge of customer, distributor, and retailer needs. (Hanan (1974) pp. 63–74)

Market centering may be particularly appropriate for marketers of industrial products where, increasingly, the emphasis is on solving customer problems rather than merely supplying individual products. A market manager will be responsible for bringing together a package and because he will possess a detailed knowledge of customers and the way in which they make their profits, he will be able to calculate the financial benefits and *communicate* these to customers. This principle is embodied in the NCR approach but this is mainly confined to salesforce organisation:

> Each of NCR's sales staff is responsible for selling co-ordinated systems of numerical recording and sorting products to an industry.
>
> Before the introduction of this organisation, a salesman was responsible for a specific product line. This meant that a client might have to liaise with several NCR salesmen in order to meet his full requirements. With the new arrangement, 'the same retail industry salesman who sells an NCR cash register to a department store can also search out and serve the store's needs for NCR accounting machines, data entry terminals, and a mainframe computer. If he needs help, he can organise a team with other NCR salesmen that can bring the required strength to his proposal. The product groups he sells are still manufactured separately; the centralised sales approach is the innovation that makes the difference.'
>
> NCR believes 'it can prescribe systems that solve comprehensive problems which would otherwise remain immune to single product solutions. Management also believes it can expand its profitable sales volume by selling larger packages and insulating its position against competition'. (Hanan (1974) pp. 63–74).

A full market manager structure would, however, take this approach further in that the 'market manager' would act as the spearhead for all the marketing effort in particular markets. Figure 4.6 gives a possible structure for a paint manufacturer which serves a number of major customers.

Summary

Corporate strategy is concerned with establishing the nature of the business, its objectives and the means of attaining these. Marketing strategy defines the means whereby marketing assists in meeting corporate objectives. The marketing 'programmes' for individual products and 'businesses' should be contained in a written marketing plan. This provides the framework within which the marketing effort can be co-ordinated. It has also been shown that effective co-ordination demands appropriate forms of organisation. Functional, market, and product-based marketing department structures were described.

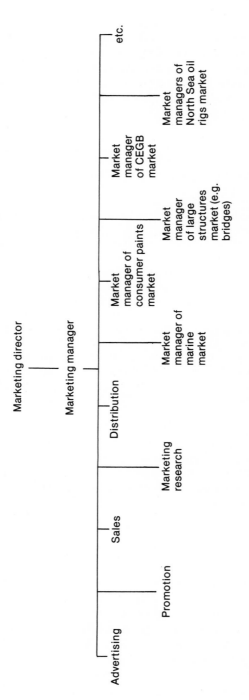

Figure 4.6 *Market Manager Marketing Organisation*

Further Reading

Chandler, A.D. (1962) *Strategy and Structure*, MIT Press.

Freeman, C. *et al.* (1968) 'Chemical process plant: innovation and the world market', *National Institute Economic Review*, No. 45.

Gilbert, N. (1981) *The Sunday Times*, 18th January.

Hanan, M. (1974) 'Reorganise your company around its markets', *Harvard Business Review*, November–December.

Learned, P. *et al.* (1969) *Business Policy: Text and Cases*, Richard D. Irwin.

Mancuso, J.R. (1973) 'How to manage products', *Management Today*, January.

Schon, D.A. (1967) *Technology and Change*, Pergamon Press.

Simmonds, K. (1968) 'Removing the chains from product strategy', *Journal of Management Studies*, 5.

Stanton, W.J. (1967) *Fundamentals of Marketing*, McGraw-Hill.

Uyterhoeven, H.E.R. *et al.* (1973) *Strategy and Organisation*, Richard D. Irwin.

Review Questions

(1) Select a large company. Define the business in which you think it should operate.

(2) What is meant by 'corporate strategy'?

(3) Why do you think that planning might be important for firms in (a) the office equipment market and (b) the automobile components market?

(4) Describe the major strategic alternatives that are open to a company. Give examples in each case.

(5) Give the possible structure of a marketing department of a firm making confectionery products that is organised on product manager lines. What do you consider are the major advantages and disadvantages of the product manager system?

Face-to-face interviewing: a direct gauge of market opinion

5

Information for Marketing Decisions

It is, by now, clear that marketing involves a wide variety of decisions on topics ranging from the markets the company should enter to the most appropriate package for a product experiencing a decline in sales. One approach to problem solving is, of course, to rely solely on intuition and judgement; indeed, this form of entrepreneurial decision making was the basis of much commercial practice in the past and was often successful — although not necessarily optimally so. Of course, life then was much simpler. Yet, even in today's complex and sophisticated environment, businessmen are often apparently compelled to resort to instinct or some form of managerial clairvoyance because it appears there is no other firm foundation on which to make a decision. To be effective, this requires a special breed of executive, a sort that is all too rarely encountered. In practice, though, it is possible to subject instinct to rigorous assessment by systematically gathering information which supplies the decision maker with a clearer view of what is happening and what may happen. It is now believed that most business decision making can be improved by having data on the market, and on the possible consequences of future marketing decisions. The importance of such data gathering increases, the greater the cost of making a 'wrong' decision. 'Marketing research' is the term employed to embrace such information-collecting activities.

This chapter considers, in some detail, the approach to planning marketing research projects; the different uses of marketing research; and the various means of collecting the data. It is obvious that marketing research can be a time-consuming and expensive exercise: it demands scarce skills, time and money. Moreover, the greater the accuracy sought, the higher the costs. Decision makers therefore need to weigh up very carefully the advantages to be derived from marketing research before embarking on exercises that might incur more costs than they yield benefits. The 'worthwhileness' of marketing research needs always to be considered by the decision maker.

The Need for Marketing Research

XYZ developed a new convenience food and was unsure of the optimum price to charge. The accountants suggested basing the price on the costs of the raw materials and its manufacture plus a ten percent mark up. The marketing manager, however, argued that since the new product was highly innovative, housewives may be prepared to pay a considerable premium for the superior quality and greater convenience that it offered. He suggested undertaking exploratory studies with groups of housewives. The results supported the marketing manager's view. More systematic interviews with a large group of potential consumers also led to this conclusion. As a result, the company set a much higher price than the accountants had originally recommended; the product was highly successful and generated considerable profits for many years.

The newly-appointed marketing manager of a chemical company that manufactured and sold a diverse range of industrial chemicals noted that the sales of one of the major products was declining. He commissioned research to investigate the possible reasons for this.

An advertising agency had been commissioned to develop an effective means of advertising a snack product aimed specifically at children. By holding discussions with children, it identified themes which would capture children's interest. It devised three different television advertisements; by assessing the reaction of groups of children to each of these, it felt it was able to select the one that had the highest probability of attracting attention.

All the above examples are possible (although hypothetical) cases of the way in which marketing research can increase the likelihood that the marketers will make the optimum decision. For example, XYZ, by undertaking research into consumers' reactions to its new product, felt able to charge a higher price and therefore considerably increased its profitability. Similarly, the advertising agency, by undertaking a detailed analysis of children and what interested them, was able to formulate advertisements that had a better chance of success. In the case of new products, we have already seen the importance of attempting some assessment of market size and company share before undertaking costly developments; but as will be seen in more detail in Chapter 7 marketing research can have a crucial and valuable role to play in discovering consumers' reactions to the evolving product throughout its development. In this way, then, marketing research lessens the risk of making an expensive mistake; it also reduces, but not necessarily eliminates, the uncertainty about the consequences of making specific decisions.

Marketing research, then, is the systematic gathering and analysis of information aimed at assisting marketers in making optimum decisions on target markets, products, pricing, promotion and distribution. By supplying relevant data it helps to reduce the risks and uncertainties associated with such decisions.

Some of the reasons for the increasing importance of marketing research have already been discussed in Chapter 1: they include the nature and extent of competitive activity; the greater discretionary purchasing power of consumers and the increase of psycho-social wants; and the high costs of product failure. An over-riding reason is the increased spatial separation between the suppliers of goods and services and their customers that has attended the development of mass manufacturing and marketing, and self-service retailing. Production is undertaken in large factories away from the market they serve; customers buy products often in large impersonal superstores. The manufacturer is remote from the people who actually have contact with the customers; in any case, there is often little personal rapport between customers and retailers − something that is increasingly the case with the demise of the small retailing units that are more likely to have an element of personal service. There is a heavy onus on the producer to actively seek out information on what is being purchased, by whom, when, where, and how frequently.

Development of Marketing Research

The techniques of marketing research have their origins in the social surveys of Seebohn Rowntree, Professor Sir Arthur Bowley and Charles Booth, all of whom were social researchers carrying out investigations into the physical conditions of the labouring classes in the nineteenth century. Perhaps the most famous survey was that performed by Booth on the *Life and Labour of the People in London, 1892 to 1897*. During the Second World War, concern about the diet of the population resulted in the introduction of the *National Food Survey* in 1940 with an initial aim of investigating the eating habits of the urban working class; its brief was later extended. The first commercial marketing research agency was probably established in the USA in the early part of the twentieth century; the introduction of research agencies to the UK occurred later. Today, however, there are a large number of marketing research agencies which vary considerably in size. Many are attached to, or are spin-offs from, advertising agencies; others have been established by entrepreneurial individuals. The expenditure on marketing research commissioned from agencies amounted to over £60 million in 1980. This is significantly augmented by companies' research performed in-house. Nevertheless, the amount spent on marketing research is over-shadowed by the huge expenditure on advertising, currently in excess of three billion pounds per annum.

The Uses of Marketing Research

Marketing research has a wide range of uses. Some of its specific applications are listed in Table 5.1; some of these applications will be considered in more detail in subsequent chapters.

Categories of Marketing Research

For each of these many uses, marketing research can assist on at least four levels:

(1) in exploring the nature of the problem; this is termed exploratory research;
(2) in describing what is happening; this is called descriptive research;
(3) in identifying the possible reasons for what is happening; this is termed explanatory research;
(4) in predicting what might happen; this is called predictive research.

In all cases there are two possible types of information: primary data which have to be collected for the first time usually by one or more of the following — surveys, observation, or experimentation; and secondary information which is already available to the marketer in the form of published reports, articles, statistics, and so on. For example, the government is a rich source of much information on the economy, various markets, output of various industries, etc. There are, in addition, a wide variety of other data sources including trade and research associations, consultants' reports, Economist Intelligence Unit, Mintel and the United Nations. The firm will also have a plentiful supply of information on its own market, its output and its competitors. Obviously, the marketer should first examine secondary sources to obviate the expense of undertaking research which yields information that is already available. The remainder of this chapter is concerned with primary data collection.

Exploratory Research

This is research of a qualitative nature that is undertaken to ascertain whether or not there is a problem and what the 'true' nature of the problem is. It is preliminary to setting the specific research objectives. It can involve free-ranging discussions with selected individuals; an examination of secondary sources of information; or a study of analogous situations from the past. The hallmarks of exploratory research are flexibility and the ability to recognise approaches to the possible problems.

> VINO, a well-established importer of wines and spirits, was considering launching a range of wines aimed at the mass market. It needed to devise a brand name and an effective marketing strategy. However, it knew little about consumers' attitudes to wines or their taste preferences. From exploratory discussion with groups of consumers it was able to identify associations with wine that could be employed as the basis of its marketing strategy. From reactions to the tasting of existing wines, VINO was able to formulate wines that it felt were more likely to have the widest appeal. More systematic research was commissioned to ascertain the most frequent associations with wine drinking and to test reactions to the product.

> Zincron is a manufacturer of 'Lustre', a brand of hairsprays that had had a dominant share of the market for many years. Recently, its market share had declined as the result of the intrusion of a new range of hairsprays called 'Freelet', having the novel non-stick ingredient TXT. The immediate response of top management was to ask for a reformulation of its hairspray to make it comparable with the competition, even though it was known that this would be expensive and take some time. The marketing manager suggested that it might be appropriate to undertake some research aimed at probing housewives' attitudes to 'Lustre' and the new brand. The results of these exploratory discussions suggested that housewives were not persuaded to purchase the new brand because of its non-stick formulation; rather, they felt that 'Lustre' seemed poor value in comparison with 'Freelet' which had been packaged in such a way as to give the appearance of being better value for money — even though the price per cc was the same. Zincron repackaged its product, slightly increased the contents, and marketed it as the Big Value hairspray. As a result sales rocketed.

Descriptive Research

As its name suggsts, descriptive research is primarily concerned with

Table 5.1 *Uses of Marketing Research*

(1) *Performance Analysis*

Sales analysis	Trend of sales for individual products
	Factors affecting sales performance
Brand share analysis	Current market share
	Changes in market share
	Factors influencing market share
Cost and profit analysis	Profitability of individual products

(2) *Market Analysis*

Size of market	Measurement of market potential
Segmentation	Means of segmenting market
	Size of individual segments
	Factors influencing purchasing behaviour in specific segments
Influences on demand	Environmental factors influencing demand over a specific time period

(3) *Sales Research*

Sales forecasts	Predicting future sales
Sales information on competitors	Market share of competitors
Establishment and revision of sales territories	Analysis of potential sales in geographical regions
Sales call planning	Location of major customers
Effectiveness of salesmen	Assessment of sales per sales representative
	The costs incurred per sales representative
Establishment of sales quota	Assessment of likely sales per sales area, given various assumptions
Retail audits	Assessment of actual sales per given period per product

(4) Product Research

Identification of opportunities for new ideas	Scanning market for new ideas
	Exploratory surveys to assess wants of customers
Product concept testing	Qualitative discussions with potential customers to assess their reaction to possible new product ideas
Product testing	Customer trials of new products to assess reactions and how the product performs in actual use
Packaging and labelling research	Evaluation of customer reactions to packaging; intelligibility of instructions on the pack
Purchase frequency	Investigations of how frequently the product is purchased and by whom
Customer satisfaction studies	Investigations of customer attitudes to existing products and how they are perceived relative to competitors
Test marketing	Launch of a new product in a microcosm of the market to assess the market response to the marketing mix

(5) Advertising Research

Formulating advertising themes	Identifying the influences most likely to stimulate customers' interest
Copy research	Assessing the comprehensibility and effectiveness of written material included in advertisements
Advertising effectiveness	Measuring the results of exposure to advertising campaigns
Evaluating effectiveness of different advertisements	Comparing the reactions to different advertisements
Selecting advertising media	Measuring the size and determining the composition of the audience to various types of advertising media

(6) Distribution Research

Retail audits	Sales of specified products from individual retail units over a specified period
Appropriate stock levels	Cost of not having the product in stock
Effectiveness of distribution outlets	Examining sales per distribution outlet and calculating the cost of servicing them

finding out what is happening, without specifically aiming to find out the underlying explanation. In contrast with exploratory research, it commences with a clear statement of research objectives. Examples might be:

   (a) examining the market share of brand X over the last ten years;
   (b) determining the age, sex, and income of existing purchasers of brand X;
   (c) finding out the attitudes of existing consumers of brand X.

The results of such research will often act as a basis for formulating hypotheses to be tested by means of future research.

   Descriptive research may, in addition, be concerned with determining the degree of association between two variables; for example, it might be found that there is some relationship between sales and economic growth, sales rising steadily with increase in GDP. It might be helpful to determine the extent of the variation between the two.

Explanatory Research

Descriptive research might indicate that brand X's share of the market is declining; exploratory research might be concerned with assessing the possible reasons why this is occurring. Various possible explanations may emerge; explanatory research might then be commissioned to ascertain whether or not any of these 'hypotheses' are valid.

Predictive Research

This aims to provide systematic data to enable estimates to be made on the future sales of a product, or on what might be the results of future marketing decisions. Sales forecasting has already been considered in Chapter 3. In the case of the latter, this type of research will strive to provide information on the likely reaction to a new product, one form of advertising as opposed to others, different levels of price, and so on.

Pragmatic, Continuous and Programmed Research

Marketing research can be undertaken as a one-off project, as a pragmatic response, to obtain background information to a specific problem; thus, Zincron commissioned a research project to investigate why the sales of its hairspray were declining.

   Marketing research can also be of a continuous nature, aimed at monitoring various facets of the firm's environment or its products (such as sales) over time. Much of the data is gathered using representative groups or a panel of consumers who note their purchases of selected products in a diary. A more objective means of obtaining information is by a 'bin analysis' whereby the panel is asked to place empty packages into a separate container, which is then analysed by the research agency. Television audience research may involve the monitoring of a panel of viewers by the use of meters attached to the set; these record the time the set is switched on and the channel to which it is tuned. The *Nielsen Retail Audit* is a means of continuously recording deliveries, sales and stocks of various products for grocery and chemist retail outlets. The Retail Audit gives an accurate indication of actual sales and inventory levels for any period. In all these cases manufacturers gain access to the data by paying a subscription fee.

It is evident that continuous research can usefully act to pin point specific problem areas; for example, a rise in stock levels could suggest a sales decline, although this would not be immediately apparent to the manufacturer whose ex-factory sales during that period may be increasing as stocks are built up by retailers.

Finally, marketing research may be undertaken in the form of a programme of specific research projects with the aim of meeting some overall goals, such as the effective launch of a new product. Table 5.2 gives a possible programme of marketing research in the case of the development of a new convenience-food product.

Planning Marketing Research

Before commencing a marketing research project it is advisable to decide on:

(a) what one is trying to do
(b) why one is trying to do it
(c) how one is going to do it
(d) how long it will take
(e) how much it will cost
(f) the form of the results
(g) what accuracy is required

In answering these questions, the company increases the chance that it will obtain the relevant information at an acceptable cost at the right time. The answers may be embodied in a document called the **Research Design** which is devised after preliminary agreement between the sponsor and those commissioned to perform the research on the parameters of the research i.e. the broad objectives, the costs, time to completion and the accuracy of the results. These may be first written-up as a **Research Brief.** Such pre-research preparation is a

Table 5.2 *Programmed Research*

Specific research project	Aim of project
Exploratory research	To assess consumer's attitudes to convenience food and to assess reactions to the notion of the new convenience-food product.
Product testing	Reaction of a random sample of consumers to various formulations of the product.
Attitude survey	Questionnaire survey of a sample of consumers to determine attitudes to convenience foods.
Advertising research	Tests of various developed advertisements among selected groups of consumers.
Test marketing	Launch of the product in a representative area of the UK to find out the reaction to the total marketing strategy in a 'real' situation.
Awareness tests	Surveys to find out whether people in the test market area had heard of the product and seen the advertising.
Special retail audits	Specially-commissioned retail audits to find out how quickly the product was selling.
Repeat awareness studies	After the launch of the product in other areas, surveys to find out public awareness of the product and the advertising.
Monitoring activity	Continuous research to identify possible problems with the product. In this way, the manufacturer hopes to keep the product up to date.

form of insurance for all the parties involved; it avoids misunderstandings, and obviates the risk of post-research recriminations about what the research was intended to yield.

Figure 5.1 depicts, in simplified form, the possible elements in the research planning process. It can be seen that it involves a continuing

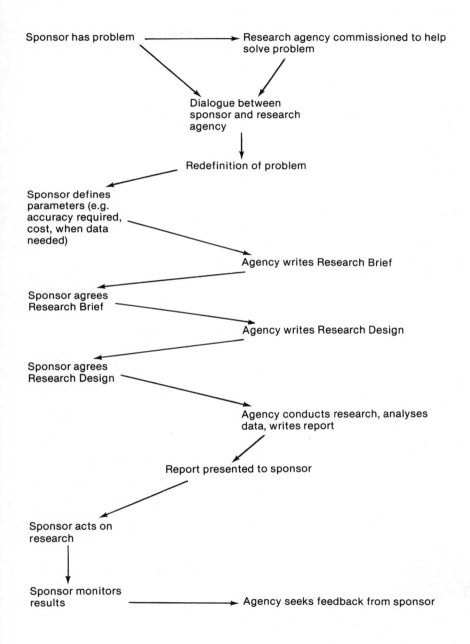

Client   *Marketing Research Agency/Department*

Sponsor has problem ⟶ Research agency commissioned to help solve problem

Dialogue between sponsor and research agency

Redefinition of problem

Sponsor defines parameters (e.g. accuracy required, cost, when data needed)

Agency writes Research Brief

Sponsor agrees Research Brief

Agency writes Research Design

Sponsor agrees Research Design

Agency conducts research, analyses data, writes report

Report presented to sponsor

Sponsor acts on research

Sponsor monitors results ⟶ Agency seeks feedback from sponsor

Figure 5.1 *Marketing Research Planning Process*

dialogue between the researchers and the sponsor. Also, it should be noted that there are usually considerable interactions between the various stages. For example, when devising the objectives it is more efficient to bear in mind how the data are to be analysed; this avoids the risk of exhaustively collecting information that cannot be effectively analysed.

Statement of Objectives

All research should start with a clear definition of objectives. These should be operational: this means that the data required are either accessible or can be gathered within the time, and with the resources, available. At first glance, it might appear that the statement of research objective(s) is a fairly straightforward exercise. This stage may, however, be a trap for the unwary, since what might appear to be the problem may only be the symptom of the problem. In other cases, a first obvious line of enquiry may, in fact, lead down a cul-de-sac. It is, therefore, important to explore as fully as possible the true nature of the problem before embarking on the detailed planning and execution of any project.

Determining the 'True' Nature of the Problem

In 1979 Coco-Nuts launched a new chocolate bar, Chocobits, which was initially well received by the retail trade. However, consumer sales did not proceed as well as expected and after fifteen months its market share was well below the initial target with the result that significant unbudgeted losses were being made. In the inevitable crisis analysis, the marketing director noted that it was known that the product was satisfactory – product tests before the launch of Chocobits had resulted in an extremely favourable reaction from consumers – whilst the advertising employed had been the most preferred of the three advertising campaigns that had been pre-tested among a selected sample of individuals. However, he was dissatisfied with the selling effort; he felt that the point-of-sale literature lacked impact and similar comments had been made by a number of retailers with whom he had discussed this. In addition, he suggested that more attention needed to be directed to the management of the sales force, with a reappraisal of sales areas and quotas. In the first instance, it was decided to test the impact of three different point-of-sale approaches.

A manufacturer of industrial chemicals was concerned about its lack of success in winning bids for contracts. It believed that the major reason was because its market information on possible forthcoming contracts was inefficient, so that the time between the invitation to tender and the closing date for the bid was too short for it to prepare an adequate marketing package, based on the best information open to it. The consequence was the high failure rate. It decided that the most appropriate means of tackling the problem was to improve its means of obtaining information, so that it would have more time between learning of a future opportunity to bid and the closing date for the tender.

It appears that in both of these examples, the causal factor had been decided on without any exploration of other possible explanations. In the case of Coco-Nuts, the marketing director focused exclusively on the promotional effort as the factor responsible for the failure of Chocobits to achieve the pre-established targets. But perhaps the cause was more deep-seated than this. He blindly accepted that the initial product trials were satisfactory and that the fact that one advertisement was preferred out of three meant it was the most effective. There may have been many reasons for the failure of the product, including the subsequent introduction of a more acceptable rival product; an increase in promotional expenditure by competitors; customer dislike of one or more elements of the marketing mix. A consideration of all these alternatives was ignored.

Similarly, in the second example there was a range of possible reasons for the firm's lack of success that an improvement in environmental scanning would not necessarily rectify. It would have been easy for the researchers to latch onto the problem as defined by the sponsor. However, in this case, the researchers suggested that a possible starting point might be to approach the problem in a more eclectic way. They held preliminary discussions with selected industrial users from whom they elicited a comprehensive list of criteria that might be employed when selecting a paint supplier. A large sample of customer firms were then asked to rank these. Finally, users were asked to rank the company and its competitors on each of these criteria. From this, the areas of the company's relative strengths and weaknesses, in the eyes of potential customers, were identified and action was then taken to improve its market performance.

Data Collection

It has already been emphasised that sound marketing research practice is always to investigate what data are already available before embarking on any primary data collection.

Where primary research is necessary, three main approaches to collecting the information are available, namely survey, observation, and experimentation. Surveys are, of course, the most widely employed, and here the researcher has available a variety of research instruments.

Surveys

Before carrying out a survey, the researcher has to decide on:

(a) who is to be questioned (this usually involves the selection of a sample);
(b) the method(s) employed in gathering the data.

It is the latter which are considered first. The main research instruments are:

(i) postal questionnaires
(ii) face-to-face interviewing
(iii) telephone interviewing

A summary of the major advantages and disadvantages of each approach is listed in Table 5.3.

Postal Questionnaires A postal questionnaire is obviously an economical means of obtaining information from a large number of consumers or firms, over a wide geographical area, at a relatively low cost. One of the problems with postal questionnaires is that it is difficult to test the accuracy of the replies; furthermore, it is impossible to probe the replies unless there is follow-up by means of a further questionnaire, by telephone or even by personal visit. Perhaps the major problem with postal questionnaires is the extremely low response rate; response rates of between 20 to 30 per cent are common. Although various methods of improving response have been suggested (for example, telephoning before the despatch of the questionnaire in order to elicit co-operation, the inclusion of a stamped addressed envelope, and the promise of a free gift), their impact can vary significantly. A low response rate could lead to inaccurate results since only those particularly concerned about the subject may reply. Postal questionnaires need exhaustive pre-planning, including:

(a) Careful selection of the sample, with the identification of the specific respondent where possible. This is particularly important when sampling organisations.
(b) The design of the questionnaire and any exploratory material to be included with the questionnaire.
(c) The means of overcoming the problem of a low response rate.

Questionnaire design is an extensive subject in its own right; it is critical to ensure that the questions asked seek the information pertinent to the aims of the research project, that they are easily understood by the respondents, that they are unlikely to result in ambiguous replies, and that they are not phrased in such a way as to lead the respondent to give the desired response. Table 5.4 points out some of the mistakes that can be made in question formulation.

The researcher has a choice between closed-ended questions where the respondent is given the options from which to answer, or open-ended questions, where there is complete freedom in answering. Closed-ended questions embrace both dichotomous questions, where a straight 'Yes' or 'No' answer is required, and multiple choice questions, where the respondent makes a selection from several alternatives. Although dichotomous questions are easy to answer and analyse, they fail to give shades of meaning — important when exploring attitudes. Moreover, a large number of dichotomous questions may be needed to obtain the information sought. Multiple choice questions are not only easy to answer and record, but they can also enable one to measure the strength of opinion and they make the collection of 'sensitive' data on personal details easier. The major disadvantage is that the respondent may limit himself to the options presented. Finally, open-ended questions are useful where it is difficult to list the alternatives or where the aim is to remove any element of suggestion by the interviewer. They can, however, be difficult and expensive to analyse. Most questionnaires will tend to be a blend of all types of questions. Table 5.5 gives examples of the different types of questions.

Face-to-Face Interviewing   Personal interviewing is used widely in both consumer and industrial marketing research; it has the advantage of being more flexible, since it is possible to follow up and probe the answers, whilst the problem of bias through low response can be reduced as a skilled interviewer is often able to overcome much initial resistance. In addition, the interviewer can often augment or check the information obtained from the interview by observation (for example, noting the reactions to questions, features about the person, the house, or firm, etc). Personal interviewing is, however, extemely expensive whilst the accuracy of the results is highly dependent upon the skills and honesty of the interviewers. For example, with unskilled interviewers there can be inaccurate recording of answers or phrasing of questions.

Personal interviewing can take one of several forms. These include:

(i)   structured interview
(ii) semi-structured interview
(iii) non-directive interview
(iv) the 'depth' interview
(v)   the group interview

Table 5.3 *Comparison of the Different Means of Obtaining Survey Data*

Method	Advantages	Disadvantages
Face-to-face interviewing	(1) Facilitates the asking of complex questions together with supplementaries. It is possible to probe answers.	(1) Can be an expensive means of collecting information, and involves considerable pre-planning (briefing of interviewers, planning of interviews, etc).
	(2) The problem of bias through 'no-responses' can be reduced since a skilled interviewer can overcome resistance to being questioned.	(2) Need to have skilled and conscientious interviewers to avoid inaccurate phrasing of questions and recording of information; otherwise obtain interviewer bias.
	(3) Interviewers can often obtain information additional to that from the interview – through observation, e.g. noting non-verbal responses, etc.	
Postal questionnaires[a]	(1) Often regarded as a relatively cheap means of collecting information. But in terms of cost per response it can be comparatively expensive because the response rate is often very low.	(1) Often have a very low rate of response, and this can introduce bias as a result of self-selection, e.g. only those interested in the topic being investigated may reply.
	(2) Permits the coverage of a wide geographical area for little extra cost.	(2) Cannot 'probe' answers.

(3) Eliminates interviewer bias.

(4) Can be an effective means of obtaining information from individuals who move around a lot.

(3) Difficult to use to obtain complex sets of information; for example, complex information collection may necessitate lengthy questionnaires, and the longer the questionnaire the lower the response rate is likely to be.

(4) Bias may be introduced because respondents can see all the questions before answering the questionnaire.

Telephone interviewing

(1) Generally cheaper than face-to-face interviewing where respondents are spread over a wide geographical area because it eliminates the need for travelling.

(2) Can expect a higher response rate and obtain information more rapidly than is the case with postal questionnaires.

(3) It is possible to follow up answers by asking supplementaries.

(1) Only people with telephones can be interviewed. May be biased against those from lower socio-economic groups (who are less likely to own telephones) and those who move more.

(2) Telephone interviews may be regarded by those contacted as an intrusion of privacy.

(3) Those questioned may be reluctant to supply information of a confidential nature to interviewers whose identity is unproved.

(4) It may be possible to ask only short questions, as opposed to questions requiring a considered response.

Note: (a) Of course, questionnaires can also be used in both 'face-to-face' and telephone interviewing; the difference is, of course, that in these cases it is used *personally* by the interviewer.

Table 5.4 *Some Possible Mistakes in Question Formulation*

(1) Asking two or more questions in one; for example:
Which do you find the cheapest and cleanest to use – electric or gas cookers?
The respondent cannot logically answer this question if he finds one cheaper and the other cleaner.

(2) Not defining the terms employed; for example:
Do you visit the cinema frequently?
Respondents will have different interpretations of 'frequently'. The researcher needs to specify what is meant by frequently (such as 'more than once a week').

(3) Using leading questions which predispose the respondent to give a particular response; for example:
Do you care enough about your health to have a medical check up once a year?

(4) Asking questions which can lead to an inaccurate answer; for example, because the answer relies heavily on the respondent's memory:
When did you last buy a tyre for your car?
or because the question demands a knowledge that the respondent is unlikely to have:
What brand of tyre did your husband last purchase?
Under these circumstances the respondent may, under the pressure of the interview, volunteer an answer on the spur of the moment. The answer may bear little relation to the truth. Similarly, respondents can refuse to answer questions of a personal nature (such as those pertaining to income).

In the structured interview, the interviewer works using a pre-planned questionnaire and has no discretion over the phrasing or the order of questioning. Not only does this obviously place less reliance on the skills of the interviewer, but it also permits pre-coding for ease of analysis – a factor that may have been an important consideration in devising the questionnaire in this way. The structured interview is common in consumer market research, but is rarely employed in industrial marketing research:

> The structured interview is essentially a tool of consumer marketing research and is effective and cheap to use where massive interviewing is taking place, where the quality of interviewers is highly variable and not always assessable, and where respondents are subject to a relatively superficial examination. In an industrial situation the structured interview can rarely take in all the information

Table 5.5 *Examples of Question Types*

Dichotomous questions
Do you own a microwave cooker?
Have you bought a drink in a pub in the last seven days?
Do you smoke?

Multiple choice questions

How frequently do you go to church?
- never
- once a year or less
- more than once a year but less than once a month
- once a month but less than once a week
- once a week or more

What do you consider is *the* main benefit of microwave ovens?
- they save on energy
- they are easy to use
- they cook faster than ordinary cookers
- they are clean to use
- other

What is your annual salary or wage; is it
- less than £4,000
- between £4,000 and £5,499
- between £5,500 and £6,999
- between £7,000 and £8,499
- between £8,500 and £9,900
- above £10,000

Do you agree that smoking should be banned in public places?
- strongly disagree
- quite disagree
- neither disagree nor agree
- quite agree
- strongly agree

Open-ended questions
What do you associate mainly with wine drinking?
What do you consider are the major benefits of home ownership?

> needed at an interview where expert opinion is being probed; its use tends to block off the respondent when additional remarks are of value... (Wilson 1973)

The semi-structured interview overcomes these criticisms since it is often a check list of points with the interviewer having some discretion over both the phrasing of the questions and the order in which they are asked. It needs to be pointed out, though, that in order to be useful this demands highly-trained interviewers. Non-directive interviews go one stage further since, in essence, they are a free-ranging discussion between interviewee and interviewer. There is the danger that the interviewer will be highly selective in what he records, so the answers should be recorded verbatim to obviate the risk of bias. In the group interview a number of people are invited to discuss some particular topic, with the interviewer often adopting a relatively passive role. The mutual stimulation of the participants can generate a wide range of ideas and insights. Because of their free-ranging nature, both the non-directive and group interviews are especially useful in exploratory research. Finally, the 'depth' interview is generally a means of exploring the subconscious motives of the individual through the use of a variety of psychoanalytical techniques. Such motivational research has been increasingly criticised because of the highly subjective nature of much of the findings.

Telephone Interviewing Telephone interviewing combines the advantage of flexibility of personal interviewing with a lower cost. It suffers from three main disadvantages: first, only those with telephones and who are listed in a directory can be contacted; this can exclude not only those from lower socio-economic groups but also those who are highly mobile or have moved home recently. Secondly, there is the problem of identity; the interviewer is anonymous to the respondent and there is no means of proving who he is. This can be a particular disadvantage where the disclosure of confidential information is required. Thirdly, interviewees may not only be suspicious of receiving anonymous calls, but may also resent what might be construed as an unwelcome and unsolicited intrusion into their homes.

However, telephone interviewing can have some important uses particularly in industrial marketing research; for example, as already mentioned, it can be employed to obtain co-operation in a mail questionnaire, or to make advance appointments for personal interviews. In both cases, efficiency can be considerably improved.

Sampling Unless it has been decided to conduct a census − in which all units of the target population are questioned (e.g. every household in the UK) − surveys will involve some form of sampling. The selection of a sample that is representative of the target population can give a highly accurate result and will save time and expense. It can be costly to obtain a high degree of sample representativeness: it demands considerable care in the specific identification of the units to be sampled and in ensuring that only the selected units are questioned. For example, ensuring an accurately representative sample may necessitate the clear naming of those to be questioned, and several 'callbacks' should they be out; substitutions can reduce the representativeness of the sample.

Sample representativeness is a function of the size of the sample − the larger the sample size, the greater the degree of accuracy of the results. Unfortunately, accuracy varies inversely as the square root of the sample size, and this means that an extremely high accuracy can demand disproportionate increases in cost. Decision makers will have to weigh up very carefully whether or not the much higher cost involved is worthwhile.

For all these reasons, marketers will often decide on a 'second best' approach: they will limit the sample size and use methods of sample selection that are quick, easy and convenient to use, but which, unfortunately, are not amenable to sophisticated statistical analysis.

The two main approaches to sampling are **random sampling,** in which the units are selected by chance, and **non-random sampling.** The distinction between the two is most clearly seen if one leaps to the stage when the interviewer is being given his instructions before going out to conduct the interviews. If the interviewer is given specific details of the respondents, for example their names and addresses, then this is more likely to be random sampling. On the other hand, if the interviewer is merely given broad descriptions of the types of informants required, being then allowed (subject to certain restrictions) to interview anyone fitting that description, then this is non-random sampling.

Random sampling necessitates a comprehensive and up-to-date compilation of all the members of the target population – this is the **sample frame.** There is obviously no point in deciding to take a random sample of under-25-year-old mothers if there is no list accessible. It is also important that management ensures that replacements, as a result of interviewees being away or out, are minimised and that where inevitable a person of close characteristics is substituted. In fact, interviewers are usually instructed to make a number of 'callbacks'.

There are several ways of selecting a random sample, the most common being the use of random number tables or the interval method. The latter (which only approximates to a random sample) involves taking every 'nth' name in a list (e.g. every thousandth name in a telephone directory). The size of the interval is determined by the required sample size.

In the case of non-random sampling, samples may often be selected purely on the criterion of convenience when speedy and cheap indications of possible reactions are required. Such convenience sampling (using, for example, volunteer employees) is often used in initial product testing or pre-exploratory discussions. Where more systematic sampling is required, firms employ quota sampling. This involves dividing the target population into subgroups or strata according to some appropriate criteria (such as sex, age groups, etc). The sample is composed so that the proportion of, say, males or 20–30 year olds in each stratum is the same as its proportion in the total population. The resulting sample is then divided into quotas for each interviewer.

The interviewer obviously has to exercise considerable judgment and it is consequently not surprising that this method leads to significant unrepresentativeness unless strict controls are employed. For example, there is a natural tendency to interview the better-dressed individuals since these appear more approachable; yet these can have different attitudes and forms of behaviour that may distinguish them from the not so well dressed. There can also be considerable inaccuracies: results obtained from different interviewers can vary significantly because of the personal and often subconscious preferences of the interviewers.

There are several potential sources of sampling error (see Figure 5.2):

(1) The list or sample frame from which the sample is taken is not exhaustive or up to date so that it does not contain all the target population; this is termed *sample frame unrepresentativeness.*

(2) There may be discrepancy between the selected sample and the sample that should have been selected in order to be fully representative of the target population; this is *sample unrepresentativeness.*

(3) The sample that is actually questioned may differ in important ways from the planned sample; this may be due to *non-response.*

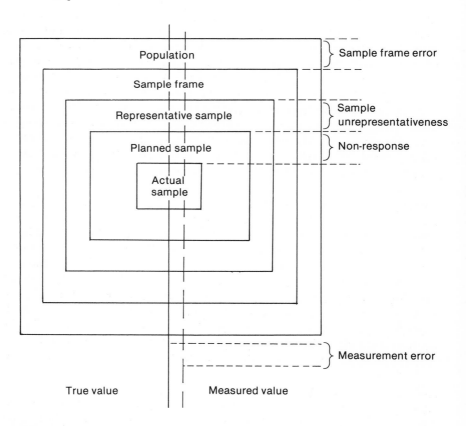

Figure 5.2 *Sources of Error in Sampling*

(4) There may be differences between the true value of the characteristics being examined and the value as measured; this is *measurement error.*

Observation

Much valuable information can be gained by observing people under various situations, using concealed human observers or hidden cameras. Such procedures can supply an accurate picture of overt behaviour; it overcomes the problems of recall and dishonesty and the other difficulties that attend more traditional methods. It is, however, extemely costly, with observers spending a lot of their time waiting for something to happen, whilst it can give no insights into why people behave the way they do or what their attitudes are. Nevertheless, it can be usefully employed to provide information on, for example, the way people shop; whether or not people notice street advertisements; the way people use various facilities, and so on.

One of the first research studies using observation was performed in the USA; it examined purchasing behaviour in supermarkets. The results contradicted the belief that supermarket shopping was carried out by housewives acting alone. In fact this was found to be so in only 39 per cent of the cases; in 32 per cent of cases the housewife was accompanied by another person who often apparently participated in the purchasing decision; in the remaining 29 per cent of cases the housewife was not present. The study also gave interesting insights into the product categories where children had an influence, the role of the adult male in some purchasing decisions, and the influence of price and packaging (Wells and Sciuto (1966) pp. 227–233).

Experimentation

Scientific experiments generally involve the study of the relationship between two variables (such as temperature and volume) under conditions when all other variables are strictly controlled. From this it is possible to derive functional or causal relationships between variables. Similarly, marketing experimentation strives to discover the effect of different elements of the marketing mix on sales by controlling extraneous influences. The difficulties are formidable, and to be sure of obtaining meaningful results — without the impact of any external 'noise' — elaborately-planned experimentation is necessary and this is expensive.

> *An example of a simple experiment would be a company that wanted to learn whether or not an increase in the price of its product would have a significant impact on sales. It selects*

two areas which are matched in terms of number and size of retail outlets, and demographic and socio-economic characteristics of populations. In one area the price is increased; in the other, the price is kept the same. The sales in both areas over the same period are then noted. The difference in sales between the two areas is the change in sales that could be attributed to the price change, assuming that the external factors affect both areas equally. However, this may not be the case; for example, a retail store in one area may embark on an aggressive promotion of a rival product or competitors may increase their advertising effort in one area only.

Summary

Marketing research aims to collect information which can assist the marketer in making the best decisions. There are two main types of information; primary data and secondary data. Secondary information is that which is already available and accessible, whereas primary information has to be collected, usually with some research objective in view. There are different categories of research: exploratory, which is often qualitative in nature and is usually concerned with obtaining more information on the background to the problem; descriptive research, which strives to find out what is actually happening; explanatory research, which focuses on the underlying reasons for what is happening; and predictive research, which attempts to provide information on, for example, the possible results of future marketing decisions. In planning a market research project, it is important that agreement is reached between the sponsor of the research and the researchers over the objectives of the research; the time when the results will be required; the cost of the research; and the accuracy and form of the results. There are several means of collecting primary information: by means of surveys; observation; and experimentation. Surveys are, by far, the most commonly employed means and the major survey research instruments used are: telephone interviews; postal questionnaires; and face-to-face interviews. Samples for surveys can be randomly or non-randomly selected. There are several main sources of error in survey work, including inaccuracies resulting from the interviewers themselves and from the sampling procedure.

Further Reading

Wells, W.D. and Sciuto, L.O. (1966) 'Direct observation of purchasing behaviour,' *Journal of Marketing Research*.

Wilson, A. (1973) *The Assessment of Industrial Markets*, Associated Business Programmes.

Review Questions

(1) Give the main reasons why you think that the marketing manager of a manufacturing company needs marketing research data.

(2) Give examples of (a) exploratory research; (b) descriptive research; (c) explanatory research; and (d) predictive research.

(3) Give details of the main sources of secondary information. What secondary information is a manufacturing firm likely to have available?

(4) The manufacturer of a range of pharmaceutical products requiring a prescription has noted that the sales of one of its major brands, which accounts for 16 per cent of its total revenue, are declining. What marketing research would you recommend him to undertake?

(5) The manufacturer of a new dry shampoo wants to find out the attitudes to his innovative product. How would you go about devising (a) a random sample; (b) a non-random sample?

(6) Say whether you agree, or disagree, with the use of the research instruments proposed in each of the following cases, and give your reasons:

    (a) a survey on household's consumption of alcohol using telephone interviewing;

    (b) a postal questionnaire to find out the reasons for the purchase of diesel-propelled lorries;

    (c) personal interviewing, using a quota sample, to find out the reaction to a series of commercials for a new product that were shown throughout the previous evening.

(7) Devise an experiment for assessing the sales response to a reduction in price of a branded soap powder.

(8) How would you attempt to reduce the errors in a random survey of attitudes using personal interviewing?

(9) What data would you expect a manufacturer of textile machinery to collect on a continuous basis?

First introduced in 1909, Persil has retained its position as a leading brand through constant modernisation. Today Persil and Persil Automatic account for 42% of the washing powder market

6

The Product

In today's highly-competitive marketing environment, companies employ a variety of strategies to distinguish their products from those of the competition. Product differentiation is founded on the assumption that customers may purchase a product for a variety of reasons. On a visible level, customers may be attracted by design, colour, packaging and technical attributes; on a more intangible level, they may be attracted by the image they have of the brand and by the reputation of its manufacturer. Finally, they may be attracted by the guarantees, the availability and price of spare parts and the back-up service. These non-price factors are, as has already been noted, increasingly important in winning orders and maintaining market share.

The product, then, can be regarded as a composite of tangible and intangible features. It is, of course, the function of marketing to assess what attributes the consumer seeks from the product and to combine these to make the most attractive product offering that, in turn, will optimise the company's profits. After all, it is a realistic premise that customers will often pay more for a product that more closely matches their requirements.

In general, each product has its own life cycle over which it grows, matures and dies. On the simplest level, companies need to ensure that they have new products coming on stream to profitability to replace those which are suffering from declining sales and profits. In addition, companies need to have an effective means of identifying problem products; then, they need to make appropriate decisions on their modification and elimination.

The Product Concept

The product of a company can, in general, be viewed as an item of its output; it is usually offered for sale. The products of manufacturing firms are obviously tangible. However, a product may also be intangible, as is the case with the output of service industries. A household insurance package is an example of a product which is a service.

133

The concept of a product becomes more complex if one accepts that it often consists of much more than those elements which can be seen, heard, tasted or felt.

> The buyer of a can of lager may be seeking several benefits from his purchase in addition to quenching his thirst. He may seek the convenience of a ring-pull can. He may prefer a brand that has certain associations that will generally have been built up by advertising and experience.

> The purchaser of a colour television set may be persuaded to buy the product of a particular manufacturer because of its physical features and the quality of its picture. In addition, he may also have been persuaded by the fact that the manufacturer has a reputation for innovation, reliability and an effective and speedy repair service.

For simplicity, it is suggested that a product can be considered as consisting of one or more dimensions.

First, there is the **generic dimension**, which is the key benefit (or benefits) that the product satisfies. For example, lorries may be regarded as satisfying the need for convenient transport; baked beans may be viewed as a nutritional food; and cameras may be seen as providing memories. A product may symbolise certain wants sought by consumers such as status, freedom, and sophistication.

Secondly, there is the **sensual dimension**, which embraces the texture, colour, taste, design, and so on, of the product. A particular tomato soup may be preferred for its colour, another for its flavour.

Thirdly, there is the **extended dimension,** which includes the *additional* benefits of the product, such as the maintenance, guarantees, and technical advice. A manufacturer of textiles could be expected to be concerned about the technical advice offered by the suppliers of textile machinery, as well as the reliability of the machine and the quality of the finished textiles produced on it.

A **brand** is the name and other features − such as label design and pack shape − that are employed by manufacturers to distinguish their products from those of their rivals. Customers can build up strong associations with a brand that not only assist in repeat purchasing, but can also aid in the launching of new brands. Cadbury, for example, cleverly employed the quality associated with the Cadbury name to market two new products, 'Marvel' and 'Smash', and thereby probably overcome much possible customer resistance to dehydrated products which (because of wartime experiences with dried milk and potato) had traditionally a low-quality image. The way in which strong associations are built up with particular brand names is emphasised by the following:

> Take for example, the idea of an instant cream dessert with fruit, something which may or may not be technically possible at present. Were such a product to be developed by a dairy company such as Unigate, it would be judged very much as an 'instant CREAM dessert with fruit'. Just the presence of the Unigate or St. Ivel names on this label would lead the consumer to expect a dairy-based product — and such a product would be more appropriate for the company itself. Because of this, the competition for the new brand would be likely to be of a particular sort; it would need to look more like a dairy product, and — most important — the 'creamy' taste would have to be quite near to natural.
>
> Now assume the same product were to be launched under the Del Monte label. Immediately the perception is different. It now becomes an 'instant cream dessert with FRUIT'. Such a brand would be judged differently, would have slightly different products as its prime competition, and would need to have a good fruit taste. In this context, the idea might, or might not, prove to be suited to that particular company. (Broadbent (1980) p.30)

The reader can test the strong connotations of certain brands by considering the viability of Persil chocolate, Esso orange drink, Mars skin cream, and Heinz disinfectant.

Branding is only one way of differentiating a product from its competitors; in fact, it would be more accurate to argue that the brand is the actual embodiment of the differentiating features, referred to as the *non-price factors*.

Product Life Cycle

As noted in Chapter 1, most products can be viewed as having a life cycle. The idealised life cycle consists of four stages: introduction; growth; maturity; and decline. Profits can be expected to increase and then fall as shown in Figure 6.1.

In the *introduction* stage, sales will be low since not many people will have heard of the new product, or if they have they will be reluctant to try it out because of its novelty. They may be unsure of its features: its fitness for purpose, its reliability, its 'true' costs . . . In this sense, then, potential customers perceive a risk in its purchase. Sales may also be limited by production capacity; the market may be supplied by a small pilot plant while the company waits either to see the market response or for the full-scale plant to be completed.

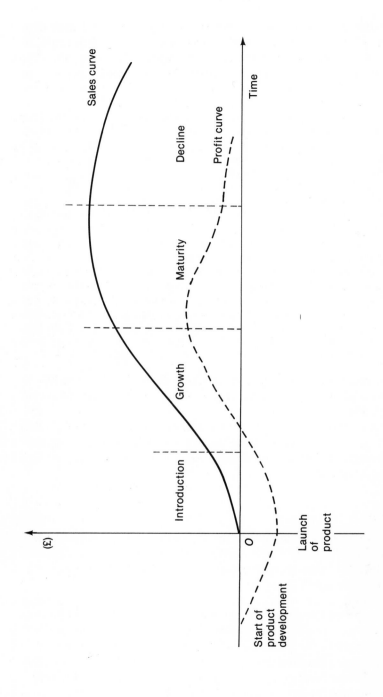

Figure 6.1 *Product and Profit Life Cycle*

One of the main purposes of advertising and promotion is to create awareness of the product and stimulate trial. Consequently, advertising and promotional expenditure will generally be high, both absolutely and as a percentage of sales. Other costs may also be high: there may have been large research and development costs which have to be recovered, whilst investment in manufacturing capacity may be necessary. Overall, then, the net losses of the product will intensify during this period.

During the *growth* stage, however, sales will take off as more people learn of the product, try it out, and disseminate information about it. Perceived risk will lessen as consumers learn of the actual effects of using the product. Sales should theoretically follow an exponential growth pattern, similar to that of an infectious disease. Although advertising and promotional expenditures will remain high, they will decline as a proportion of total product price. Unit costs in general will decline substantially as output increases, and the product should make profits. During this stage competition will enter the market, but as long as total demand increases there should be enough room for everyone. The emphasis in the advertising will shift from 'Buy this product' to 'Buy my brand'. Although prices will probably fall over time in order to stimulate sales, price competition will not be general.

In the *mature* stage, there is a deceleration in sales growth, the market becomes saturated and there is little, if any, growth in the market. Demand, for the most part, consists of repeat sales with any growth stemming from increases in population in its market segments. Consequently, competition intensifies, prices tend to fall, and selling effort becomes aggressive. Profits then are squeezed. Finally, in the *decline* stage, actual sales begin to fall under the impact of new-product competition and changing consumer tastes and preferences. Prices and hence profits decline.

Some firms may delete mature products from their range, and reallocate their resources to other, more profitable, activities. Others may decide to retain the product with the minimum of marketing support; they will be content, provided it covers its variable costs and makes some contribution to overall company profits and overheads. Alternatively, companies may try to stimulate sales by modifying the product in some way such as improving its design or its technical features.

The product life cycle is a conceptual representation. This cycle is not inevitable since it can be rejuvenated by modifying the product as suggested above. Indeed, several products or brands have maintained their market position over many years precisely because their manufacturers have pursued a policy of periodically reappraising the product and 'modernising' it where appropriate.

Nylon is an ideal example of a product whose life cycle was extended by product and market development. Nylon was conceived, developed and marketed by the large American chemical company, E.I. du Pont de Nemours. It was first employed primarily for military applications, in particular for parachutes, thread and rope. It was then used in, what is termed, the 'circular knit market' where it came to dominate the women's hosiery business. Eventually, this market became saturated and Du Pont sought to stimulate sales by introducing new shades and patterns: 'Hosiery was to be converted from a "neutral" accessory to a central ingredient of fashion, with a "suitable" tint and pattern for each garment in the lady's wardrobe'. Du Pont also developed new uses that ranged 'from varied types of hosiery, such as stretch stockings and stretch socks, to new uses, such as rugs, tyres, bearings, and so forth'. In fact, it has been suggested that without an active policy of innovation designed to create new applications for nylon, consumption would have reached a saturation level of 50 million pounds annually in its original military, circular knit, and miscellaneous uses. In fact, in 1962 consumption exceeded 500 million pounds. (Levitt 1963)

Persil — first introduced in 1909 — obtained its name from the perborate and silicate from which it was made. It quickly secured its place as a leading brand in the market place, and over the years has maintained that position; today Persil and Persil Automatic account for 42 per cent of the washing powder market that is worth some £270 million per annum.

What are the reasons for the brand's ability to retain its market lead in such a highly competitive market? Probably a distinctive blend of a sound product, a policy of constantly modernising the product formulation, and heavy and effective advertising.

When Persil was first introduced by Crosfield most washing was still performed using bar soap, so that the new 'amazing oxygen cleaner' was a significant advance. When Lever Brothers took over Crosfield in 1919 washing methods were changing from the old 'dolly tub and washboard' to the much less laborious method of soaking, using these powerful soap-based detergents. The merits of Persil were heavily advertised, and the 'Persil washes whiter' slogan soon helped the product gain a lead over its main rivals, Rinso and Oxydol.

However, in the early 1950s, Tide — the first of the new breed of synthetic, non-soap detergents (NSD) — was launched by Lever Brothers' arch rival, Procter and Gamble, and it quickly secured market leadership. These NSDs had a significant advantage in that they were equally suitable for both soft and hard water and left no nasty scum. Lever Brothers reacted by reformulating Persil to make it suitable for hard water, and it regained its market position.

Since then, a policy of reformulation to take account of new requirements imposed by the introduction of new types of fabrics has been actively pursued. However, another major challenge came in 1969 when P & G introduced the biological detergent Ariel. Persil's share fell from 26 per cent to below 20 per cent. Lever Brothers immediately reacted by emphasising Persil's gentleness in order to capitalise on what was perceived to be housewives' concern that the new biological detergents might harm fabrics – and perhaps certain skin types. This campaign, combined with the long association of Persil with 'caring', resulted in Persil recovering its market lead by 1972 as Ariel's market share fell to below 20 per cent.

Perhaps one of the most important decisions by Lever was to launch a powder specially for use in automatic washing machines under the Persil brand. Lever decided in 1968 that it should produce a low-suds detergent suitable for automatics even though only 4 per cent of UK households at that time owned automatic washing machines. The first marketing attempt was called Skip – a powder which had a completely different formula from the existing high-suds Persil – but test marketing gave disappointing results. The product was renamed Persil Automatic. Persil's brand manager suggests:

> That was probably the most important decision behind the success of Persil Automatic today. Simply by doing that they invoked all the heritage of Persil, which by then was enormous.

Currently 35 per cent of households have automatics, and this has had favourable consequences for the demand for low-suds powders because housewives with automatics tend to use twice as much detergent as those with twin tubs. The explosion in the size of the market has justified Lever's early efforts. Today, Lever spends heavily on advertising Persil – around two million pounds annually – and also on promotion to ensure that the brand maintains its share of supermarket shelf space. Despite its market supremacy, Lever Brothers is aware of the dangers of complacency. As its existing brand manager commented: 'Changes in technology can make previous history irrelevant. Procters are extremely professional competitors, even if they happen to have been not particularly successful in the last few years'. (Braham (1982) pp. 16–18).

A second point to note is that the length and pattern of product life cycles can vary significantly from product to product. There is no reason to believe that all products inevitably pass through all four stages; some might, for example proceed straight from growth into decline because, say, of the introduction of some superior new product. Other products may have a prolonged introduction stage before coming into wide acceptance.

It is also important to note that there is a distinction between the life cycles of a product class (such as cars, beer, canned food), product type (e.g. sports car, lager, canned peas), and brands (e.g. Triumph TR7, Skol, Batchelors). The product life cycle of a class can last

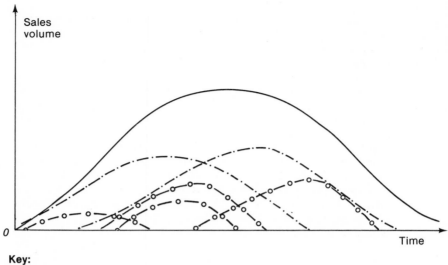

Key:
—— product class
—·— product type
–o– brand

Figure 6.2   *Life Cycles of Product Class, Type and 'Brand'*

several or even more decades. Within the class life cycle there can be several product-type life cycles. Brands will, on the whole, have even shorter life cycles. (See Figure 6.2).

At first glance, it would appear that the product life cycle could act as an invaluable planning tool to marketers: it would enable them to predict when, for example, a product's sales would stabilise and to plan appropriate marketing programmes. Moreover, it could be employed as the basis for timing the development and launch of new products. In fact, its usefulness for strategic management is suspect: the forecasting of the turning points (e.g. from growth to maturity) is hazardous and usually inaccurate. Indeed, management may only be aware of a product's position in its life cycle when it is well into a particular stage. However, the concept of the product life cycle does serve to remind management of the tenuous nature of much product success and thereby of the evils of complacency.

Product Planning

The product life cycle suggests that management needs to monitor the performance of existing products, to devise appropriate policies for

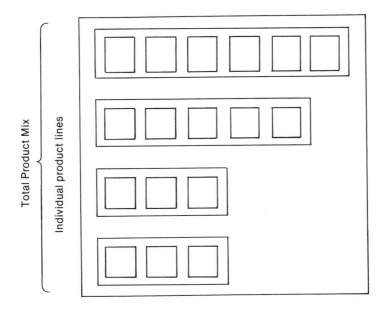

Key:

Individual products

Figure 6.3 *The Product Mix*

those products, and to develop new products where necessary. All this is the essence of product planning. **Product planning**, then, involves ~portfolio~ devising procedures to evaluate the performance of products, and planning the modification, where necessary, of existing products aimed at extending their lives; the deletion of those products which have reached the 'terminal' stage of their lives; and the development and marketing of new products. Overall, the aim is to ensure that the company has, and will continue to have, a mix of products that maximises its objectives.

The Product Mix

The **product mix** is the complete range of products that a company markets. Nowadays, many companies have wide and highly-diverse product mixes; others have extremely focused and harmonious product mixes.

A product mix, in turn, may consist of one or more product lines (see Figure 6.3); a **product line** is composed of variations of a basic product.

Philips, the electrical giant, produces a wide range of products aimed both at the consumer and industrial market. For example, it markets washing machines, radios, radio-cassette players, music centres, hi-fi units, refrigerators, video recorders, video-disc players, radar equipment, and so on. In some cases, it produces several variations of each product.

Simon-Rosedowns supplies a wide range of vegetable-oil extraction and processing plant. The products of their customers include salad and cooking oil, as well as ingredients for such products as ice cream, and margarine. Simon-Rosedowns markets screw-processing equipment, solvent-extraction-process plant, deodorisers, and oil-processing plant. The aim is to meet, as fully as is possible, the special processing requirements of their customers.

Companies should strive to ensure that they have a 'balanced' product mix or product portfolio in the sense that there are new products being developed or marketed to replace or augment those in decline or maturity, and that there are products with a positive cash flow which can be used to finance the development of new products. In addition, as we shall see later, it is important to ensure that there is a balanced portfolio of new products so that those which are highly risky (but offer the prospect of a high return) are balanced by those which have a low element of risk but also a corresponding low return.

Portfolio Analysis

One approach to analysing the product portfolio, to ensure that it is 'balanced', was devised by the Boston Consultancy Group (BCG). It was based on the experience curve principle which states that the unit costs of adding value decline as the cumulative production increases.
The gains in efficiency with greater experience stem from:

(1) productivity improvements as a result of technical change and learning effects;
(2) increasing specialisation and economies of scale;
(3) displacement of less-efficient factors of production, especially investment for cost reduction, and the substitution of capital for labour;
(4) modifications and redesign of products to reduce costs.

BCG argued that the cost reductions obtained from the above could be quite significant, amounting to a decline of approximately 20 to 30 per cent in real terms for each doubling of accumulated experience. This experience curve phenomenon (see Figure 6.4) is quite universal,

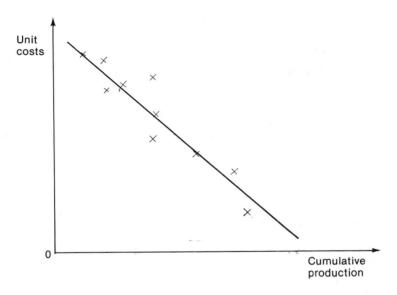

Figure 6.4   *A Generalised 'Experience' Curve*

being demonstrated for a wide range of products including transistors, float glass, and even insurance.

It is important to note that such 'experience effects' do not occur naturally with increased production; rather, companies have to act to ensure that they are realising the full gains in efficiency – that they are on the experience curve for their industry – by introducing new techniques, redesigning products, and so on. Companies which have greater experience and have adopted active managerial policies aimed at realising the consequent cost reductions will have a significant competitive advantage. They may take advantage of their lower costs to reduce prices (and thereby possibly gain a higher market share); or they may enhance their profitability (and hence the flow of cash for investment in new products) by maintaining prices, or by reducing them by only a proportion of the total cost reduction.

One conclusion of this analysis is that the greater an individual company's cumulative experience relative to its competitors, the greater its cost advantage. This suggests that companies should strive to increase their **relative market share** – defined as the ratio of the company's market share to that of its largest competitor. It is this, rather than absolute market share, which is important because it provides a truer indication of a company's competitive strength in a particular market. For example, a company may have a 40 per cent share of the market but be faced with a rival also having a 40 per cent share, in which case it does not have an obvious dominance of the market.

As a company increases its position of leadership in an industry, and thereby gains experience, its ability to reduce costs faster than its rivals is enhanced. In fact, BCG argue that if a company has a market share twice as large as its nearest rival, it generally has a cost advantage of at least 20 per cent.

In summary, then, it is suggested that in a given market or product field, profitability of competing products is a function of their market share. Products with a high market share, which dominate their market sector, have high margins and thus generate substantial cash. This relationship between market share and profitability is explained by the experience curve effect.

BCG argue that a second dimension is important in the analysis of a product portfolio: that of market growth. The faster the growth of the market, the greater will be the costs necessary to maintain the company's position because of the need to invest in working capital and in capital plant and equipment in order to ensure that production capacity keeps in step. Moreover, the high growth rate will attract competitors into the market so that aggressive product development, pricing and promotion will be essential. This is the second general rule: the investment required to maintain market share in any given market is a function of the growth rate of that market. If the growth rate is high, a high level of investment in plant, equipment, inventory, advertising, and research and development is needed if the product is to grow as fast as the market and thus retain its position.

Using these two general rules, BCG devised a product portfolio matrix as shown in Figure 6.5 (Hedley (1977) pp. 9–15). Four main classes of products are identified: 'prospects'; 'yielders'; 'question marks'; and 'dogs'. The 'prospects' are those products which are in rapidly-growing markets and which, therefore, absorb large amounts of cash. However, because they are also market leaders they are generating high revenues. The result is that they generally produce a neutral cash flow since they generate as much cash as they require for investment. These are the products which the company hopes to develop into the 'yielders' of the future.

The 'yielders' have a high market share in a low-growing market — a market where total new demand is slowing down and reaching maturity. These products demand little investment in plant and equipment, although the company may feel it necessary to spend on advertising, promoting and modifying them in order to ensure that they retain their high market share. Such products generate substantial net revenues, and they can be 'milked' to produce far more cash than can effectively be reinvested in them. 'Yielders', at least, 'pay the dividends, pay the interest on debt, and cover the corporate overhead'.

The 'question marks' have a low market share in a fast-growing

Relative market share / Market growth	High	Low
High	Prospects	Question marks
Low	Yielders	Dogs

Figure 6.5 *Product Portfolio Matrix*

market. They have the potential of being the stars of tomorrow but in order to do so they need substantial financial commitment. The company knows that unless it invests heavily in them it will eventually be compelled to withdraw them from the market at a loss. Yet there is no guarantee that they will ever catch up with the leading products in the field. A company may well find that it has several 'question marks', but it will only be able to afford to support a few of them. It must have the means of identifying those with the best promise of success. These 'question marks', then, constitute a considerable gamble, and probably most of them end up as failures.

Finally, the 'dogs' are those products with a low market share in a low-growing market. The company, then, is at a considerable cost disadvantage in a market that has no potential; generally, the effort required to sustain their position is greater than the net returns, whilst the resources required to secure the leading position in the market would, undoubtedly, be more effectively invested elsewhere. BCG recommend that such products be withdrawn from the product portfolio.

A balanced product portfolio could be said to be one where the net revenue from the 'yielders' is sufficient to offset the losses from the 'question marks', to provide enough resources to move at least the more attractive 'question marks' into the 'prospects' category, and yield a profit on total company operations sufficient to satisfy shareholders (see Figure 6.6). The positive cash flow from the 'yielders' should be directed to converting the 'question marks' to prospects. In turn, these should become 'yielders' as their demand slackens.

In recent years, many criticisms have been made of this BCG

Relative market share / Market growth	High	Low
High	Neutral cash flow	Large negative cash flow
Low	Large positive cash flow	Net losers

Figure 6.6   *Cash Flow and Dynamic Product Policy*

approach to product-mix analysis. In particular it has been argued that:

(1) There is no definition of 'the market'. A market may consist of several segments, and although a company may have a low share of the total market, it may have a high and very profitable share of a particular market segment. For example, BMW has only a low share of the total car market, but has a significant share of the premium-priced, luxury segment. It is also very profitable. Companies can successfully pursue a strategy based on catering for the wants of smaller, specialised segments.

(2) The analysis is often interpreted as suggesting that it is low price (achieved by lower costs as a result of greater 'experience') that assists in winning greater market share. This may be true in certain markets, but in other markets, non-price factors such as design and technical specifications may be equally, if not more, important. In these cases, the exclusive pursuit of the lowest cost structure will not be successful.

(3) Companies may aggressively pursue policies aimed at winning the highest market share in the hope that when they do, there will be a sufficiently long and uninterrupted period when they can collect their rewards. In fact, there is no guarantee that this will be the case: new competition may enter the industry with more efficient plant; or market demand may slacken or disappear because of technological innovations or changes in customer tastes and preferences.

(4) The terms 'high' and 'low' are not defined.

(5) The elimination of the 'dogs' may not necessarily be the most appropriate option, as we shall discuss under the product elimination decision later.

The original BCG approach has, then, been criticised as being over simplistic: there are many qualitative influences that may need to be considered. Other analyses have attempted to take some of these into account. For instance, Shell (1975) has devised a matrix using 'prospects for sector profitability' (which embraces market growth rate, market quality, industry situation, and environmental aspects) and 'the company's competitive capability' (which includes market position, product research and development, and production capability).

Product Review Procedure

Companies should periodically review their existing product mix and take action, where appropriate, to modify or even delete those products which do not meet some pre-established criteria of adequate performance. This suggests the need to have some systematic method that enables them to identify quickly and easily those products requiring managerial action. Figure 6.7 depicts the outline of a possible simple procedure.

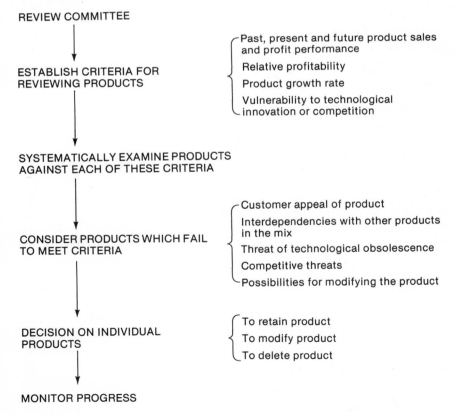

REVIEW COMMITTEE

ESTABLISH CRITERIA FOR REVIEWING PRODUCTS
- Past, present and future product sales and profit performance
- Relative profitability
- Product growth rate
- Vulnerability to technological innovation or competition

SYSTEMATICALLY EXAMINE PRODUCTS AGAINST EACH OF THESE CRITERIA

CONSIDER PRODUCTS WHICH FAIL TO MEET CRITERIA
- Customer appeal of product
- Interdependencies with other products in the mix
- Threat of technological obsolescence
- Competitive threats
- Possibilities for modifying the product

DECISION ON INDIVIDUAL PRODUCTS
- To retain product
- To modify product
- To delete product

MONITOR PROGRESS

Figure 6.7 *Product Review Process*

The first stage might commence with the formation of a review committee. This might consist of representatives of marketing, finance, production and research and development in order to obtain a fuller picture of all facets of individual products. From marketing, a senior marketing member might be involved, such as the marketing manager (who has an overview of the product mix and is not specifically committed to one or more products), as well as marketing-research personnel. Their objectives would be to establish criteria for appraising the product mix in order to identify those products demanding further detailed consideration. Consequently, the committee would have to decide on whether or not to maintain the product in the mix without any alteration, to modify the product, or to eliminate the product.

Criteria for Appraising Product Mix

In the first instance, a simple check list of criteria is required in order to sift out quickly those products which either merit immediate action or are likely to demand action in the future because of the possibility of changing environmental conditions. At this stage, then, the committee might decide that some or all of the following criteria are appropriate:

(a) sales and profit history of the product;
(b) profitability relative to other products in the mix;
(c) future profit growth;
(d) vulnerability to technological developments, competitors' actions, changes in tastes ...

Sales and Profit Performance   If sales and/or profits of a product have stabilised or deteriorated then this suggests that the product might have reached the mature or even decline stage of its life cycle. However, the product may only be undergoing a temporary setback; nevertheless, the reasons for this need to be investigated further. It may not be sufficient, though, to consider a product's current performance; products may be generating considerable revenue but still be highly susceptible to competition or external technological innovation and a quick assessment of this vulnerability may be desirable at this stage.

One easily applied criterion that can be employed is based on the product's relative profitability. All those products that have a below-average profitability might, according to this principle, merit further consideration. A further simple diagnostic aid, based on the growth rate of the product relative to that of the market in which it is competitive, might also be helpful at this early stage of product analysis. From Figure 6.8 it can be seen that products which lie above the

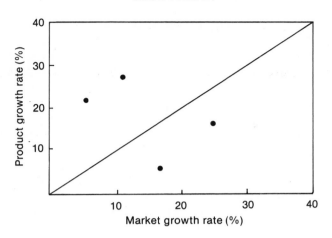

Figure 6.8 *Product Growth Rate and Market Growth Rate*

diagonal are growing at rates faster than the market, so that in each case the product is increasing its market share. They would appear to be in a healthy position but this may be being maintained at considerable investment cost. The company needs to ask, then, to what extent this position can continue to be maintained.

'Weak' Products Those products which fail to satisfy these predetermined criteria have been termed 'weak'. They are those products which, given the present marketing formula are absorbing resources that could yield a higher return if allocated elsewhere. By altering the marketing formula (i.e. modifying the product in some way) or by deleting the product from the mix where the modification is unlikely to be successful, overall corporate profitability is likely to be improved.

Many of these 'weak' products can often be a heavy burden, both in terms of the financial resources they consume and the managerial effort they demand. As Alexander (1967) noted:

> The old product that is a 'football' of competition or has lost much of its market appeal is likely to generate more than its share of small unprofitable orders; to make necessary short, costly production runs; to demand an exorbitant amount of executive attention; and to tie up capital that could be used more profitably in other ventures.

In a careful detailed examination of the weak products, the review team needs to consider a number of important questions before making the critical decision of whether or not to eliminate such products from the mix. These might include the following:

(1) What is the customer appeal of the product? It may be that a product has no distinctive appeal because of the introduction of new products or improvement of its main rivals. By simply reformulating the product, repackaging it, and modernising the advertising, it might be possible to regain its former competitive edge.

(2) What are the possibilities of modifying the product? For example, can the functional aspects be improved? Has it a perceived low quality relative to its competitors, and can its quality be improved?

(3) What is the vulnerability of the product to technological innovation and competition? It has already been noted that such external changes pose a very real danger to all products. The company needs to assess carefully the susceptibility of the product to such threats.

(4) What are the interdependencies between the product and other products in the mix? There are two types of interdependencies: cost interdependencies, and demand interdependencies.

Cost interdependencies exist when the product shares facilities (such as manufacturing and distribution) with other products. Consequently, the product may be making a contribution to the total cost of the facilities; its removal from the mix will mean that the total costs have to be borne by the remaining products. When considering the deletion of a product, then, the company needs to ask: 'What will be the effect of the removal of this product on the cost structure?'

Demand interdependencies exist where there are cross elasticities of demand between products; a product may, for example, be regarded as a complement to other products in the mix. The removal of the product from the mix will compel customers to seek alternative sources of supply, and they may take some or all of their other custom as well, particularly if they prefer to deal exclusively with one manufacturer.

The Product Elimination Decision

Given that a company decides to eliminate a product from its product mix, there are important factors that should be taken into account in phasing it out: the need to retain customer good will, minimise costs, and at the same time ensure the optimal reallocation of resources.

First, the company needs to consider its obligations to existing customers. This may mean building up adequate stocks of replacement parts and advising customers of the impending withdrawal of the product so that they can make suitable alternative arrangements. However, customers 'should be advised about the elimination of the product sufficiently in advance so that they can make arrangements for a replacement, if any is available; but not so far in advance that they will appoint new suppliers before the deleting firm's inventories of the product are sold' (Alexander 1967). Considerable customer illwill can be engendered if such precautions are not taken.

Secondly, the timing of the withdrawal of the product is important. This can be especially true where the plant and equipment used in its manufacture have not fully depreciated. Two considerations may be taken into account: first, whether or not this plant and equipment can be employed in the manufacture of other products (if so, it is important to ensure that such a transfer is efficiently effected); and secondly, whether or not the plant and equipment have fully depreciated (if not, it is easy to allow the desire to recover the full costs to influence the deletion decision, with the result that products may be prolonged at further cost to the company). The amount already invested should be disregarded in such decisions; it has already been spent and should be written off.

Summary

The 'total' product can be said to consist of the generic, sensual and extended product. All products have a life cycle which conceptually consists of four stages: introduction, growth, maturity and decline. Companies need to plan for (a) the modification of existing products in order to stimulate sales as products approach the later stages of their life cycles, and (b) the replacement of products whose sales are stabilising.

Companies should establish a review system for identifying 'weak' products. A number of questions need to be answered before deciding to withdraw a product, including 'what would be the effect of the withdrawal on the costs of and the demand for the remaining products?'

Further Reading

Alexander, R.S. (1967) 'The death and burial of "sick" products', *Journal of Marketing*, April.

Braham, M. (1982) 'Why Persil keeps its lead', *Marketing*, 12th August.

Broadbent, D. (1980) 'Give new products a chance', *Marketing*, 27th August.

Hedley, B. (1977) 'Strategy and the business portfolio', *Long Range Planning*, February, Vol. 10, No. 1.

Levitt, T. (1963) 'Exploit the product life cycle', *Harvard Business Review*, November–December.

Shell International Chemical Company (1975) 'The directional policy matrix: a new aid to corporate planning', November.

Review Questions

(1) What 'wants' do you think that the following products satisfy?
    (a) Porsche automobiles
    (b) Instant-picture cameras
    (c) A business micro-computer
    (d) Chanel perfume

(2) Why do companies employ branding?

(3) Analyse the major factors that are likely to affect the future demand for:
    (a) photocopying machines;
    (b) calculators;
    (c) canned foods.

(4) It is often argued that the length of the life cycles of products is declining. Do you agree? Give your reasons.

(5) Select a well-advertised brand and define the 'personality' of that brand.

(6) What do you think *should be* the major factors influencing the number of product lines in the product mix (the 'width' of the product mix)?

(7) How would you decide on which 'question marks' to retain and support?

(8) Summarise the major factors that you consider should be taken into account before deciding to withdraw a product from the product mix.

The Yorkie image: a key factor in the product's success

7
New Product Development

*He that will not apply new remedies
must expect new evils, for time is the
greatest innovator*

(*Francis Bacon,* Of Innovations)

*NOW, HERE, you see, it takes all the
running you can do to keep in the same
place. If you want to get somewhere else,
you must run at least twice as fast as
that*

(*Lewis Carroll*, Alice's Adventures in Wonderland)

Companies need to have a dynamic product development policy to guarantee their future growth and indeed their very survival. Those that do not innovate will either ultimately be compelled to do so in the wake of pioneering innovations of their competitors, or be forced out of business. There is, however, a high risk associated with product development: most new products are abandoned during the course of development; and a significant proportion of those new products that are marketed have to be withdrawn because they fail to satisfy commercial criteria of success. Against this background, experienced companies will adopt a policy of having a stream of new products under development in order to be sure of some new product success.

The product development process itself can be complex and usually involves the participation of all the main corporate functions. This in itself can pose formidable organisational problems. In this chapter, the factors that are likely to increase the probability of successful product development are outlined and a case study of a successful new product development is described.

The Need for New Product Development

The importance of new products is by now clear: the company concerned to ensure its future growth, or faced with constant threats of competitive innovative developments, saturated markets for existing products, and changes in customer tastes, needs to have in hand a programme of new product launches. The importance of product innovation has been repeatedly stressed. For example as was emphasised by the OECD (1971):

> Because of sales decline and price erosion of older products, a firm must − in addition to making relatively minor innovations − successfully launch new products if it is to maintain its growth targets... these products will sometimes be based on new technologies or radically new markets for the firm.

Numerous studies have pinpointed the importance of new products to sales and profit growth. For example, investigations of the grocery industry have shown that this industry − in which technological innovation has, for the most part, been minor rather than radical, but in which competition is intense and the consumer increasingly fickle − has tended to concentrate on the development of new products and brands as a means of maintaining and increasing sales. As can be seen from Table 7.1, which details the results of two studies, *new* food products or brands have accounted for a high proportion of total sales increase (around 70 per cent in some cases) and for an important proportion of total sales.

Companies alert to external threats to their existing products pursue a policy of constant product appraisal, modification and development. Product innovation may be stimulated by:

(a) Obsolescence of existing products as a result of changes in technology etc. There may be little, if any, scope for modification; or it is felt that such a course will yield only marginal benefits not commensurate with the costs involved. Under such circumstances, it will be more effective to reallocate resources to the development of new products which will not only be more competitive but will also offer the promise of significantly higher returns.

(b) The inability of the existing product range to generate sufficient sales and profits to satisfy corporate objectives. Product innovation will be one means of filling such a gap.

There are different types of product innovation: some may demand only minor changes in technology, whilst others may involve more

Table 7.1 *Effects of Distinctly New Products and New Brands on Sales Growth*

	% increase in total sales 1958–1964	Sales of distinctly new products introduced since 1958[1]	
		% of total sales increase: 1958–1964	% of 1964 sales
Average for high-growth companies (weighted)	43.3	72.7	22
Average for moderate-growth companies (weighted)	20.3	47.3	8

	% increase in total sales 1966–1970	Sales of new brands introduced since 1966[2]	
		% of total sales increase: 1966–1970	% of 1970 sales
Average for whole sample	30	50	11
Average for moderate- to high-growth companies	49	67	> 10
Average for moderate- to low-growth companies	16	15	< 10

Sources: (1) Buzzell, R.D. and Nourse, R.E.M. (1967) *Product Innovation in Food Processing 1954–1964*, Harvard University Press.
(2) Mandry, G.D. (1973) *New Product Development in the UK Grocery Trade*, Manchester Business School Retail Outlets Research Unit.

substantial innovations in technology and, in turn, create totally new markets. For simplicity it is possible to distinguish between two polar extremes of innovation based on the degree of technological change involved (Littler 1978).

Evolutionary innovations are the result of a process of continuous modification to and improvement on existing technology. This form of change is, for the most part, an on-going activity in the modern, large, industrial corporation; consequently, evolutionary innovation may be 'routinised' and, in the case of new products, the marketing function will often be the major initiator. Most product innovations are of this nature.

Radical innovations generally involve discontinuities, both in trends of existing technologies and in patterns of consumption. Although they offer the promise of high payoffs, these have to be balanced against the high risks and uncertainties associated with such developments.

Most product innovation is inevitably of an evolutionary nature. The reasons are obvious: first, the opportunities for radical technological breakthroughs are limited; secondly, companies in any case would prefer, wherever possible, to keep within the technological and market areas with which they are familiar; thirdly, radical innovation often involves risks and uncertainties which can act as a significant deterrent.

Risks and Uncertainties

New product development presents a dilemma: it often involves risks and uncertainties that management would consciously like to avoid; yet decision makers are aware that the very survival of the firm can be dependent on a dynamic product-development activity.

The risks associated with innovation are well known in that many new products, once marketed, have to be withdrawn because they fail to meet predefined market goals and may make appreciable losses. It has been suggested, for instance, that approximately 50 per cent of products which are launched have to be withdrawn. For UK food manufacturers, the risks are much higher: it has been estimated that only 3 to 4 per cent of new food brands are successful (Ramsey (1981) pp.4 – 6; Madell 1981). Such figures underestimate the true risk involved because most new products will be abandoned at some stage during their development. Such product failure can be expensive:

> Du Pont developed a leather substitute called Corfam which was withdrawn from the market at an estimated cost of 150 million dollars.

> The Ford Edsel was a major product disaster that cost the company hundreds of millions of dollars.

Watney's Red Barrel, a keg bitter heralding the 'Red Revolution', flopped at a significant cost to the company.

The major cigarette manufacturers and other large 'market-oriented' companies, such as ICI and Courtaulds, invested heavily in the development of tobacco substitutes. Several new brands containing these materials were launched; all failed.

Given that the advertising costs alone of many consumer products can amount to many hundreds of thousands of pounds, it is not surprising that companies aim to minimise the risks as much as possible. However, the risks of losses are offset by the chance that the product may be highly profitable:

Pilkington developed a new, revolutionary method of producing high-quality flat glass that involved floating the molten glass on liquid tin in an inert atmosphere of nitrogen. Millions of pounds were spent on developing and perfecting the process. It has since been marketed worldwide, with most major, flat-glass manufacturers licensing the technology. The resulting licensing income has contributed significantly to Pilkington's profits, enabling investment in the development of new products.

Rowntree Mackintosh developed a new solid chocolate bar in competition with Cadbury's Dairy Milk which had long dominated the solid chocolate-bar market. The resulting product, Yorkie, achieved sales of £40 million within four years of being marketed.

Uncertainty arises because of the difficulties of predicting what is likely to happen. Although it stems from a wide range of sources, it is sufficient to note two main types: market uncertainty and technological uncertainty.

Market uncertainty ranges from the difficulty in forecasting whether or not competing technologies, which might inhibit the demand for the innovation, are being developed, to the uncertainty concerning the reaction of users and customers and therefore the possible market size of the product. Thus, uncertainty surrounds the future income stream.

Technological uncertainty results from the difficulty of predicting the nature of the technical problems which might arise during the course of development. These often demand novel technical solutions, the cost of which will often inflate the initially estimated development costs.

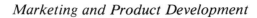

(Costly
Risk)

The fact that such uncertainties can have a dramatic impact has been indicated by the findings of a number of empirical investigations. In general, there are deviations between initial forecasts of costs, benefits, and time for project completion, with cost and durations being underestimated, and benefits overestimated. Uncertainty is one plausible explanation of such deviations between predictions and outcomes.

Product Development Process

The process of developing new products embraces a variety of different tasks and functions. For ease of description, it can be viewed as a series of distinct stages; in practice, some of the tasks are performed simultaneously, and most activities are carried out continuously. For example, marketing research should be carried out throughout the development to ensure that the emerging product continues to satisfy market wants; similarly, the commercial prospects of the product should be continuously reviewed in the light of changing environmental conditions, since there may have been dramatic changes that could, for example, undermine the originally-conceived prospects for the innovation.

Some of the ingredients of the new product-development process are listed in Table 7.2. The process starts with the development of a 'bank' of ideas which then pass through a series of stages as they are evaluated and developed. It is argued that the number of ideas that fall by the wayside as they progress through this process is high (see Figure 7.1). According to one famous study of 51 companies, for every 58 ideas, about 12 pass the initial screening. Only seven of these survive after evaluation, and only three pass through to test marketing. Two are eventually marketed, and only one could be said to be commercially successful (Booz, Allen and Hamilton (1968) p.9). In another study of product development in the food manufacturing industry (Buzzell and Nourse 1967), it was concluded that of every 1000 new product ideas:

  810 were rejected at preliminary screening;
  135 were rejected on the basis of product tests;
  12 were discontinued after test marketing;
  43 were introduced to the market on a regular basis;
  36 remained on the market after introduction.

Generation of Ideas

The first vital step is to generate ideas. Unfortunately, 'good' ideas are generally not as plentiful as is often believed and they may well have to

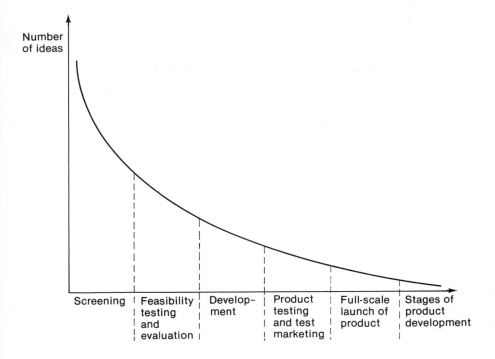

Figure 7.1 *Rejection of New Product Ideas During the Development Process*

be actively and painstakingly sought. Even the most conscientious searching may yield few bases for practical product development. Ideas can arise haphazardly and from many sources, including:

(1) marketing: for example, active market analysis can help to pinpoint unfulfilled gaps in the market; in addition, customer complaints and requests can be powerful indicators of possible product opportunities;
(2) salesmen: they are in everyday contact with customers, and are thus in a good position to note unfulfilled wants;
(3) technological developments: patent searching, monitoring the technical literature, and the extrapolation of technological trends can suggest possible ideas for new products;
(4) 'creativity' sessions: increasingly, firms are using brainstorming and other methods for stimulating the generation of new ideas. In essence, these involve groups of people in a relaxed, uninhibited environment being given the freedom to voice ideas spontaneously.

In some cases, the process of product development is initiated by an

Table 7.2 *Product Development Process*

Generation of ideas	Build up a bank of ideas. Sources of ideas might be: Market studies of customer wants 'Creativity' sessions Technological forecasting Corporate management Research and development Salesforce
Preliminary screening	Elimination of those ideas which obviously have no potential. Criteria used might include: Corporate fit Translatability into core-benefit proposition Technical feasibility Market potential Competitive advantage Possible profitability
Feasibility testing	Development and evaluation of concept: Formulation of core-benefit proposition Concept testing Technical studies
Evaluation	Examination of the commercial feasibility of the projects: Cost−benefit analysis
Development	Development of a tangible product: Design Development of actual product Development of manufacturing technology

Pilot production	The manufacture of small quantities on small manufacturing plant to test the feasibility of the manufacturing process
Preliminary product testing	To examine the qualities of the product: Technical tests to measure durability and reliability under extreme conditions Consumer usage tests
Marketing strategy formulation	Devise the full marketing mix: Agreement on advertising theme, pricing, product name, distribution, selling
Test marketing	Testing the market reaction to the marketing strategy: Launching the product in a representative area of the country
Production plant development	The scaling up from pilot plant to full production plant
National launch	Marketing of the product on a national basis
Diffusion	Process of adoption by the market

unpredicted research discovery or an invention, and not as a result of a systematic idea-search process. Often, also, companies do not seek, or are not able, to build up a bank of ideas from which they make a choice.

Preliminary Screening

Only a few of the ideas that are actually produced will merit further effort. If the company generates a large number of ideas, it will need to have a formal set of criteria against which each idea can be assessed. These might include:

(1) Corporate 'fit' — the extent to which the idea is compatible with the company's objectives, builds on its strengths, and overcomes its weaknesses.

(2) Customer benefit: is the idea convertible into a product concept that offers a real benefit to customers?

(3) Technical feasibility: is the technology to make the product easily available or, if not, can it be developed?

(4) Market potential: is there likely to be a sizeable market for the product?

(5) Competitive advantage: will competitors be able to copy the product, and are any competitors, to the knowledge of the company, already engaged on the development of a rival? The possibility and benefits of patenting the product need to be explored.

(6) Possible profitability: given the above, is it likely that the company will be able to establish a price and gain a sufficient share of the market to make it a worthwhile proposition?

Feasibility Testing

If the idea passes through this initial assessment, then much more work needs to be carried out on refining the idea, converting it into a more concrete concept which can be tested (initially in qualitative discussions with customers), and in ensuring that it is possible to manufacture the product at a profitable price.

In particular, Urban and Hauser (1980) have argued that it is important to express the concept in terms of its **core-benefit proposition** or **CBP.** The CBP is a concise and explicit statement of the essential differentiating features of the new product. It, in turn, acts as the cornerstone for the design of the marketing strategy:

> It (the CBP) should specify exactly what we are offering to the consumers, what they will get from it, and how this is important and possibly unique. It is not simply an advertising appeal, but rather a

basic description of the overall strategy in terms of consumer benefit. It is more than a description of the physical product because it specifies the benefits the consumer derives from the product ...

This approach, so it is argued, guides the development of the idea: research and development formulates a physical product to meet the specifications of the CBP; advertising devises copy to emphasise the benefits, and so on.

Some possible examples of core benefit propositions might be:

(1) a soluble analgesic that is quickly absorbed into the bloodstream, has no adverse aftertaste, and does not irritate the stomach;
(2) solid, weatherproof doors which require no maintenance and can easily be fitted, even by the amateur;
(3) odourless, quick-drying paint, easily applied;
(4) cheap, portable, easy-to-use computers.

Evaluation

Already, many ideas may have been rejected on the grounds that they are not compatible with company objectives, that it is not technically possible to manufacture them, and that consumers do not perceive that they offer significant advantages. The company is now faced with the decision on whether or not to develop them further. At this juncture, a detailed economic assessment may be undertaken for these two reasons:

(a) Once it is decided to develop the tangible product, costs begin to rise appreciably (as can be seen from Figure 7.2). Firms will wish to minimise their risks and ensure that such a commitment is likely to be worthwhile.
(b) The company may be faced with a number of product proposals but have insufficient resources to support them all. It will wish to invest in those which offer the best prospects of a higher-than-average return.

A number of methods for evaluating new product proposals have been suggested; perhaps the most simple is the breakeven method. Given that a decision has been made on the price at which the product will be sold, and that data on the fixed and variable costs are known, it is possible to calculate the volume that will have to be sold in order to break even.

At breakeven point, revenue equals costs ($R = C$); but revenue also equals price times volume sold ($R = P \times Q_b$) and total costs equal fixed costs plus variable costs times volume ($C = F + Q_b V$).

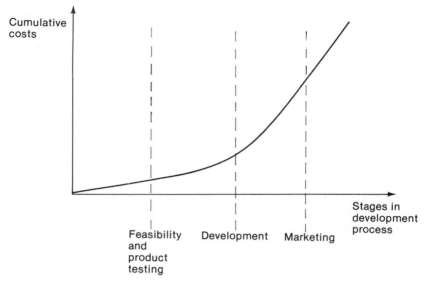

Figure 7.2 *Costs of Development and Stages in Product Development*

Thus it is possible to calculate the breakeven volume:

$$P \times Q_b = F + Q_b V$$

$$Q_b = \frac{F}{(P-V)}$$

Companies can begin by asking themselves whether they are likely to achieve this breakeven volume, and if products fail to satisfy this simple criterion, then there seems little point in proceeding further. However, as has already been noted, companies may be more concerned with the potential benefits (however measured) and with ranking the various product proposals.

Benefits are a function of a large number of variables:

$$B = F(P,D,N,I,C,V,\ldots)$$

where

B is the benefit such as return on investment, unit profitability, profit as a proportion of sales, etc.

P is the price charged

D is the quantity demanded at this price

N is the lifetime of the product

I is the investment costs of capital equipment required

C is the other costs such as R & D and marketing

V is the variable costs of production

These benefits will arise over a number of years.

It is obvious that evaluations at such an early stage in the development can involve a considerable degree of guesswork, and will consequently need to be refined as the development proceeds and more information about costs, pricing, and possible market reaction becomes available.

Development

During the development stage, the product idea is converted into the tangible physical product. This will involve the design and formulation of the product and the development of a technically and commercially appropriate method of manufacture. Often, profound technical difficulties can be encountered, and considerable expenditures may be required to overcome them. For example, in the case of Pilkington's float glass process, the technological problems were 'formidable'.

> Upon exposure to the atmosphere the tin (which in its liquid form was the medium on which the glass was 'floated') oxidised and produced a crystalline scale on the glass surface. A carefully selected and maintained inert atmosphere slowly began to alleviate this problem. But other technical challenges rose to take its place. Because of the company's expertise in forming a glass ribbon through rollers, the team initially chose this method to flow the molten glass onto the tin surface. But tin vapours condensed on the water cooled rollers, which then imparted surface imperfections to the tin. Unless the tin was extremely pure it also reacted with the glass. Ultimately the team had to purify the tin well beyond the highest specifications for laboratory quality tin ... (Quinn 1978)

Preliminary Product Testing

It is important to ensure that the product satisfies the criteria of usage: for example, in the case of a washing machine, that it is reliable, durable and 'washes well' without spoiling clothes; in the case of food products, that they can be easily used, that they have no harmful side effects, and that they have an acceptable taste and appearance when prepared under actual, as opposed to laboratory, conditions. Manufacturers have devised a complex set of methods of subjecting their products to various tests and they will often commission outside agencies to carry out such work: for example, a new washing machine may be kept running for many thousands of hours; a new material may be washed hundreds of times to test its durability, colour fastness, and degree of shrinkage. Industrial products should be tested by existing manufacturers under actual operating conditions. Thus, a new synthetic shoe-upper material should be used by footwear manufacturers to test its technical performance.

Marketing Strategy Formulation

In theory, the decision on the market targets and marketing mix should have been made at the outset of the development. Certainly, a company should have a clearly-defined market target before development proceeds, even if this does have to be revised later on because of changes in circumstances or new information that comes to light. Decisions on many of the details of the marketing mix, such as advertising themes, promotional material, and distribution channels to be used, will be made as the development proceeds. At this juncture, though, it is critical that a fully integrated marketing strategy is agreed before continuing with the actual launch of the product.

Test Marketing

In the case of high-volume, rapid-turnover consumer products (such as many grocery items), manufacturers will often **test market** the product. This involves the launch of the product in a small, representative area of the country using the agreed marketing strategy. If the results obtained are to mirror exactly what might occur on a national scale, it is critical that the effort expended in the test market is directly proportional to the relative size of the test market to the national market. For instance, if the test market accounts for 10 per cent of the total potential market, then advertising expenditure should equal (with some qualifications) 10 per cent of the total proposed national advertising expenditure. Similarly, the sales achieved will be 10 per cent of those it can be expected to obtain nationally. Obviously, test marketing is a means of minimising the risk of a national launch. Not all products, though, are test marketed. For instance, products may not be test marketed where the product is easily copied and competition is intense. In any case, test marketing provides competitors with the breathing space to develop a rival which they may even launch nationally before the innovating firm. In other cases, the new product may involve little risk, and the company may not feel that the delay and cost of test marketing is worthwhile.

Production Plant Development

In many cases, particularly where the production plant ties up huge amounts of capital, the decision on whether or not to proceed with the construction of the large-scale manufacturing unit may be postponed until fairly late in the development process – until, for example, there is some clear indication of the likely market reaction as a result of test marketing. Up until this time, the product may have been supplied on a batch basis or from a small pilot plant. The scaling up from pilot plant is not inevitably an easy transition; there can be formidable engineering problems that considerably delay the availability of the product in quantity.

National Launch

It is such problems that may delay the full national launch of the product, and companies may, in such circumstances, decide on what is termed a 'rolling launch' whereby the product is marketed progressively in different areas of the country, usually working outwards from the test market area. However, a company may adopt such a policy out of choice, since it can minimise risks.

A full national launch of a new product, itself, often involves a complex set of activities which may be geared to generating maximum impact, particularly in the case of a consumer product. Ford's launch of the Mustang in the USA is not an untypical example of what might be involved in the launch of a new car.

Launch of Ford Mustang[1]

Ford had planned the full launch of the Mustang for April 17th.

The company's 'first objective was to convey the enthusiasm ... for the Mustang to our dealers and salesmen. To do this we held major live shows for dealers in 13 cities across the country and followed with hour-long film shows in 37 district cities for salesmen'.

On April 13th, representatives of the press were invited to the Ford Pavilion at the New York World's Fair, where they were shown the Mustang. Afterwards, reporters were paired, given a set of road-rally instructions, and told to drive a Mustang to Detroit. This resulted in extensive coverage of the new car, with leading stories in 'Life', 'Newsweek' and 'Time'.

Ford bought simultaneous advertising 'time' on the three national television channels on the 16th April and on the following day advertising announcing the launch of the Mustang was included in over 2,600 newspapers. In this advertising, Ford emphasised the 'unexpected' theme – unexpected in terms of styling, and an unexpected low price! In addition, there were advertisements in 24 of the highest-circulation magazines. Mustangs were placed in the termini of 15 major airports, and in the lobbies of 200 Holiday Inn Hotels.

1 Summarised from Marshak (1970) pp.149–150

Not all new product introductions are as ambitious as this, but all should have the close-detailed integration of marketing activities — from selling to distributors to ensure there is widespread availability of the new product, to the development of a promotional and advertising programme aimed at maximising impact.

Diffusion

The final stage of the new product development process is the diffusion or adoption by customers/users. Companies are interested in the level and rate of diffusion because the ultimate level of diffusion is a limit on the total sales of the company, whilst the rate of diffusion affects how quickly the company covers its costs and begins to make a profit. In some cases, companies will strive to secure a rapid rate of diffusion, particularly where there is a threat from competition. In certain markets, the need to have quick acceptance may be important in view of the argument that the 'honeymoon' period (the period between the launch of a new product and the launch of rival products) is shortening. In other cases, companies may, at first, price products high in order to tap the premium price and therefore more profitable segments of the market, then gradually reduce price. Such a policy may, of course, inhibit the rate of diffusion in the early stages. As has been seen, most products are believed to have S-shaped diffusion curves (see Chapter 6). Readers should ensure that they fully comprehend the reasons for this before proceeding further.

The notion of diffusion suggests that some people will adopt a new product before others; that is, that people vary in their degree of innovativeness. One means of classifying people according to their innovativeness is based on the normal distribution curve (Rogers and Shoemaker 1971). Using the mean, and standard deviations, it is possible to categorise adoptors into the following main categories (see Figure 7.3).

(a) *Innovators*   These are the first 2½ per cent of adoptors. They tend to be risk takers, be better educated, be more cosmopolitan and have above-average income. They are less integrated into local groups than are, say, the early adoptors.

(b) *Early adoptors*   These are the next 13½ per cent of adoptors. Although they are not the first to adopt the innovation, they tend to be among the first within their local community or peer groups. Like the innovators they too tend to be wealthier and be better educated. They may also have a greater technical knowledge of the product class to which the innovation belongs, than has the rest of the population. The major feature that distinguishes them from innovators is, however, that they are well integrated into the community and therefore tend to

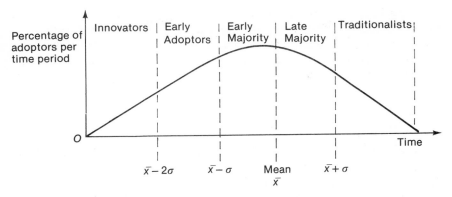

Note: σ is the standard deviation

Figure 7.3 *Adoptor Categories*

have a significant influence there. They are often the people
that the rest imitate or turn to for advice. This group then has a
high degree of *opinion leadership*.

(c) *Early majority*   This group, which accounts for the next 34
per cent of adoptors, tends to be more cautious before adopting
an innovation, waiting until its benefits and other features have
been clearly demonstrated before adopting it.

(d) *Late majority*   This is the penultimate group which contains,
again, 34 per cent of the adoptors. They are more conservative
and may respond to innovations only because a high proportion
of the population appears to have accepted them. Another
possible reason for their apparent reluctance is that because the
innovation may have been initially highly priced they may not
have been able to afford it; however, by this stage, economies
of scale and competition may have brought the product to
within their price range.

(e) *Traditionalists*   These are said to account for the remaining
16 per cent. This group is not further subdivided because, so it
is argued, very little is known about them. They will often only
consider adopting an innovation as a last resort.

It is important to note that these are what is termed 'ideal types' and
it may, in practice, be difficult to identify individuals that specifically
match the features of particular innovator categories.

Success in New Product Development

Given the high costs of product failure, companies should try and
maximise the probability of successful new product development. A

large number of studies have been carried out into the factors which promote success. Although the process of product development is complex, being affected by no simple combination of variables, it is possible to extract a number of broad facilitating factors. One study has summarised these in what can be regarded as five general rules for product success (Science Policy Research Unit 1972).

(1) Successful innovators pay close attention to the requirements of the market: they will carry out market research to identify market wants, and maintain close liaison with potential users during the development.

(2) Successful innovators pay close attention to all the facets of marketing such as advertising, promotion, selling, packaging, technical literature, and so on.

(3) Successful innovations tend to have received the support of a person high up in the corporate hierarchy. Such 'product champions' are more likely to have the power to overcome organisational inertia and other factors that can impede the development.

(4) Successful innovators have good external communications, being in contact with institutions in science and technology (universities, polytechnics, research associations, etc). These not only act as a good source of the original ideas for new products but they can also help in the rapid and effective solution of technical problems that occur during the development. The ability to solve such problems in a cost-effective way can be a crucial factor in success.

(5) Successful innovators tend to perform their development work more efficiently than failures, but not necessarily more quickly. They eliminate technical defects from the product *before* launch, and they have bigger development teams and spend more money on development.

A Case Study of a Successful Product Development

The Development of Yorkie

The British are renowned for having a 'sweet tooth' and this is reflected in the sales of confectionery − a market worth £1,250 million, equal to a volume of 650,000 tonnes, in 1977. Of this, chocolate confectionery was worth a massive £800 million, or 350,000 tonnes. The market is dominated by three large companies − Rowntree Mackintosh, Cadbury-Schweppes, and Mars, which together account for approximately 80 per cent of chocolate confectionery sales.

Rowntree Mackintosh is a well-entrenched company in this market with very successful products such as Kit Kat, Rolo, After Eight, and Aero. For many years, it has pursued an active policy of product development. In the early 1970s, the chocolate solid block sector of the market was actively examined as a possible opportunity for new product development since the sector was big (approximately 70,000 tonnes) and Rowntree Mackintosh's share was relatively small. There was, however, one drawback: widely-accepted brands had captured a major portion of the market; in particular, Cadbury's Dairy Milk seemed to have an almost impregnable position. Rowntree Mackintosh baulked at taking on this highly successful market leader. However, it might be that there was a market niche attractive enough for the company which would not bring it into direct competition with the Cadbury brand. In its aggressive search for new products, it was certainly a market that merited further investigation.

Rowntree Mackintosh already had detailed statistics on the sales of the various products; it supplemented these with a number of exploratory discussions on the attitudes to these existing brands. Among the various findings, it emerged that there was a degree of dissatisfaction with these products: there were comments that the lower-priced chocolate bars appeared too thin, an obvious consequence of the manufacturers' response in reducing weight to obviate the need for significant price increases as raw material costs rose. This interpretation was reinforced by the knowledge that the sales of the larger thicker sizes were increasing, whilst the previously dominant lower-priced bars of Cadbury's Dairy Milk were experiencing a sales decline. It seemed that consumers might prefer a more substantial chocolate bar — something they could 'bite into'.

In collaboration with its advertising agency, J. Walter Thompson, five product concepts were devised, each representing a distinct attempt to meet a 'separate consumer motivation and need, hypothesised from the analysis of the existing market'. Each concept was embodied in an edible product that was given a name, package, and advertising approach. They were then presented to four groups of consumers who tasted the product and discussed the total presentation. As a result, one concept emerged as favourite: 'Rations', a thick, milk chocolate block presented as a sustaining food to be eaten in the open air.

The 'Rations' concept had, however, generated a number of criticisms; in particular that it had connotations of wartime austerity, of a mere utility product with no associations of enjoyment. As a result, new names were examined to see if they could be registered and new presentations were devised. Each was tested by means of group discussions. At the same time, different chocolate types and block designs were tested in large-scale surveys. In consequence, the product concept was defined as a solid, thick, block of chocolate that was nourishing as well as enjoyable.

Decisions still had to be made on the details of the marketing mix. Rowntrees wanted to price the product competitively, but there was a major obstacle in that the surface area of the top of the block was less than that of competitors; even though it was thicker, it might not appear such good value for money. In addition, as a result of the defined product concept, it was a heavier block since it had to be chunky and satisfying to eat. It was priced higher than the competition, although its value was approximately equivalent (see Table 7.3).

Table 7.3 *Comparison of 'Value' of Yorkie with its Main Competitors*

	Weight (gms)	Price (p)	Value (gms/p)
Yorkie	62.0	11	5.6
CDM	48.4	9	5.4
Galaxy	50.0	9	5.6

Distributors were encouraged to sample Yorkie themselves in order to convince them that it was worth the higher price. The advertising was to use a lorry-driver theme with the implication that the product must be satisfying if he found it so. This was probably one of the most important factors in the product's ultimate success, as reflected in the cult image that has followed.

The product was test marketed from March 1976 in the London ITV region, which accounts for 25 per cent of the country. The major reason for the decision to use London was that, since it was felt that the product could be easily imitated, it was important to establish a foothold in a major market from the start. The experience gained from the test marketing would enable Rowntree Mackintosh to assess the rate of sale and the necessary production level and stock holdings.

The major emphasis of the sales effort was on the major national multiples. At Rowntree Mackintosh's Annual National Sales Conference, territory salesmen were given the background information about Yorkie, including the market analysis, the objectives of the project and the market research results. Salesmen were supported by a comprehensive range of selling and display aids.

Twenty weeks after the launch, Yorkie was stocked by over 90 per cent of retail confectionery outlets. In 1976, Yorkie sales totalled 1,750 tonnes, representing £3 million in retail sales, and on this basis Rowntree Mackintosh launched the product nationally in 1977, and total sales for that year amounted to 7,500 tonnes (£18 million). By 1980, Yorkie had sales of £40 million, giving Rowntree Mackintosh a

30 per cent share of the market (see Table 7.4). Since the launch of the original milk chocolate Yorkie, two variations have been introduced: a Raisin and Biscuit, and a Peanut Yorkie. Both have been widely accepted, and they in turn have increased Rowntree Mackintosh's share of the 'milk ingredient block' market to 21 per cent.

Table 7.4 *Rowntree Mackintosh's Share of the Chocolate Confectionery Market — 1975 and 1980*

	Volume (tonnes)		RM's share (%)	
	1975	1980	1975	1980
Milk solid blocks	35,000	35,000	10	30
Milk ingredient blocks	21,000	18,000	—	21
Plain solid blocks	5,000	2,000	1	—

The competition has not relaxed either: both Cadbury and Mars have revamped their products (Cadbury's Dairy Milk and Galaxy) in line with Yorkie, making them thicker and slimmer.

Summary

New product development becomes increasingly necessary in a fast-changing environment if companies wish to ensure that their product mix continues to be compatible with the wants of customers. Short-sightedness in innovation can result in a product mix that is 'tired', with the majority of products reaching maturity and decline with all the disadvantages that suggests. Unfortunately, product development is risky, with many ideas falling by the wayside. The innovation process should start with the clear definition of the wants of the specific target groups the new product will satisfy and throughout the development there should be continuous market research to ensure the product meets the wants of the consumers. Five guidelines for successful product development have been listed.

Further Reading

Booz, Allen, and Hamilton (1968) *Management of New Products.*
Buzzell, R.D. and Nourse, R.E.M. (1967) *Product Innovation in Food Processing 1954–1964*, Harvard University Press.
Littler, D.A. (1978) *The Management of Industrial Innovation*, School of Business Studies, University of Liverpool.

Littler, D.A. and Pearson, A.W. (1972) 'Uncertainty and technological innovation', *Management Decision,* Vol.10, Summer.

Madell, J. (1981) 'Where do successful brands come from?', Boase Massimi Pollitt Univas Partnership.

Marshak, S. (1970) 'The Mustang Story', in J.T. Gerlach and C.A. Wainwright *Successful Management of New Products,* The Pitman Press.

OECD (1971) *The Conditions for Successful Innovation.*

Quinn, J.B. (1978) *Pilkington Brothers Ltd,* Centre d'Etudes Industrielles, Geneva, Switzerland.

Ramsey, W. (1982) 'The new product dilemma', *Marketing Trends,* Vol.1, A.C. Nielsen Company Ltd.

Rogers, E.M. and Shoemaker, F.T. (1971) *Communication of Innovations,* Free Press.

Science Policy Research Unit (1972) *Success and Failure in Industrial Innovation,* Centre for the Study of Industrial Innovation.

Urban, G.L. and Hauser, J.R. (1980) *Design and Marketing of New Products,* Prentice-Hall International.

Review Questions

(1) Why do you think it is argued that new product development is increasingly necessary?

(2) A manufacturer of rubber tyres for automobiles is searching for new product ideas. Where do you think it might look for new ideas?

(3) What is meant by the new product ideas screening process? Discuss what you consider are the important criteria in screening.

(4) A manufacturer of petfoods is considering developing a semi-moist 'beefburger' for dogs. This would be packed in a new protective film and sold in cartons. How would you go about testing the concept?

(5) A manufacturer of specialised industrial tools is evaluating the commercial prospects of a new product. He estimates that the unit labour costs will be £350, and the unit costs of raw materials, energy, and transportation will be £500. The total cost of the plant and equipment needed is approximately £150,000 which he will depreciate over five years. He aims to spend £35,000 in the first year on advertising, and £20,000 in the second year. Two salesmen will be employed at a total cost of £40,000 per annum. He calculates that the total size of the market is approximately 1,000 units, although a German competitor will undoubtedly take some of these sales, and some conservative manufacturers will not adopt the new product. He has set a price of £1,450. Given that he

aims for a payback of two years, should he proceed with the development?

(6) What factors should a manufacturer take into account when deciding whether or not to test market?

(7) Why do you think 'Yorkie' was a success?

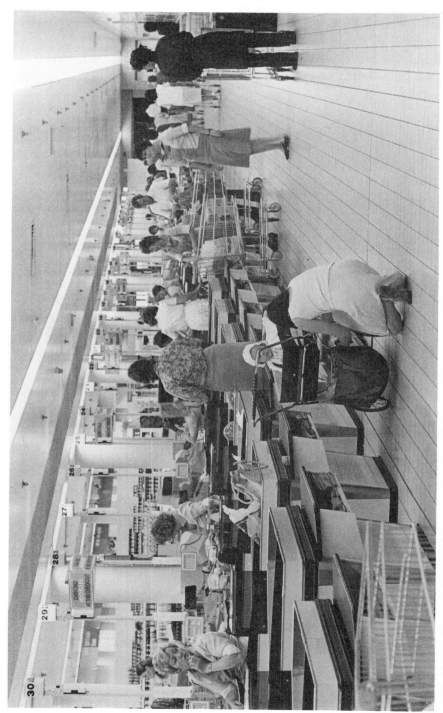

Supermarket checkouts: the pricing decision for a new product is ultimately determined by the price customers are willing to pay

8
Pricing

*A man who knows the price of everything and the
value of nothing.*

(A definition of a cynic—Oscar Wilde)

Traditionally, pricing has been stressed as the critical factor affecting
the demand for goods and services. Neoclassical economics stresses
the 'equilibrating' role of price. However, as we have seen, in contemporary markets there is much emphasis on the use of non-price
factors. Indeed, companies will strive if possible to make the demand
for the products relatively price inelastic, that is, they will endeavour
to *differentiate* their products, through the use of good design,
technical features, convenience, back-up service, and so on.

Getting the price 'right' is, of course, still crucial: whether or not the
company makes a profit and if so, just what level of profit is made,
depends on it. There are two main types of pricing decision: setting the
price for a new product; and changing the price of an existing product.
Many factors will influence the pricing decision. Several approaches
to pricing are discussed.

Pricing in the Marketing Mix

In many markets, price is no longer the only major weapon of
competition for, as we have seen, customers may make purchasing
decisions using non-price criteria; indeed, such factors can often sway
the decision in favour of a particular product. This does not mean, of
course, that price is insignificant: in many instances customers will
strive to secure the best product offering at the cheapest price.
Although in some luxury-goods markets price may be relatively
disregarded, in general customers will seek the optimum combination
of price and non-price variables; in many cases they are prepared to

spend more for differentiating product features. Price, then, is often seen as only one of several factors affecting demand. Indeed, the trend towards the increasing concentration of industry—with a major proportion of the output of many industries being accounted for by a few producers or oligopolists—has, according to some economists, assisted the decline of pricing as a prime marketing tool. Oligopolists, so the argument runs, will avoid prime competition since it will more likely result in all being worse off; instead, they will tend to concentrate on product differentiation through incremental product modifications and advertising.

> It has been noted that oligopolists do not often tend to change price, possibly because any price change they make will be evident to competitors. They may regard any price cut as a serious and direct challenge and a price war (the oligopolist's counterpart of a nuclear war) is likely to break out. The result is that price cuts, like nuclear weapons, will only be employed by oligopolists rarely, if at all.
> ... the fact that nuclear weapons are so powerful that they are rarely used makes it more, not less, likely that smaller-scale military activity and, even more, espionage will occur. The same is true in business. Many firms which are reluctant to alter prices, spend a great deal of money on market research, advertising, cut-price offers, and other forms of sales promotion. The fact that a price war is unlikely makes it more, not less, important continually to probe the rival's position, to erode his market, and (through market research) to be well informed about his market share and his general competitive position. (Hague 1971a pp. 289–290)

It is frequently argued that price is of diminishing importance, with other marketing-mix variables assuming greater significance in purchasing decisions. However, it is important to remember that price is one of the marketing-mix factors and as such is an important component of the product offering.

Setting correct price levels is, of course, critical to ensuring that ultimately a company's total costs are recovered, and that in addition the company makes an adequate return. In any case, in many markets demand may still be highly sensitive to price. This is likely to be the case where:

(a) there is little difference between the products of competing suppliers;
(b) it is relatively easy, with little cost involved, to change the source of supply (it is much easier for a housewife to buy a different brand of grocery product than for a company to change the supplier of its computers);
(c) brand loyalty is not significant.

Risks in Pricing

There are, in fact, two types of risk in pricing: opportunity-forfeited risk, and loss risk. The risk of forfeiting an opportunity arises when the company has lower total profits from a product than it could have obtained either because:

(a) it set a price too low, such that it did not reflect the true value of the product to the customer and as a result had a lower income than it could have obtained; or

(b) it underestimated the potential demand available and set too high a price. Given a high price elasticity of demand, the company would have generated more income by setting the price at a lower level.

The risk of loss occurs when the company has set a price such that the revenue does not cover the apportionable costs of the product. This could mean that the company over estimated the demand for the product or that in the first instance it set the price too low and found it difficult to increase this later, often because of intense competition.

Pricing Objectives

It is generally assumed that companies price their products so as to maximise profits. However, some empirical studies have cast doubt on this premise. For example, an in-depth investigation of fourteen pricing decisions carried out in the 1960s (Hague 1971b) found that firms often did not have full information on their own internal costs, nor did they have an understanding of the prices of competing products. With such inadequate data, companies would not know whether they were maximising their profits. In general, short-run market share tended to be used as the best guarantee of long-run profit, a policy which accords well with the recommendation of the Boston Consultancy Group (see Chapter 6).

A study performed in 1958 (Kaplan, Dirlam and Lanzillotti) of the pricing objectives of twenty American companies found that pricing objectives could be diverse; among those identified were:

(a) pricing to achieve a target return on investment;
(b) pricing to maintain or improve market position;
(c) stabilisation of price and margin;
(d) pricing to meet or follow competition;
(e) pricing related to product differentiation.

These studies were carried out some years ago, and it could be argued that the increased use of professional expertise (qualified accountants and graduate economists) together with advances in information technology have resulted in improved cost data and a generally more profit-conscious approach.

Of course, the fact that management does not clearly specify profit maximisation as its prime objective does not mean that its pricing behaviour necessarily leads to dramatically different results. A company may, for example, adopt an aggressive low-pricing strategy in order to ward off competition and ensure its survival in the long term; in such instances its approach agrees with an aim of securing, in the long term, the best profit that it can. In such cases, though, it is essential that short-term tactics are undertaken with some long-term strategy in view. Gabor has suggested that much pricing behaviour is not in conflict with the objective of profit maximisation:

> If asked, they (businessmen) will usually say that they are striving for a reasonable rate of profit, not maximum profits. However if we press the issue further, and ask why they are not charging higher prices, the answer is likely to be that this would have a detrimental effect on sales. If now we ask why don't they reduce their prices, they will say that this would not help either. In some cases they will be afraid of starting a price war, in other cases the belief will be expressed that the customers would welcome the decrease in price but would not thereby be induced to buy more. Summing up, what the businessman has told us is that he can see no way in which he could increase his profits and that is, of course, exactly what the economist means by profit maximisation. (Gabor 1967 pp. 28–33)

Within the overall objective of pricing, 'to achieve the best profit that one can', companies may have several shorter-term objectives as means of reaching this longer-term goal. The pricing policies adopted will obviously be affected. Companies may, for example, engage in pricing to promote the product (promotional pricing), pricing to make it uneconomic for competitors to enter or stay in the market (destroyer pricing), 'skimming' pricing, and 'penetration' pricing.

Promotional pricing may involve temporary reductions in price that are usually well advertised. It may be a reaction to competitors' pricing moves, an attempt to induce trial in the case of a new product, a means of stimulating sales, etc. The main problem is that there is no guarantee that retailers will pass on the full value of the price reduction.

Destroyer pricing is where companies adopt a low pricing policy in order to warn off possible entrants or to compel competitors to leave the industry. In the case of the latter, such a policy is more likely to be successful where the competitor has higher costs, where the product concerned accounts for a high proportion of the profits and when the price adopted is near the competitor's marginal costs. In such a case, the main motivation for destroyer pricing may be to reduce the capacity in the industry where there is overcapacity, and/or a desire to raise the general level of prices over the longer term.

Penetration pricing involves setting a low price to generate sales volume and secure a high market share. In the case of new-product pricing, such a policy may be important where there is a large potential market and competitors can be expected to enter quickly. Under these conditions, a manufacturer may wish to entrench itself firmly by setting a price at the expected long-run level. The conditions which favour penetration pricing can be summarised as:

(1) a high price elasticity of demand; the company is depending on a low price to attract customers to the new product;
(2) economies of scale, since the large sales volume will mean lower unit costs; provided the company anticipates large sales it can price at a level that covers such high volume costs;
(3) a strong threat of competition; a low price can ward off potential entrants to the market;
(4) sufficient available production capacity, for there is obviously no point in establishing a price that results in high demand if the company is unable to meet it;
(5) the absence of segments of the market that will accept a high price.

Skimming pricing (or market skimming) is a diametrically opposite policy whereby the company establishes a high price in order to capitalise on the fact that there are people who are prepared to pay more for the new product; in this way the company is taking advantage of a surplus of consumers. As this segment is saturated, the manufacturer gradually lowers the price to tap other segments of the market, until eventually a mass-market price is reached. It is, essentially, a low-risk strategy and may be used where the manufacturer has difficulty in ascertaining the customer-perceived values of the new product, something which is particularly likely to apply in the case of radical product innovations. By setting a high price initially, the manufacturer is unlikely to make the mistake of foresaking revenue by misreading the appeal of the product to the market; moreover, an initial price that is too high can be reduced easily, and price reductions may even be used to promote the product.

Market skimming is likely to be favoured where:

(a) demand is relatively inelastic because consumers know little about the product, and close rivals are few;
(b) the market can be broken down into segments with different price elasticities of demand;
(c) little is known about the costs or price elasticity of the product; market skimming is favoured because it minimises the risks, and also because it is much easier to lower price than to raise it.

Pricing Decision

There are two main types of pricing decision: the pricing of a new product; and changing the price of a product. In the case of the pricing of a radically new product, the manufacturer may have little, if any, experience or information on which to make a pricing decision, whereas in the case of new brands consumers will have usually built up expectations about price, based on experience with existing brands. During the lifetime of the product, companies may be periodically faced with altering the price, say, in response to changing costs or competitors' actions.

In theory, at least, there are several influences affecting the pricing decision. These include: costs; competitors' reactions; and the sensitivity of customers to price (that is, the price elasticity of demand). Information on one or more of these may be unavailable, or difficult or expensive to collect. In some instances, management may attempt to simplify the pricing decision by focusing on just one or two factors which it considers 'critical'; whilst in others, a particular influence may dominate, such as a competitor's price reduction, or the increase in the cost of an important raw material or component.

There are several broad approaches to pricing; these include:

(a) cost-based pricing;
(b) contribution pricing;
(c) competitive pricing;
(d) customer-value pricing.

Cost-Based Pricing

This approach commences with the product's costs, usually the average total costs of manufacture, with a mark-up added for profit. For this reason, it is often referred to as **cost-plus pricing**. It involves the estimation of all the direct costs incurred in the manufacture and marketing of the product, together with the apportioning of indirect costs, such as general overheads. The latter can be quite arbitrary.

The cost-based method is probably widely employed in industry for two reasons. Firstly, costs are easily calculable, so that this method simplifies the pricing task. As Hague (1971b) comments:

> The firm argues this way. Cost is what we have data about, and market information is what we look for. Therefore we tend: (a) to begin with what we have; (b) concentrate on what we have; (c) to ignore what we do not have.

Secondly, decision makers have the misconceived belief that because this method starts with costs, it guarantees that a loss will not be made. There is, however, a major flaw in this approach: the company's costs are calculated assuming a forecasted sales volume, but with little regard to the effect that price can have on demand. Cost-plus pricing may, for example, result in the setting of too high a price, leading to lower sales than anticipated, and therefore to a failure to cover average costs. On the other side, because there is no attention to the market, the firm may charge a lower price than people would be prepared to pay, resulting in a sacrifice of profits.

Overall, cost-plus pricing can lead to strange pricing behaviour; for where demand is greater than expected, average total costs will be lower than estimated, and consequently it may be felt that prices can be lowered. On the other hand, where demand is lower than forecasted, average costs will be higher than anticipated and the accountants may press for higher prices. Thus, cost-plus pricing could mean that prices are raised in bad times and reduced in good times.

Too great an emphasis on costs will usually result in a company fully reflecting any cost change in its prices. This can result in a considerable loss in revenue if, in the case of a cost increase, a competitor does not increase its price as much, if at all.

Contribution Pricing

Contribution pricing can be said to be a form of cost-based pricing; however, since it focuses on the direct costs of a particular product or service, it can often lead to different and more sensible decisions.

This approach is based on the fact that two broad categories of costs can be identified:

(1) *Direct costs* embrace costs that vary directly with the level of production (such as raw materials, energy used in production, labour — with some qualifications), and other costs incurred *directly* as a result of producing and selling the product or service (such as plant that is only used in the manufacture of the specific product).

(2) *Indirect costs* embrace, among other things, general costs of administration, certain general marketing expenses, management salaries and importantly, in many cases, the costs of plant and equipment which is employed in the manufacture of several products. Indirect costs, then, include overheads and similar expenses which are not directly attributable to a particular product.

Contribution is the surplus remaining after the individual product's direct costs have been subtracted from its revenue. The total contributions of all the products should be sufficient to cover the indirect costs and satisfy the company's profit objective (see Figure 8.1).

If average total costs are employed as the basis for pricing then all

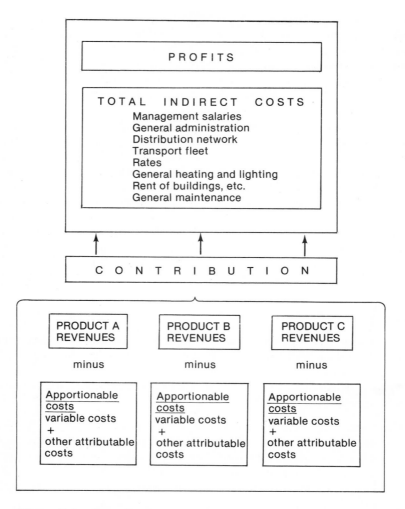

Figure 8.1 *Contribution*

costs, whether direct or indirect, have to be allocated to particular products. For direct costs this is quite easy, provided there is a sound accountancy system; but the calculation is more difficult, quite arbitrary, and often ludicrous in the case of indirect costs where, for example, the company's rates bill may be divided among different products on the basis of the number of man hours or amount of floor space involved in their production. Moreover, the apportionment of indirect costs in this way can make a product appear unprofitable, leading to its withdrawal; yet it may be that the product was not only covering its direct costs, but was also making some contribution to total overheads and profits (even though it was not fully covering its average total costs). Unless the company can reallocate the resources used by the product in a more efficient way, it can actually be worse off if decisions are made on the basis of average total costs. In general, the use of average total cost can mean loss of revenue, as the following examples illustrate:

> A company decided to abandon the development of a new product because it would not yield a profit. Although the new product would have used existing distribution facilities, a proportion of their costs had been arbitrarily allocated to the product; without this extra burden, it would have been extremely profitable. In this way, the company not only lost revenue, but perhaps abandoned a product innovation that might have facilitated its entrance into a new market.

> A large firm abandoned exporting because it claimed it lost money. In fact, what it meant was that the unit revenue did not cover average total cost. Yet exports would make a considerable contribution without the allocation of indirect costs, which would be incurred irrespective of whether or not the company exported. In this case, then, as long as there was no prospect of the company increasing its sales in the domestic market and exports made some contribution to overheads, it paid to export.

Consequently, it can be seen that contribution pricing is more rational than a traditional cost-oriented approach: it is likely to *facilitate* the optimisation of revenue, and it obviates the need for the arbitrary apportionment of certain types of costs. It is not, however, a pricing panacea, for its strict application can lead to prices that are considerably out of tune with those the market finds acceptable. Moreover, the company must, of course, ensure that the total contribution from all its products covers overheads and gives a profit.

Competitive Pricing

In this case, prices are mainly influenced by competitors' prices. In particular, prices may be set according to some prevailing price, and firms may not wish to deviate significantly from this for fear of losing sales. Indeed, firms may maintain their prices, even though costs change, because their competitors do not change their prices. This should only happen where there is considerable demand elasticity. Under such conditions, companies should strive to differentiate their products to make them individually relatively price inelastic.

Companies may also fix their prices according to some prevailing market price because they regard this as a just price, since it has been set by the industry as a whole. It may also be that customers have become accustomed to this level of price and would regard any significant difference as unjust or the reflection of an inferior product. Furthermore, such pricing is likely to be least disruptive and may, therefore, be favoured by companies.

Different facets of competitive pricing are manifested, in particular, in oligopolistic industries — those where a high proportion of the output is in the hands of a few firms. Perhaps the most common is **price leadership** whereby one company, because of its marketing expertise or its market share, is viewed as leader, and all the remaining follower companies will postpone any price change until it makes the first move. Certainly there often tends to be an outstanding uniformity in the prices of oligopolists.

A particular form of competitive pricing is **sealed-bid pricing** which is used in industrial and institutional markets where large orders are put out to tender. Usually, companies are invited to submit bids for the order by a closing date. In this case, the companies have to pay close regard to the prices that a competitor may be expected to charge. Neither costs nor a fixed level of profit are usually the primary determinants. Companies will be more concerned with estimating the maximum price that they can charge in order to win the order. They must, of course, take account of costs: they cannot afford to bid below their marginal costs, unless they are prepared to accept significant losses on the order as a means of securing more orders; and yet if they bid too far above them, they may well lose the order. It is not surprising, then, that under such circumstances, companies are often tempted to collude on prices on the basis that firms take turns in winning contracts, with the other firms agreeing to bid considerably higher. In some countries, such a stratagem is illegal, and where detected can result in not only the companies being fined but also being sued by their customers for substantial damages.

When responding to a price cut by competitors, manufacturers have available to them a range of options in addition to the Pavlovian response of immediately cutting price by the same amount or even more. Figure 8.2 depicts the alternatives in the case of a branded consumer product. In this case, an important factor may be whether or not a price reduction will damage the image of the brand; if it does, then the manufacturer should consider other alternatives, depending on the size of the competitor's price cut. These include temporary price reductions, promotions, an advertising campaign, and possibly reformulating the product when the competitor's price reduction is over 10 per cent.

Customer-Value Pricing

The most efficient approach to pricing would be based on the value

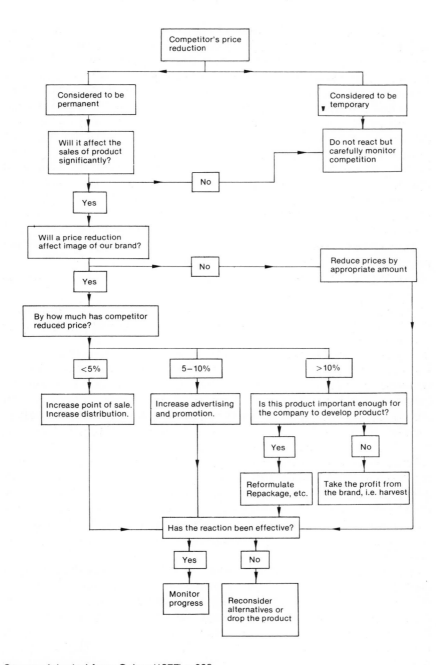

Competitor's price
reduction

Considered to be
permanent

Considered to be
temporary

Will it affect the
sales of product
significantly?

Do not react but
carefully monitor
competition

No

Yes

Will a price reduction
affect image of our brand?

No

Reduce prices by
appropriate amount

Yes

By how much has competitor
reduced price?

<5%

5–10%

>10%

Increase point of sale.
Increase distribution.

Increase advertising
and promotion.

Is this product important enough for
the company to develop product?

Yes

No

Reformulate
Repackage, etc.

Take the profit from
the brand, i.e. harvest

Has the reaction been effective?

Yes

No

Monitor
progress

Reconsider
alternatives or
drop the product

Source: Adapted from Gabor (1977) p.228

Figure 8.2 *Possible Reactions to Competitor's Price Cut: Branded
Consumer Products*

that customers themselves place on products. If such an approach could be applied effectively, then not only would it avoid the possibility of losses flowing from inaccurate pricing but it would also be more likely to result in optimisation of revenue. This is either because the company charges a premium price to take account of the considerable advantages the customer perceives in the product, or because it charges a lower price, which it recognises a considerable number of people are prepared to pay, and in this way secures a high sales volume and high total profits. It has been suggested that the hallmark of Henry Ford's genius was not in production but rather in marketing: he recognised that there was a huge potential demand for a simple automobile priced at around 400 dollars. He proceeded to devise a method of continuous manufacture that would enable him to produce automobiles cheaply. By so doing, he generated considerable demand and profits.

When considering the appropriate price for a product, management may address itself to answering three questions:

(1) How much would a customer be prepared to pay for this product?
(2) How many are we likely to sell at this price?
(3) Will the sales volume generated be sufficient to cover our direct costs and make a contribution to overheads and profits?

A number of influences may affect customers' perception of the value of the product. In certain markets customers may judge the quality of a product by its price; the higher the price the higher the perceived quality. In these cases setting a low price may have an adverse effect on demand since the customer may suspect the quality. On the other hand, there will be a price above which, for various reasons, the customer will not be prepared to go. This has resulted in the notion of a **price range** within which the customer operates. Thus, so the argument runs, the individual does not have a fixed price which he is prepared to pay, but rather upper and lower limits of acceptable prices (see Figure 8.3). A simple analysis suggests that a company may price a relatively 'uninnovative' product within range BD, and probably closer to C than D. An innovative product, on the other hand, can be priced within the range DE.

The manufacturer needs to be aware of the lowest price the consumer is prepared to pay, that is the price below which he considers the quality of the product suspect; and the highest price he would be prepared to pay (because, for example, he cannot afford a higher price or because he perceives there are superior competitive offerings available at higher prices). This has been used as the basis for ascertaining the price that is most acceptable, by asking a sample of consumers various questions aimed at eliciting the highest and lowest prices considered acceptable. Various other methods have been devised for researching into pricing. For example, customers may be taken to a 'laboratory shop' where a

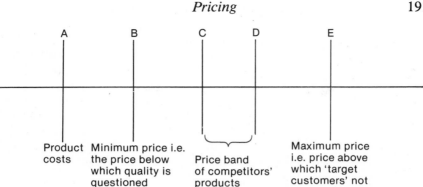

Figure 8.3 *Price Bands*

number of products are displayed, including the product whose 'acceptable' price level is being investigated. Consumers may be given a quantity of money and told to buy whatever products they want, equal to this amount. By varying the price of the subject product, the responsiveness to price can be determined. The conditions of the experiment are, of course, highly artificial.

In industrial markets, 'customer-value' may be determined by calculating, for example, the cost savings obtained from the product. However, improvements in, say, quality obtained from using the new product are difficult to quantify. In any case, price is often based much more on negotiation, and the relative strength of the respective buyers and sellers will often be a major factor influencing the final price agreed. Cost-based pricing will also tend to be important, mainly because of its ease of application.

Summary of Factors Affecting Pricing Decision

There are probably several factors that may, and perhaps should be considered when making a pricing decision. Among the more important are:

(1) *Costs*   The aim will be, at the minimum, to cover the variable costs of production. The company also has to ensure that, within a stated period, all the products will make a sufficient surplus over direct costs to pay for all overheads and satisfy profit objectives.

(2) *Customers' perceptions* of the 'value' of the product, the extent to which they relate price to 'quality' and the amount they expect to pay (based on experience, for example, with similar products). Customers' perceptions may also be important in other respects. For instance, when considering lowering prices manufacturers should take into account the way such a price cut may be per-

ceived by customers. To them, it may symbolise a reduction in product quality, or suggest a withdrawal of the product or a model change, because manufacturers are perceived as trying to reduce stocks.

(3) *Company's product range* When introducing a new product into a product line, the price of existing products in the line will set boundaries on the price that can be set. Often, companies introduce new products to fill a 'price gap' in the line; these will generally have different features, designs or quality to reflect the price difference.

(4) *Competition* The structure of the industry (such as whether or not it consists of a few major rivals with a price leader) and the relative costs and financial state of competitors may be important influences.

(5) *Distribution* Where distributors are employed (such as retailers), the company will need to take into account their margins, for which there may be a traditional minimum, and which are often based on a percentage of, say, the recommended final price. Incentives may also have to be offered to distributors to stock and, where it is considered necessary, to promote the product.

Summary

Although price is only one of the elements in the marketing mix, the decision on the price of the product is critical in the sense that it determines the revenue and, thereby, the level of profit or loss. The pricing decision for a new product is influenced by a variety of factors ranging from costs to the margins for distributors. Ultimately, though, it is the price customers are prepared to pay, in the context of the strategy for the product, that is important. When changing the price of a product, the perception of customers and the reactions of competitors need to be considered.

Further Reading

Gabor, A. (1967) 'Pricing in theory and practice', *Management Decision*, Summer.

Gabor, A. (1977) *Pricing Principles and Practice*, Heinemann Educational Books.

Hague, D.C. (1971a) *Managerial Economics*, Longman Business Series.

Hague, D.C. (1971b) *Pricing in Business*, George Allen and Unwin.

Kaplan, A.D.H., Dirlam, J.B. and Lanzillotti, R.F. (1958) *Pricing in Big Business*, Brookings Institution.

Review Questions

(1) Discuss the disadvantages of cost-based pricing.

(2) Do you think pricing a new brand in an established product class is more difficult than setting the price for a radically new product?

(3) Describe how you might approach the pricing of a new industrial product.

(4) A new consumer product to be retailed at £2.50 will have a fore-casted sales volume of 100,000 units. Total variable costs amount to £75,000. The cost of the plant amounts to £300,000 to be depreciated over ten years. General management expenses, rates, rent and other running costs of the firm amount to £1.5 million. The estimated sales volume, if attained, will account for one tenth of total company sales volume. Competitors' products are priced in the range of £2.26 to £2.70. Distributors' margins are usually in the range of 25 per cent of the ex-factory price (the price charged by the company to its distributors). Do you think the price to be charged is at the right level?

(5) A manufacturer of electricity-generating plant has been invited to bid for a contract in India. Discuss the influences that it might consider in establishing the price of its bid.

Unsightly but effective: the impact of advertising hoardings as a means of communication

9
Communications

*... there has appeared a tendency to replace
communication by a private maundering to oneself
which shall inspire one's audience to maunder
privately to themselves—rather as if the author
handed round a box of drugged cigarettes*

(*Malcolm Lowry,* Literature and Psychology)

What I tell you three times is true

(*Lewis Carroll, Hunting of the Snark*)

*I know half the money I spend on advertising is
wasted; but I can never find out which half*

(The First Lord Leverhulme)

Advertising through newspapers, magazines, television and radio seems to be the most popular means that companies employ to convey the merits of their products and persuade people to purchase them. In fact, companies have a vast armoury of techniques of communicating to the customers; among the more important are salespeople, posters, and point-of-sale displays. An effective communications campaign will be a judicious blend of these various means of communication since they can be mutually supportive in securing a favourable disposition to the firm and its products, and thereby in effecting the actual purchase of the products.

In devising its communications strategy—its target audience, its campaign theme or message, and the vehicles it will employ in conveying that message—a firm will have at least an implicit model of how communications work i.e. the way in which customers learn of products and are influenced to buy them. Nowadays, for instance, it is generally acknowledged that personal communications between individual consumers is one of the most effective means of communicating information. It is, however, the channel of communication over which companies have the least control. Consequently, in many instances they have to resort to other methods which will have a more direct effect. In deciding on its 'mix' of communications channels, a firm should start from an explicit statement of the objectives of the communications, i.e. it needs to decide on what it is striving to communicate and the results it is expected to achieve. Without this, the strategy is likely to lack direction, and there will be no means of assessing its effectiveness.

This chapter starts with an overall view of the communication process, and continues by discussing the various channels of communications, both personal and impersonal. Various models of communication are described. In the final two sections, the focus of discussion is on advertising with the vital issues in this area being outlined.

The Communications Process

In essence, the communications process can be said to involve a source, one or more communications channels, a message, and a receiver (see Figure 9.1).

COMMUNICATOR ⟶ MESSAGE ⟶ RECEIVER
via
COMMUNICATIONS CHANNELS

Figure 9.1 *A Simple Model of the Communications Process*

The communicator—generally the company or firm but may also include government, or other bodies (such as Oxfam)—will generally finance the campaign, although at least one form of communication (i.e. publicity) may be free. In devising and implementing its communications strategy, the communicator may seek the assistance of others, such as advertising agencies and outside consultants. **The message** embodies what the communicator wants to say about itself and about its 'product', given knowledge about its target audience. **The receiver** is the audience—those segments of the market the company has identified as potential purchasers of its products. Finally, the **communications channels** are those means whereby the sponsors of the message reach its audience. Each of these will now be discussed in turn.

Communications Channels

There are two main categories of communications channels. Impersonal channels include all those mass-media channels whereby the communicator can communicate directly with the audience; the major mass media are television, radio, newspapers and magazines. Generally, the use of such impersonal channels of communication implies a carefully formulated communications strategy, with a predetermined target audience and messages. Personal channels of communication, on the other hand, involve the use of a human agency, and they tend to be more flexible. The use of salespeople is, of course, the major personal channel open to the communicator.

Impersonal Channels

There are three main impersonal forms of communications: media advertising; publicity; and sales promotion.

Advertising, on which current annual expenditure amounts to in excess of three thousand million pounds, embraces all those communications which appear in the media and for which the source usually pays. Table 9.1 gives a breakdown of advertising expenditure by media type; it can be seen that over half is spent on advertising in the press. Advertising can be said to have two main components: an informative element giving basic factual information, such as technical features, prices and where the product can be purchased; and a persuasive element aimed at creating a desire for the product by, for example, emphasising its features. Generally, advertising is regarded as synonymous with communications, and there is no doubt that it is the most powerful and pervasive means of communication

Table 9.1   *Total Advertising Expenditure by Media, 1982*

Media	1982 (£ million)
Press	1,986
Television	928
Poster and transport	124
Cinema	18
Radio	70
Total	3,126

Source: Advertising Association

open to a company. Because of its importance, most of this chapter is directed to discussing how advertising works, and the important decisions involved in formulating and implementing an advertising campaign.

Publicity embraces those non-personal forms of communication which are not paid for by the source, but which provide information about the company and its products. Publicity, then, would include comments on products made in television programmes such as 'That's Life' and 'Tomorrow's World'; editorial references in technical journals such as *Tin International* and *Rubber Journal*; and mentions in the editorial pages of the press such as *Vogue, Woman* and *The Sunday Times*. Publicity can often have high credibility because readers, viewers and listeners perceive the source of information as having no vested interest in the sales of the product. Such references can be either favourable or adverse, and the company in general has little, if any, direct control over them.

Sales promotions are paid-for, non-media, and impersonal activities which embrace point-of-sale display material seen in supermarkets, competitions, special offers, money-off coupons, and so on. Trade exhibitions (such as those where companies have display stands at which they often exhibit their products, and have at hand promotional literature for possible purchasers) may also be regarded as a form of sales promotion. Sponsorship of activities, in particular of various sports, is also an important form of promotion. The expenditure on such promotional activities is vast; they will often proceed in conjunction with an advertising campaign.

Personal Channels

There are two main personal channels of communications: through personal selling which can involve a company-employed salesforce, a retailer- or wholesaler-employed salesforce, and commissioned agents; and interpersonal communications whereby information about products is passed between consumers or users. Public relations may also be regarded as a form of personal communication.

Overall, personal selling in the mass consumer-goods markets has diminished in importance with the rise of mass retailing: first, because there is more self-service; and secondly, because the general concentration in the retailing sector means that more retailers buy their goods centrally, directly from the manufacturers. Personal selling to individual retail outlets has diminished in importance. In industrial goods markets, though, there is still an important role for personal selling particularly where technical products are involved and where the salesperson can be regarded as a 'customer problem solver', such as in the sales of computers and sophisticated office equipment. In such instances, the technical sales person may be able *inter alia* to demonstrate to the potential user the specific benefits resulting from the adoption of the product.

Interpersonal communication is now regarded as a particularly influential channel of communication since consumers learn of a product via social acquaintances who will be able to speak of their actual experience of the product. Such social acquaintances will often be highly regarded and will be seen as more objective sources of information. Moreover, such personally communicated information will often be augmented by actual demonstrations of the product in a working environment, such as the kitchen or garden. Advice may also be sought and/or given by individuals who for various reasons, such as their technical expertise or their social standing, are highly regarded; such individuals have been termed *opinion leaders.* The evidence of the significance of such interpersonal channels and of the role of opinion leaders has been derived from a number of studies on the diffusion of innovations (Rogers and Shoemaker 1971). One result of this view of the communications process is that information about a product may be recieved from a number of sources and the view of advertising acting *directly* on each member of the target audience (the so called hypodermic needle model) has had to be revised (see Figure 9.2).

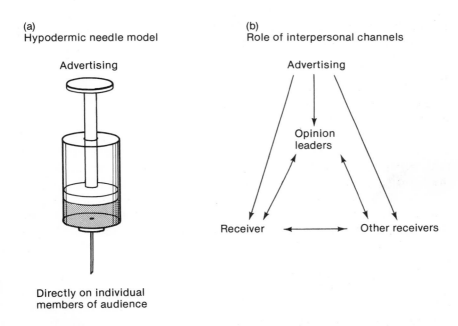

(a)
Hypodermic needle model

Advertising

Directly on individual members of audience

(b)
Role of interpersonal channels

Advertising

Opinion leaders

Receiver   Other receivers

Figure 9.2

Opinion leaders may be very influential conveyers of information, and communications could obviously be made more effective if they could be focused specifically on this group. A number of general conclusions about the characteristics of opinion leaders have been distilled from the many studies on the subject: they tend to be better educated, younger, read more, have a greater knowledge of the product in question, and perhaps have a higher social standing than the rest of their peers.

Assessment of Channels of Communications

Each of these channels of communication can have a valuable role in the total communications strategy of the company, and generally two or more will be employed with the aim of optimising impact. For example, a television advertising campaign emphasising the qualities of the product may be supported by street posters and point-of-sales material; advertisements in technical journals may be employed to create awareness of the product and maintain its visibility, thereby providing valuable support for a personal selling campaign.

It is obvious, though, that the major communication channels differ in important respects; in particular, three dimensions of comparison can be identified:

(1) *control*, which is the extent to which the communicator is able to influence directly the content of the message;

(2) *credibility,* which is the extent to which the message is believed by the audience, and this is generally assumed to be related to the objectivity of the source;

(3) *flexibility,* which is the extent to which the message can be altered to suit the particular requirements of the audience; the individual receiver can have specific problems which he wants answering or can, for instance, vary in his degree of scepticism.

Obviously, the company will want to maximise control, credibility, and flexibility. Unfortunately, no communication channel rates highly on all three criteria. Figure 9.3, which is a qualitative representation of the relationship between control and credibility, suggests that there is an inverse relationship between the two. In general, the company will have a high degree of control over advertising, but the credibility of advertising will often be low to medium. In the case of sales promotion, retailers can have some discretion over point-of-display material, although in general the source or communicator will have a high degree of control. Surprisingly enough, salespeople can often have a high degree of perceived credibility, particularly where they clearly have a deep knowledge of the technology of the product and are able to articulate feasible solutions to customer problems. As

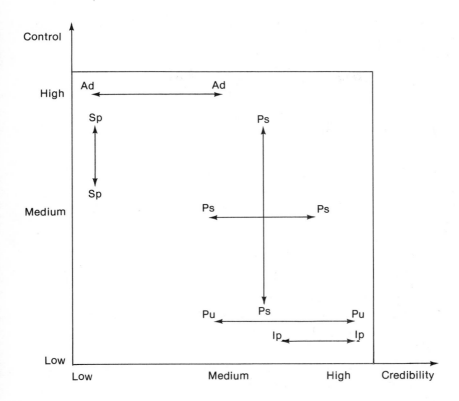

Figure 9.3 *Control versus Credibility of Communications Channels*

we have already noted, both publicity and interpersonal communications can have high credibility, but the communicator will often have little if any control over the content of the communication.

Figure 9.4 depicts the relationship between control and the flexibility of the communication channel. Mass-media channels have the minimal degree of flexibility; their use involves the imposition of a message on an audience, regardless of whether or not individual members are receptive. They depend generally on the passivity of the audience, since they cannot be adapted to suit moods, relevant wants, etc. At the other extreme, interpersonal channels will have the highest degree of flexibility. In the case of personal selling, much depends on

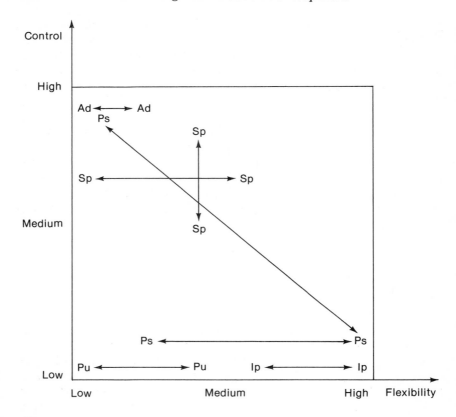

Key:
Ad = advertising
Sp = sales promotion
Ps = personal selling
Pu = publicity
Ip = interpersonal communications

Figure 9.4 *Control versus Flexibility of Communications Channels*

the proficiency and professionalism of the salesperson. Often, companies have developed standardised sales dialogues and these may often be employed unwisely, regardless of the reaction of the receptor. Obviously, the greater the discretion given to the salesperson, the less the degree of control, but given a high calibre of sales personnel, good induction, and effective training, this is not likely to present any real problems.

The Communicator

The communicator is the originator of the message; it can be a company, government, charity, and so on. In the case of advertising, the communicator will usually pay for the cost of the communication.

For the most part, it is assumed that the corporate communicator will be concerned with increasing the sales of the particular product (or products) which is the subject of the communication, and generally this will be seen as the ultimate objective. But companies may see that the means of achieving this are the following: to create awareness of the product, or to generate favourable attitudes towards it, or even to effect a change in attitudes towards this product. One or more of these may be regarded as stages along the way to persuading consumers to purchase the product, and would fit in with some of the models of the communications process depicted below. Companies may also engage in corporate advertising where the advertising focuses on the company rather than on specific products. It may do this to develop awareness of the company in general among potential customers, suppliers, financial institutions and even government.

Audience

It is widely accepted that the communicator needs to specify the audience at which the communication is to be addressed. First, it needs to ensure that it understands the behavioural and other characteristics of the target audience (which should, of course, be the market segment(s) specified as part of the total strategy for the company and its products) so that it can obtain details on the media-listening, viewing and reading habits. It also needs to ensure that it presents its communication in a form that is likely to be comprehensible and stimulating to them.

In devising its communications, the communicator needs to have an understanding of how customers make purchasing decisions. Many models of the buying-decision process have been proposed, often with the view of trying to explain how advertising works. The more popular models assume that the process consists of several sequential stages; an example is the AIDA model: Awareness, Interest, Desire, and Action. Table 9.2 depicts two of the main models of advertising based on some key assumptions of the consumer decision process.

It can be seen, then, that in the case of advertising, at least, its major task is concerned with carrying the decision maker through the major stages: at first informing him of the product; then generating understanding and interest; and finally persuading him to purchase. The model depicted in Table 9.3 is a suggested model of the decision process for the adoption of new products; it suggests a role for all forms of communication, with media advertising being important in generating needs, and personal communications becoming relatively

Table 9.2   *Two Models of How Advertising Works*

AIDA[1]	Lavidge and Steiner[2]
(1) Awareness	(1) Awareness
(2) Interest	(2) Knowledge
(3) Desire	(3) Liking
(4) Action	(4) Preference
	(5) Conviction
	(6) Purchase

Sources: (1) Sandage and Fryburger (1963) p.240
(2) Lavidge and Steiner (1961) pp.59–62

Table 9.3   *Consumer Adoption Process*

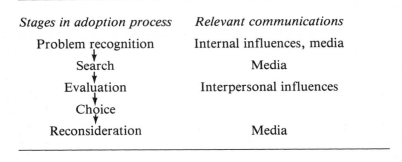

Stages in adoption process	Relevant communications
Problem recognition	Internal influences, media
Search	Media
Evaluation	Interpersonal influences
Choice	
Reconsideration	Media

Source: Engel, Blackwell and Kollat, 1978

more important as the consumer passes through to making the decision on a specific means of satisfying these needs.

It is possible that in some cases individuals have already identified their problem or 'need' before communications in general inform them of a possible means of solving the problem or satisfying their 'needs'; in such cases, the individual will have a predisposition to act, and communications provide a possible specific direction. In fact, the individual may actively seek out information. In other cases, communications may advise the individual of a possible product, that is, create awareness but at that time he has no need for it. He may neglect that information, 'store' it for future reference, or forget it. In yet other cases, the communications may have the effect of stimulating 'needs' or may consciously move the individual to identify a problem.

Selective Perception, Exposure and Retention

From what has been said above, it is apparent that communications, and in particular advertising, does not necessarily fall on either virginal or eagerly receptive minds. The individual may not be 'ready' to receive the information and he may mentally 'switch off'. Even if he consciously absorbs the information, he may, because of the barrage of other information to which he is exposed, forget it after some time. Alternatively, the individual may, for various reasons (because of, for example, strong attitudes or beliefs about certain subjects, or even previous product purchases), interpret the information in a way that agrees with his beliefs or attitudes or previous purchasing behaviour. For similar reasons, the information that is retained in the individual's memory may be very selective. It is argued, then, that there are very powerful filters that can intercede between the communicator and the audience, with the net result that the individual does not always notice the information even though he is exposed to it, or interpret it in the way desired by the communicator even when the information is absorbed. These phenomena have been termed selective exposure, retention, and perception.

The way in which selective exposure and selective perception may affect the communication of an innovation can be summarised as follows. The individual will only tend to be interested in those communication messages which accord with his interests, beliefs or attitudes. Anything which is in conflict with these will tend to be avoided; this is termed *selective exposure*. Where an individual is aware of messages on an innovation, but where the innovation is not relevant to his views or consistent with existing attitudes or beliefs, the communications will have little effect. This tendency is known as *selective perception*. 'Selective exposure and selective perception act as particularly tight shutters on the windows of our minds in the case of innovation messages, because such ideas are new' (Rogers and Shoemaker 1971). Where, for example, communications disagree with strongly-held beliefs the receiver may adopt one of several reactions:

(a) avoid the conflicting information;
(b) forget the information;
(c) distort the information;
(d) denigrate the source;
(e) argue that there are always exceptions.

For example, a strong believer in the harmful effects of smoking is unlikely to be persuaded by communications which attempt to persuade him otherwise. Similarly, a long-standing smoker will often dismiss communications that focus on the long-term adverse consequences of smoking.

It has also been noted that particularly *after* the purchase of a major item, such as an automobile, hi-fi equipment, or automatic washing machine, consumers are inclined to look at advertising relating to their purchase; it may be that they are seeking reassurance for their original decision (particularly as doubts might have crept in about whether or not the item was worth the high expenditure and possible sacrifice involved), or additional information about competing brands may have come to light. Such *dissonance* is often normal after major expenditure decisions, and the consumer will naturally often elect to adopt means of reducing it as much as possible. Advertising, pointing out the advantages of products, can then have an important role in this respect.

The Message

The message is more than what is said, or written; it also embraces scenes, symbols, and personalities involved in the communication. It could be very complex in the case of a television commercial. For example, the manufacturer of convenience-food products may devise a television commercial which defines a specific role for women as well as pointing out the advantages of his particular food product. He may be striving to reflect what he perceives are the often hidden motivations of housewives and to demonstrate how this product can satisfy these.

In devising the communications, the communicator will first have to select the major theme he wishes to communicate to the audience (for example, the economy of an automobile, the 'kindness to hands' of a washing-up liquid, the flexibility and technical superiority of a business micro-computer). The effectiveness of the communications will obviously be enhanced if such a theme offers, what has been termed, a *unique selling proposition*; this focuses on a single feature specific to the product, and relates this feature to the prospective buyer's requirements.

Secondly, the communications should attract attention and retain the interest of the audience. This applies to both impersonal and personal communications: just as a salesperson who has a mundane sales routine is likely to be ineffective, so an advertisement which has little to distinguish it from the mass of other advertisements is likely to remain unnoticed. Thirdly, it is important that the communication is understood by the audience; technical words, jargon, and rarely-used words are likely to pass over the heads of the majority of the audience. The clever use of puns may well impress—but only a minority. Finally, the communication should be memorable.

Advertising Decisions

For the remainder of this chapter, the focus shifts to advertising, not because it offers, necessarily, a unique set of problems (certainly, the problems of planning and managing the salesforce could be said to be more unique), but mainly because it tends to be the major item of expenditure in most companies' communications mixes. Moreover, it is something about which we all have experience.

Companies will generally commission advertising agencies to assist in the creation of the advertisement and to place the advertisement in the media. The agency may also undertake (or commission on behalf of the company) background market research, the pre-testing of the advertisement, and the evaluation of the 'impact' of the advertising.

With regard to advertising, a number of major decision areas can be identified:

(1) the definition of the objectives of the advertising;
(2) the amount to be spent on advertising;
(3) the formulation of the creative strategy to be employed;
(4) the selection of the media mix;
(5) the scheduling of the advertisements;
(6) the measurement of the campaign's effectiveness.

In considering these decisions, a number of points need to be made: first, each of these decisions can obviously involve a complex set of factors; here we will only be concerned with highlighting the nature of the decision and some of the major issues involved. Secondly, the decision will be considered with regard to a specific product, in isolation from other major decisions (such as those regarding other marketing-mix decisions or the competing allocation of the resources). It is obvious that in a multiproduct company decisions regarding the advertising of one product may be influenced by decisions regarding the advertising of other products.

The Objectives of the Advertising

It is, by now, apparent that advertising can have other immediate objectives than just to 'increase sales'. These might include:

(a) 'educating' the consumer, where the product involves an unfamiliar technology and perhaps different ways of doing things;
(b) generating awareness, in the case of new brands;
(c) counteracting a decline in sales;
(d) advising potential industrial customers of the company and the technical specifications of its products;
(e) increasing market share, sales, and so on.

A clear definition of the objectives of advertising at the outset is likely to assist in devising a more effective advertising campaign.

The Determination of the Advertising Budget

Ideally, of course, the expenditure on advertising will be such as to yield the optimum benefits. Unfortunately, the measurement of the effects of advertising is difficult enough in hindsight, let alone before the allocation. In practice, a number of approaches to the determination of the advertising budget have been adopted. These can be summarised in the following way:

(a) What the company can afford: the company allocates an amount to advertising based on some estimation of what it can afford. Major criticisms of this approach are that such a criterion does not take into account the other alternatives to expenditure on advertising, or the advertising elasticity of demand. If, as has been suggested, this approach is based on all that the company can afford then it '... reflects a blind faith in advertising which, though occasionally rewarding, is nevertheless a confession of ignorance' (Dean (1951) pp. 65–74).

(b) A percentage of sales: this approach is founded on incorrect logic for sales are more likely to be influenced by advertising – not the reverse!

(c) The level of last year's expenditure: there is often a tendency to build on past budgets, reducing or (more likely) increasing or maintaining last year's expenditure. Such an approach obviously minimises the amount of managerial effort involved, but it fails to take into account the fact that demand and cost factors may alter appreciably from year to year.

(d) Competitive parity: the advertising expenditure is decided on the basis of what competitors are spending. Presumably, the rationale for such an approach is that competitors collectively know the 'best' level of expenditure. Yet competitors may be spending too much; or they may have more visibility in the market (implying that our company needs to spend more); or their products may be inferior to our own; or we may be able to 'steal a march on them' by spending proportionately more.

(e) The goal and task method: this starts by asking, 'what is the profit or sales level that the company seeks to obtain for a product and what is the likely level of advertising required to achieve this?' Although it implies a consideration of the sales responsiveness of different levels of advertising, no means of doing this is advanced.

Confronted with the formidable problems of measuring the effects of advertising, it is not surprising that companies resort to methods of calculating advertising budgets which are easy to understand and operate. There is no true scientific method of deciding the advertising appropriation. Nevertheless, there has been some empirical work on branded grocery products which suggests that there is a strong correlation between the product's market share and its share of the total level of advertising on the product category of the brand (Nielsen Researcher 1979). At least for fast-moving consumer goods, then, companies might consider the market share they wish to obtain and decide on the advertising budget, given assumptions about what competitors are likely to spend. It is also argued that companies which neglect to spend on advertising can expect to lose market share, at least in the case of branded grocery products. But this says little about how one ensures that advertising expenditure is effectively allocated.

Overall, managers need to pay attention to the profit implications of advertising, and not fall into the trap of neglecting that it is advertising that affects sales and not the reverse. The question that should be asked is: 'given that we have a set objective for our product, what is the level of advertising that is most likely to produce that objective?'

The Decision on the Creative Strategy to be Employed

The company has then to decide on what it wishes to communicate to the audience (for example, the qualities of its product) and how this can be most effectively conveyed.

As has already been noted, the audience is faced with a barrage of advertising and other messages every day. The first thing to ensure is that the advertisement is noted; it needs, then, in some way to capture the interest of the audience and having done that, to retain it. This does not imply noisy or strident advertisements; indeed, these can irritate and may have the opposite effect to that desired. In gaining the interest of the audience, the advertisement may stimulate some wants and show how it can satisfy these. Often humour and tunes are skilfully employed.

In general, an advertisement should:

stimulate interest
relate to audience's wants
generate desirability
have credibility
have distinction
be memorable

Often, several advertisements will be devised, and these may be pre-tested under 'laboratory' conditions using selected groups by asking questions designed to find out preferences and memorability. Alternatively, the advertisements may undergo limited field tests by arranging for different versions of the advertisement to be run in different areas. Measures of 'effectiveness' employed might include: ability to remember the advertisement; any change in attitude towards the product; and changes in intention to buy.

Two Examples of Successful Campaigns

Concorde Qualcast   Traditionally, lawnmowers had blades which rotated around a horizontal axis and which collectively formed the shape of a cylinder. Hover rotary mowers, in which the blades rotate on a vertical axis, are a fairly recent innovation, and it is only since the introduction of electric-powered, hover rotary mowers, from the mid 1970s, that they have had a significant impact on the market.

In 1979, the major supplier of cylinder mowers, Qualcast, in line with the total market suffered a 12 per cent decline in volume sales compared with 1978. Qualcast was concerned because there was evidence of an increasing rejection of cylinder mowers in favour of hover rotary mowers, which were manufactured by the original innovator, Flymo. In fact, electric cylinder mowers had experienced a fall of 26 per cent in demand, whilst the sales of hover rotary machines had increased. Qualcast's major light, electric-powered cylinder mower, the Concorde, had only maintained its sales by increasing its share of the declining market for cylinder machines. The major objective for an advertising campaign was seen as reversing the decline in demand for cylinder mowers.

Extensive consumer research indicated that the hover mower was associated with ease of use, whilst consumers often disassociated the problems of the grass cuttings left after using hover mowers. However, after a trial with both mowers, over half of those originally favouring the Flymo machine switched their preference to the Concorde. This suggested that the campaign needed to provide a substitute for the experience of a trial of the machines.

In formulating the advertising campaign it was decided to:

    (a) focus on the undisputed advantages of Concorde—such as the fact that it cut closer and collected the grass cuttings—and to avoid using price as a competitive weapon;

    (b) educate the consumer on the advantages of cylinder mowers;

    (c) improve Qualcast's image with the retailers.

Television was employed as the main medium to demonstrate the superiority of Concorde compared with the hover mower, using the slogan: 'A lot less bovver than a hover'. The advertisements were restricted to those days leading up to the weekend. Press advertising was used to emphasise certain aspects of the television advertising.

The 1980 campaign was followed by an adapted campaign in 1981. Qualcast spent £650,000 in 1980, and £1,238,000 in 1981. Other competitors, in particular Flymo, also increased their advertising expenditure, with the result that total industry expenditure increased from £539,000 in 1979 to £2,037,000 in 1980. Concorde's sales increased by 53 per cent in 1980, and a further 9 per cent in 1981, despite a substantial increase in price in 1981 (its competitors either maintained or reduced their prices).

Campaign on Government Support for Small Businesses   In 1982 the Government financed an advertising campaign aimed at increasing awareness of its various schemes for assisting small businesses. The target audiences were the owners/managers of small businesses and their professional advisers (banks, accountants etc). The problem was to break through the known apathy and even resentment that many owners/managers in small firms, (who, by their very nature, tend to 'independent'), feel towards what they often regard as government intervention and even interference. For this reason, the advertising agency decided to base its campaign on the proposition 'Take advantage of the government!' as an extra resource to assist them to expand. Sixty-second TV commercials showed a manager climbing a cliff, each step up being made with some form of government assistance — grants, loans, advice etc. The television advertising was immediately followed by full-page advertisements in the National Press. These had such themes as 'Is the government helping your competitors steal a march on you?' and 'Take advantage of us while you can. Don't worry. We hope to get a bit back later.' Each advertisement contained a direct response coupon or a Freephone telephone number so that people could easily obtain more information. It was planned to run the campaign from mid-March to late June 1983 at a cost of £1.1 million, and 60,000 replies were anticipated. In fact, the campaign was stopped after just seven weeks, when 140,000 people had responded.

The Selection of the Media Mix

The advertiser is faced with several choices of media: how does he, for example, choose between television, cinema, posters, newspapers, magazines, and radio? There are possibly several factors that will influence the decision:

(1) *The product to be advertised* — for example, some products may require action to demonstrate their usefulness fully. Thus the advantages of a new instant cake mix may be more clearly demonstrated by using, say, a film that demonstrates clearly

how it is easily prepared and the nature of the results. Other products, for example, cannot be advertised on television, (e.g. cigarettes), so their manufacturers are compelled to use other media forms.

(2) *Relative costs of the different media* — advertisers may be influenced by the cost per thousand (of total readers, or viewers, or listeners) of different media. However, in considering unit costs the advertiser needs to take into account both the impact and the selectivity of different media.

(3) *The impact of the media* — this is the extent to which the message is effectively taken in. There is no point in advertising on television if viewers start doing other jobs during the commerical breaks, or if for other reasons they lose concentration until the main programme returns.

(4) *The selectivity of the media* — this refers to the extent to which the media cover the target audiences at which the product is aimed, to the exclusion of those for whom the product is not intended. For this reason, industrial goods manufacturers will tend not to advertise on the ITV channel.

(5) *The target audience's media habits* — this will be a very relevant factor; for example, marketers of expensive fashion products may find that very few of their target audience view commercial television. They may more effectively advertise in fashion magazines.

(6) *Reach of the media* — this is the proportion of the target market which will have at least one opportunity to see the advertisement.

The Scheduling of the Advertisement

The advertiser is now faced with the decision of how frequently to show this advertisement. The advertiser will not, of course, have unlimited funds to devote to advertising. He will have to choose between several options: at one extreme he can concentrate all his advertising into a short time period, frequently repeating advertisements for the product; at the other extreme, he may spread his advertising throughout the whole year. Furthermore, he can use several different advertisements for his product in any given time period. The schedule that is decided upon will depend on the product and its stage in the life cycle. Obviously, a product in the early stages of its life cycle will tend to be advertised frequently in a short time period, in order to create awareness and knowledge. A well-established but successful brand may be advertised in a less concentrated fashion throughout the year, to ensure that the brand name remains firmly at the forefront of the minds of the consumers. Seasonal products will, of course, be advertised near and during their peak sales periods (although advertisers can often create unseasonal demand). Products with extremely short life cycles will tend to be advertised intensively.

In considering whether or not to opt for the intensive repetition of advertising the product, there was a school of thought that argued that consumers could be conditioned to buy products provided that the advertisement was shown sufficiently repetitively, just as Pavlov conditioned his dogs to salivate or Skinner conditioned pigeons to perform some act. This 'behavioural' perspective has been criticised by a school of thought that argues that man is a thinking, rational being, and not a mere automaton. It is probably true, though, that constant repetition of an advertisement can have an impact by constantly reminding the consumer of the product, even though the total message may not be taken in completely on a conscious level. On the other hand, too much repetition may create annoyance and damage the sales prospects of the product.

The Effectiveness of the Advertising

It has already been argued that in order to allocate his budget efficiently the advertiser should, in theory, have an indication of the effects of the advertising. The difficulties of performing such an analysis before the investment are obvious. But should it not be possible to measure the effectiveness during and after the advertising campaign? In this way, first, the advertising and the expenditure on it can be altered as the campaign proceeds, and secondly, the advertiser, by examining the possible impact after the advertising has finished, may be able to use the knowledge gained in making decisions about future advertising appropriations.

Unfortunately, a number of obstacles stand in the way of these desirable objectives. First, without carefully controlled experimentation, one cannot conclude that there is any direct link between advertising and the sales/profits secured; there are too many other variables involved. Even if all the extraneous variables are controlled (which would be costly and probably impossible), there might still be some external influence, unthought of by the experimenters, that may affect the results.

Secondly, the full impact of advertising may be spread over time; some people who are acquainted with the advertising in the early stages of the campaign may react quickly; others may, for various reasons, delay a response. A further group of people may not learn of the advertising for some time after it starts. In the same way, the full effects of reducing or stopping advertising may not become apparent for some time; there may well be a 'carry over' effect. Thus, when considering the impact of advertising at any given time, it is possible to have a distorted picture of its general effectiveness. It may well be that there is a steep rise in sales stemming from the advertising, but this may be because the advertising has *brought forward* sales that, in its absence, would have been made some time in the future; the total sales may be unaffected. Of course, this may well be what the advertiser desired: he will have the advantages of obtaining, perhaps, a higher market share (and earlier); in addition, there will be a resulting higher sales revenue in the early stages of the product's life cycle — and in inflationary periods that can only be financially beneficial.

Thirdly, the effectiveness of the advertising, although undoubtedly affected by the total amount expended, will also be dependent on the creativeness of the campaign. Spending large amounts of money on advertising will not inevitably lead to substantial sales if the campaign itself leads to resentment, fails to stimulate interest, or lacks credibility. Similarly, of course, advertising will be ineffective, in the medium term, if the product is unreliable, of poor quality, or has undesirable side effects. Because of the specificity of most of the marketing variables (i.e. the creativity of a specific campaign for a specific product), it becomes difficult to make conclusions about the effectiveness of an additional pound spent on advertising in general — this is often neglected.

It is not surprising that variables other than sales are often employed as indicators of advertising effectiveness. Manufacturers may,for instance, measure the level of awareness of the brand, or of the advertising; or they may measure shifts in attitudes in order to ascertain whether or not consumers have become more favourably disposed to the product as a result of the advertising. Both are easy to determine, and although awareness of the brand and a favourable attitude towards it can be assumed to be prerequisites of purchase, neither can be regarded as a true indicator of advertising effectiveness. Awareness of a brand does not naturally lead to its purchase; and because somebody has a favourable attitude towards a product, this is no indicator of whether or not they will purchase it. It is only sales which are a true indicator of effectiveness:

> Advertising copy is good when it achieves the effect intended, when it brings in trade. There is no other standard of value outside of the ranks of the theorists. (J. Walter Thompson 1906)

The Control of Advertising

Advertisers are faced now with a number of strict controls applied by the Independent Broadcasting Authority (in the case of advertisements shown on commercial television or played on commercial radio) and the Advertising Standards Authority. Both have developed codes of practice which are strictly applied; this can limit severely what can be advertised and the way it can be advertised.

The IBA, for instance, not only controls the amount and distribution of advertising by the various programme contractors, but it also has the duty and the power (as embodied in the IBA Act of 1973):

> ... to exclude any advertisement that could reasonably be said to be misleading, and to decide as to the classes and descriptions of advertisements and methods of advertising that should be excluded from television and radio.

Its codes of practice are drawn up in consultation with its own advisory committees and it has its own staff who work with the contractors to ensure that advertisements satisfy this code. This code, for example, bans the advertising of cigarettes and cigarette products, as well as advertisements by money lenders, matrimonial agencies, undertakers, bookmakers and private-investigation agencies. It defines a set of rules regarding advertising and children. In general, these are aimed so that:

> No product or service may be advertised and no method of advertising may be used, in association with a programme intended for children or which large numbers of children are likely to see or hear, which might result in harm to them physically, mentally or morally, and no method of advertising may be employed which takes advantage of the natural credulity and sense of loyalty of children. (IBA 1979)

Summary

Four major elements in the communications process have been identified: the communicator, which is generally the company or organisation with a product or service it wishes to market; the message, i.e. the information that is to be conveyed; the communication channels, through which the message is conveyed; and the audience, which is generally the consumer or customer. Communication channels can be divided into personal and impersonal channels. Personal channels embrace personal selling, public relations and interpersonal communication; the latter, it is believed, being particularly effective since, overall, the element of partisanship is absent. Impersonal channels include media advertising and sales promotion (such as competition, point-of-sales displays, coupons, exhibitions). Media advertising is by far the most powerful and pervasive; however, the difficulty lies in scientifically evaluating its effectiveness. It has been shown that there are too many influences affecting the sales outcome for such an evaluation to be performed with any degree of confidence.

Further Reading

Dean, J. (1951) 'How much to spend on advertising', *Harvard Business Review*, January–February.
Engel, J. F., Blackwell, R. D. and Kollat, D. T. (1978)*Consumer Behaviour*, Dryden Press.
IBA (1979) *The IBA Code of Advertising Standards and Practice*.
Lavidge, R. C. and Steiner, G. A. (1961) 'A model for predictive measurement of advertising effectiveness',*Journal of Marketing* Vol. 25, No. 4.
Meers, J. and Marie – Stella, R. (1982) '*The Qualcast Concorde – an advertising case history*', Wight Collins Rutherford Scott, June.
Nielsen Researcher (1979) No. 3, A.C. Nielsen Company Ltd.
Rogers, E. M. and Shoemaker, F. F. (1971) *Communications of Innovations*, The Free Press.
Sandage, C. H. and Fryburger, V. (1963) *Advertising Theory and Practice,* Irwin.

Review Questions

(1) List as many means as you can of *promotion* for
    (a) an industrial product
    (b) a consumer product

(2) Why do you think 'word of mouth' is considered important in the marketing of consumer products?

(3) How do you think advertising 'works'?

(4) What do you consider is the main role of advertising in the marketing of industrial products?

(5) Select an advertisement. Do you think it satisfies the major criteria for an 'effective' advertisement?

(6) Outline the major objectives of advertising an innovative consumer product.

Loading up: distribution is concerned with ensuring the availability of the product

10

Distribution

England is a nation of shopkeepers
(Napoleon Bonaparte)

Distribution is the fourth variable in the 'marketing mix'. The main aim of the firm's distribution policy is to ensure that the product is where the customer wants it, *when* he wants it. Distribution has, sadly, been a rather neglected area of study, yet it can account for a high proportion of final product cost. As in other spheres, there have been significant innovations in distribution and the wise and active company needs to ensure that it keeps abreast of these developments and alert to the potential that future possible changes offer.

Distribution occurs through *channels* which usually consist of one or more intermediaries (such as agents, wholesalers and retailers) which will perform a range of functions − such as assisting in the finance of the purchase, carrying stocks, providing technical advice and service. The functions carried out by whichever actor in the channel can vary.

In this chapter, we will be considering why efficient distribution is important, the functions of the intermediaries in distribution, and some of the issues involved in the design and choice of a distribution channel. Some developments in retailing are discussed in the final part of the chapter.

Cost-Effective Distribution

In essence, a manufacturer must be concerned with ensuring that its products are where the customer expects to buy them, when he wants them, at the lowest cost to the manufacturer. The provision of a high level of customer service (for example, availability in a high proportion of possible sales outlets, or speedy delivery to the customer −

involving perhaps greater stocks, and more vehicles) may increase sales. However, the costs involved in despatching small quantities of the products to retailers who are widely dispersed geographically, together with costs of ensuring quick delivery from the manufacturer's plant or distribution depots, may exceed any marginal benefit involved. The manufacturer has to balance the marginal costs of increasing customer service against the marginal gains it obtains.

The Costs of Distribution

Distribution costs are a major proportion of total product costs, and for some companies they can account for up to 16 per cent of sales value. Table 10.1 provides data for 55 companies which tended to be the largest and probably the more efficient in their industries. These costs have increased in recent years as a result of rising fuel prices and legislation which, for instance, now restricts the number of hours drivers can work in a day. A company prepared to manage its distribution efficiently would obviously secure a significant competitive advantage.

Sales Responsiveness to Customer Sales

Figure 10.1 indicates how sales can vary with availability of the product. This generalised customer service level—sales response curve is relatively inelastic at the extreme: after a certain level is achieved,

Table 10.1 *Distribution Cost Elements as a Percentage of Sales Value*

	Food, drink and tobacco	*Chemical and allied products*	*Distributive trades*	*All groups*
Transport	4.30	3.37	1.85	3.54
Warehousing and storage	2.52	2.70	3.26	3.01
Administration and other costs	3.90	2.22	1.50	2.88
Inventory	1.65	2.49	2.30	2.57
Totals	12.37	10.78	8.91	12.00

Source: Centre for Physical Distribution Management, March 1982. Quoted in 'Distribution management' (1972) *Financial Times Survey*, November 1st.

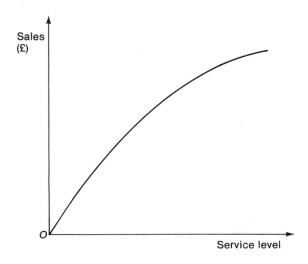

Figure 10.1 *Sales – Service Level Response Curve*

further increases in service level will only generate small increases in sales. Saturation has, in effect, been achieved. For many products (for example, fast-moving consumer goods) the curve will be highly elastic: for example, housewives not finding a particular brand of grocery product in the supermarket, may well substitute the brand that is available. In the case of consumer durables, some consumers may be prepared to 'shop around' on the basis of price, but even here there will be a limit to the extent to which they are prepared to seek out a product. In industrial markets, the level of availability of a product may well be a critical factor; shortages of components and materials can, for example, close down production processes, at great cost to the producer. Recently, manufacturers have attempted to lower their costs by holding lower stocks; this places greater onus on the suppliers' ability to provide at short notice.

Costs and Service Level

The manufacturer has then to relate the sales level at specific 'customer service' levels to the costs of providing those sales. Figure 10.2 gives a possible generalised relationship.

This indicates that costs may rise steeply at greater levels of customer service. Having a large transport fleet which mobilises stocks, and many depots to give widespread, quick delivery, can obviously be expensive. Management has obviously to consider whether the increased sales resulting from high service levels are worth

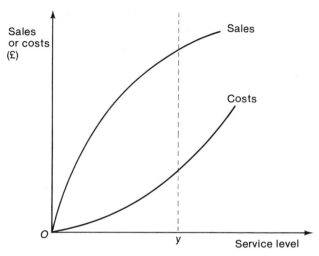

Figure 10.2   *Optimum Service Level*

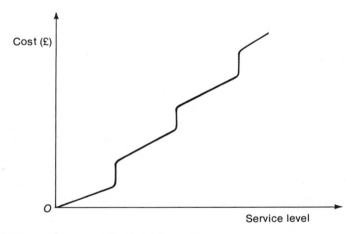

Figure 10.3   *'Stepped' Cost Increase*

the marginal costs involved. The relationship between costs and sales depicted in Figure 10.2 suggests that the *optimum* service level is *y*, where the margin between sales and costs is at a maximum. Higher service levels may, however, be considered if maximum profit is replaced by maximum market share as an objective. In practice, the cost function may not be smooth as indicated, since this assumes that all costs are variable. There will, in fact, often be a considerable fixed-cost element (see Figure 10.3). Fixed costs (e.g. a new warehouse) may be incurred as service levels are increased and these will give rise to step-like increases in the total costs.

In general, it will be difficult to forecast the sales associated with particular service levels; a blend of experience and judgement will usually be employed in evaluating the sales associated with specific service levels.

Distribution Channels

The distribution channel is the means which a manufacturer employs to get its product to its customers. The channel may be simple, such as when the manufacturer sells directly to its customers (through direct mail, or the selling of custom-made industrial propducts), or it can be considerably more complex, involving the use of retailers, wholesalers, agents, manufacturer's depots, etc. The nature and complexity of the distribution channels employed depends on the product (its perishability, bulk, frequency of purchase, whether or not it is an industrial or consumer product), the customers for the product, and their geographical dispersion.

> The marketing of aeroplanes involves close liaison between manufacturer and airline: negotiations are performed directly between the two parties and delivery is direct.

> The distribution of milk in the UK is a complex operation. A national agency (the Milk Marketing Board) is responsible for collecting the millions of gallons of milk produced per day from thousands of farmers. This has to be stored and pasteurised and speedily delivered to distributors. The perishability of the product and the fact that the main market is usually some considerable distance from production makes the operation complex.

Direct Marketing versus the Use of Intermediaries

Why does a manufacturer use intermediaries? It may simply be that it is following the industry in using the traditional methods of distribution. Apart from the fact that there is always a potential competitive advantage to be gained from innovating, the manufacturer may gain specific advantages from the use of intermediaries; in other cases direct marketing may prove desirable or necessary.

Direct marketing, as the name implies, involves selling direct to the end user without the use of intermediaries. Inevitably, it is employed by firms selling particular categories of industrial products, such as expensive capital goods (e.g. chemical plant, electricity-generating plant, ships) or bulk raw materials. The sales involve high-value dispatches, relatively infrequent purchases, and special pre-sale negotiations on price and technical specifications. Of course, direct marketing is also employed by manufacturers of consumer goods; for example, Avon Cosmetics employs saleswomen to sell to housewives; whilst many companies may sell direct from their factories through mail order, the medium being used to solicit orders.

Where independent middlemen are used, a distinction can be drawn between those who merely act on behalf of the manufacturer (for example, selling and distributing the product) without purchasing the product (that is, they do not take title), and those who take title and undertake all further responsibility for distribution and perhaps other aspects of marketing. Intermediaries who do not take title include brokers and manufacturers' sales agents. A broker will attempt to find possible purchasers of the product and bring the manufacturer and these potential customers together. A manufacturers' sales agent fulfils a similar function, although he will often employ his own sales staff, carry stock on consignment and provide ancillary services such as financing, installation, and so on. Both brokers and agents receive a commission on any sales.

Among intermediaries which do take title are the large wholesalers, and retailers. These both buy and sell. Wholesalers will collect a range of goods from various manufacturers and usually sell them to other intermediaries (for example, small retailers). Wholesalers are used when, for example, the amount sold per customer is relatively small, or when customers are widely scattered geographically. Generally, wholesalers sell to other companies or to retailers. Retailers, which carry out a similar function, mostly sell to the final customer. Large retailers will generally take delivery direct from manufacturers. Figure 10.4 gives some possible general channel structures.

The Use of Intermediaries

It is obvious that the greater the number of intermediaries, the less the degree of control the manufacturer may have over distribution and the other aspects of marketing, such as the extent of 'sales push' pricing, and promotion of the product. In addition, the longer the chain between manufacturers and customers, the less likely there will be full, fast and accurate feedback on demand and customers' reactions. One of the major problems in using intermediaries is that where they are responsible for a range of merchandise from several manufacturers, the amount of effort devoted to a particular line may be considerably diluted; it will inevitably be affected by the profitability and ease of selling of the particular products.

Given such apparent disadvantages, why are intermediaries employed at all? First, the use of intermediaries can minimise the

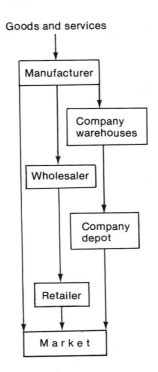

Figure 10.4 *Possible Channel Structures*

number of transactions involved for the manufacturer. For example, in the case of 4 manufacturers selling directly to 10 retailers, there will be 40 contact lines between the two groups. If one wholesaler is used by both manufacturers and retailers, only 14 contact lines will be necessary. Delegation of distribution means that the manufacturer can devote attention to manufacturing and other elements of marketing.

Secondly, the use of intermediaries can offer considerable economies. Manufacturers may have to bear heavy unit-distribution costs because sales volume is low; this could make them uncompetitive. Intermediaries, however, assemble the lines of many producers into an assortment of potential interest to buyers so that the costs are more evenly spread. Thirdly, the manufacturer may have more profitable investment outlets for its capital. Money that would be necessary for establishing a channel network could then be more fruitfully employed. Fourthly, intermediaries may be able to offer a wide service which the manufacturer would not otherwise be able to afford. This may include market research, service back up, etc. Moreover, the use of intermediaries may mean that the manufacturer has a more

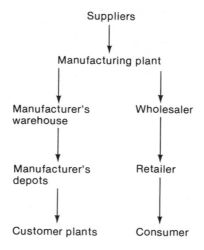

Figure 10.5   *Physical Goods Transfers*

favourable cash flow and this can be particularly advantageous for the small manufacturer.

It must be added that the manufacturer does not inevitably have to relinquish control for the marketing of his product where intermediaries are used: he can, for example, employ his own promotional salesmen to work within, say, the retail outlet; or he can use merchandisers to ensure that the product is correctly and adequately displayed within the store. There is, in fact, great scope for innovation in intermediary—manufacturer relationships.

Channel Transfers

There are transfers between the different elements of the distribution chain. Five types of transfers can be identified.

(1) Physical goods transfers: the movement of goods, ranging from the initial raw materials, through components and sub-assemblies, to the final product. Possible physical goods transfers are depicted in Figure 10.5.

(2) Ownership transfer: as the product passes through the chain, the ownership of the physical goods can change. Manufacturers will purchase supplies, and will sell from their factories to, for example, other manufacturers or retailers. They may, however, deliver to intermediaries who then sell the products without themselves taking ownership. These intermediaries may collect

payment, deduct their commission for effecting the sale, and transfer the remainder to the manufacturer.

(3) Payment transfers: the movement of money for the payment of goods and services. Generally, payments will be made between adjacent elements in the chain (e.g. between manufacturer and wholesaler). There can, however, be considerable delays in payment. A manufacturer may transfer goods to its depots, from where they are transferred to a wholesaler's warehouse. The wholesaler may be given credit of, for example, thirty days from delivery to him by the manufacturer. In this case, the manufacturer may wait in total a considerable period before receiving payment.

(4) Information transfer: the flow of information between different stages in the chain. Usually, there is a two-way flow of information between adjacent stages, but the manufacturer may, for example, wish to supplement the information it receives from its own customers with additional information obtained by, for example, market research.

(5) Influence transfers: the way in which different elements in the chain attempt to promote themselves and thereby influence other elements in the chain. For example, component and raw-material suppliers can be expected to promote themselves to their purchasers using advertising and other forms of promotion. In some cases, suppliers of materials may consider it advantageous to advertise to the final consumer. For example, ICI advertised Tereylene and Du Pont Teflon.

Channel Design Decisions

In deciding on the form of distribution channel to adopt, the company should take into account several factors:

(a) the customer;
(b) the nature of the product;
(c) cost and service level;
(d) degree of control.

In some cases, the customer may expect to purchase a product from a particular type of outlet, although the evidence suggests that customers are quite prepared to accept innovation in distribution where the advantages of change are significant. Perhaps more important to the decision are existing geographical concentrations of customers and the way these are likely to change in the future. Some customers may, of course, insist on a certain form of distribution. For example, ASDA superstores require many of their suppliers to deliver directly to their stores. Other grocery retailers accept delivery at their own warehouses.

Some products, by their very nature, require speedy delivery, and this suggests a shorter distribution chain. This would appear to be the case for perishable products. However, advances in the technology of preservation are such as to be able to prolong the life of many perishable products. Frozen foods, of course, demand their own form of distribution channel: refrigerated warehouses, depots, and delivery vehicles. Many bulk items of capital equipment will be delivered directly from manufacturer to customer.

The degree of service necessary against the cost of providing this service needs to be measured. For example, if the customer expects speedy service, the manufacturer may have to have extra depots near the user, and perhaps a high level of stocks; both can be costly. The manufacturer also has to balance cost against control. Ideally, the company would like to have the maximum degree of control over the marketing of its products, but it has to weigh this up against the costs involved.

A final point that should be considered is the possibility of future innovations in distribution. Companies do not want to become committed to an expensive system of distribution that is likely to be superceded in the near future.

Retailing

In general, it is argued that retail distribution development is governed by the wheel of retailing. This suggests that new retailing forms start as low-status, low-margin, low-price operations and thereby act as powerful competitors to existing retailing forms. Over time, the competition between the 'new' and 'traditional' retailers intensifies; gradually, the 'new' upgrade their facilities, resulting in higher costs and consequently prices. The 'new' in turn become susceptible to new, low-cost retailing operations.

There is nothing inevitable about this cycle. It assumes that price is a primary factor, which may be true for certain segments of the markets in a recession. It is, however, not unrealistic to assume that some innovative retailing developments may be aimed specifically at customer segments concerned more with other aspects — quality and service, for example.

Changing Pattern of Retailing

There is no doubt that there have been some dramatic changes in the nature of retailing in the last 25 years; self-service is now a prominent

Table 10.2 *Retail Trade: Single and Multiple Outlets 1976 and 1979*

	1976			1979		
	Outlets (number)	People employed (000s)	Turnover (£ million)	Outlets (number)	People employed (000s)	Turnover (£ million)
Total retail trade	390,512	2,503	34,171	351,187	2,429	52,065
Single-outlet retailers	231,187	1,000	11,657	207,530	888	16,498
Small multiple retailers	78,674	392	5,004	69,465	358	7,364
Large multiple	80,651	1,111	17,509	74,192	1,182	28,203

Source: Business Statistics Office

feature, whereas it was virtually nonexistent in the 1950s; large supermarkets selling a wide variety of grocery and hardware products have
advanced at the expense of the small independent shop; chain stores
such as Littlewoods, British Home Stores, Marks and Spencer and
W.H. Smith have gained an increasing proportion of sales, whilst
department stores have declined in importance. Large hypermarkets
on the outskirts of cities are now familiar.

Table 10.2 indicates the increasing concentration of power of multiple retailers: for example, large multiple retailers accounted for 51 per
cent of total retail turnover in 1976; this had increased to 54 per cent in
1979. Single-outlet retailers, on the other hand, had 34 per cent of
total retail turnover in 1976 and 32 per cent in 1979.

Grocery Retailing

In the case of grocery retailing the number of outlets has declined
markedly in the last twenty years, whilst multiple chains (those with
ten or more retail shops under common ownership) have increased
their share of the total market. For example, taking the decade 1971 to
1981, the number of grocery outlets fell by 46.2% (a net reduction of
48,694), and as can be seen from Table 10.3, the number continued to
fall in 1982. In fact, the multiples themselves are now reducing the
number of their own outlets, and concentrating in general on developing bigger stores. This is reflected in the turnover per outlet of the

Table 10.3 *Number and Percentage Share of Grocery Outlets in Great
Britain, 1971–1981, 1982*

	1971[a]	1981[b]	1982[b]
Cooperatives	7,745 (7.4)	4,467 (7.9)	4,096 (7.3)
Multiples	10,973 (10.4)	4,789 (8.5)	4,599 (8.2)
Independents	86,565 (82.2)	47,334 (83.6)	47,334 (84.5)
All grocers	105,283 (100)	56,590 (100)	56,029 (100)

Sources: (a) Business Statistics Office 1971
(b) Nielsen Researcher (1981) No. 3
Note: percentage shares are shown in brackets

multiples which increased fourfold between 1971 and 1981 (whilst turnover per independent outlet remained almost constant during this period). In 1981, the multiples had 62.7 per cent of total grocery sales, compared with 44.3 per cent in 1971 and 20 per cent in 1950. This increase had been obtained at the expense of the independents (23.6 per cent in 1981, 42.5 per cent in 1971 and 57 per cent in 1950) and the cooperatives (13.7 per cent, 13.2 per cent and 23 per cent respectively).

These major multiples exert significant buying power which has become centralised in the headquarters of the major chains. Independents have reacted: under the leadership of some wholesalers they have formed themselves into groups such as SPAR. The independent retailers agree to purchase their supplies from the SPAR wholesaler which consequently has greater purchasing power. SPAR undertake promotion and commission own-label products.

The net result of the rationalisation of the grocery retailing business is that today there are of the order of 275 large buying units which account for 82 per cent of total grocery sales (Table 10.4). Obviously, these large buying units wield considerable power: they can exact special terms and promotions from the manufacturer, and in turn have put manufacturers' profit margins under considerable pressure.

Table 10.4 *Concentration of Buying Points in Grocery Retailing: (1975 and 1980)*

Number of	1975	1980
Cooperative societies	227	186
Major multiple head officers	6	6
Other multiple head officers	56	43
Major symbol wholesalers[a]	55	40
Total	344	275
Proportion of grocers' business controlled or influenced (%)	75	82

Note: (a) Symbol wholesalers include groups such as 'Spar' and 'Bob'. Groups of independents purchase their supplies from wholesalers which negotiate with manufacturers, undertake promotion and commission own-label products.

The Future

Technological developments are likely to have a marked impact on the nature of retailing over the next few years. These may include:

(a) Cashless transactions, which will become more frequent, particularly as it is likely that there will be increasing acceptance of 'electronic funds transfer' enabling funds to be transferred directly from a customer's bank account to that of the retailer at the time the purchase is being made.

(b) Home shopping, whereby information about a retailer's or manufacturer's products will be displayed on a television screen and, by means of a computer terminal, customers will be able to communicate with the advertiser and order the goods directly.

(c) The increasing use of laser light beams to scan information (including price) which is stored in the form of a code on products. This information can be conveyed back to a computer which enables, for example, stricter stock control and automatic reordering.

Summary

Distribution is an important component of the marketing mix; it is concerned with ensuring the availability of the product. In deciding on the extent of the availability, the company has to consider the cost and weigh this against the extra profits flowing from the provision of the higher customer service level. There are a number of approaches, or channel structures, that a company can employ, including distribution direct to the customer or via a number of intermediaries. The choice of the channel design will depend on a number of influences. Retailers are an important element in the distribution channel, and there have been significant changes in the structure of retailing in the last three decades with, in particular, a significant trend towards concentration in the ownership of outlets.

Further Reading

'Distribution management' (1982) *Financial Times Survey*, November 1st.
Grattuna, J. (1978) 'Channels of distribution,' *European Journal of Marketing*, Vol. 12, No. 7.

Review Questions

(1) What should be the main distribution objectives of:
    (a) a manufacturer of household cleaning products (e.g. washing-up liquids, lavatory cleaners, etc.)
    (b) a manufacturer of industrial chemicals

(2) Describe the major tasks of a wholesaler.

(3) Outline a possible distribution system for a major national retailer, giving your reasons.

(4) Discuss the major influences that you consider will affect distribution over the next five to ten years.

Since its launch abroad in 1981, over 150,000 Metros have been sold overseas.

11
International Marketing

*To found a great empire for the sole
purpose of raising up a people of
customers . . .*

(Adam Smith, The Wealth of Nations)

*Every Englishman has to survive one insult
the moment he lands on foreign soil: he is
called an 'alien'.*

(J.E. Morpurgo, American Excursion*)*

Britain has long been involved in international trade: its Empire was developed from a striving to extend markets for British goods and from a search for novel products that would find a profitable welcome at home. During the early history of industrialisation, Britain dominated the world market for manufactured goods, but as other countries have developed their industries and entered international markets Britain's share of world trade has steadily declined to around 9 per cent today. Nevertheless, Britain is still a formidable international trader; for example, it exports a higher proportion of its gross national product than other major countries. It does, of course, need to export services and manufactured and semi-manufactured products in order to pay for the huge quantities of raw materials and agricultural produce that it is compelled to import. Perhaps unfortunately, Britain also has a great propensity to import foreign manufactured products, which have consequently gained a significant share of the British market. Although, for most of the post-war period, there has been concern about Britain's export performance − a reflection of this concern being the introduction of the Queen's Award for Export Performance in the late 1960s, as a 'reward' for 'good' exporters − Britain has been successful, and outstandingly so, in certain areas, in particular insurance, banking, and specialised manufactures.

235

This chapter aims to provide an appreciation of international marketing. First, we will examine how it differs from domestic marketing and see that it is not necessarily synonymous with exporting. Secondly, we will consider why companies engage in international marketing; generally, the saturation of domestic markets, the imperatives of technology, and the opportunities for making an additional profit overseas are all possible explanations. Thirdly, the various means of 'entering' overseas markets are discussed, ranging from exporting to the establishment of a fully-fledged, multinational organisation. Finally, alternative international marketing strategies are outlined.

The Nature of International Marketing

Why is a distinction generally drawn between international and domestic marketing? At least five possible areas of difference exist:

(1) long distance involved;
(2) environmental factors;
(3) culture;
(4) government regulations;
(5) control and co-ordination.

Where goods are exported, they may often have to be transported over longer distances; there may in turn be problems of control of the marketing operation as a result of the remoteness of corporate headquarters from the markets in which it is selling its goods. Yet, for instance, the distance over which a Swedish manufacturer, based in Stockholm and selling his goods in the North of Sweden, may have to transport his goods may be far greater than that involved for a London-based manufacturer selling in Paris.

Environmental factors often vary significantly between countries; there may, for example, be climatic differences that demand alterations in packaging and product formulations, whilst variations in discretionary income will affect the demand for goods and services. Distribution systems, too, may differ.

Cultural dissimilarities may mean that what is acceptable in one country may be considered with disbelief and even contempt in another. A complete disregard for such overseas cultural influences can affect the success of the company's products; for example, on a mundane level, the bright red colour of tomato soup, so favoured by the English, would be considered repulsive by the Germans. Similarly, linguistic differences affect the translatability of slogans; too literal a translation can affect their meaning in the foreign country. For example, Colgate-Palmolive introduced Cue toothpaste in French-speaking countries; unfortunately 'cue' was a pornographic word in French.

A country may have its own regulations relating to foreign trade and corporate investment. There may be regulations governing prescribed ingredients, on the proportion of domestically-manufactured components that have to be in the final product, on the maximum share of foreign ownership of manufacturing operations, and on the proportion of indigenous nationals the company has to employ. In addition, governments often offer sizeable incentives to attract foreign investment; whilst the use of tariff barriers and quota restrictions can affect the transnational shipment of goods.

Although there may be differences along many of these dimensions within countries, the domestic-based manufacturer will often, through experience, be acquainted with them. In the case of international marketing, many of these differences can combine together to create an environment that is unknown and therefore uncertain to the prospective marketer. Against this background, though, it should be remembered that the principles of marketing are the same: successful marketing will be founded on an understanding of market structure, of the influences affecting purchasing behaviour, and of the 'wants' of the market. The identification of market segments and the development of marketing mixes aimed at meeting the wants of these segments remain essential marketing practice.

However, international marketing may require that special attention is given to the control and co-ordination of overseas operations. In particular, the company will be anxious to ensure that company targets are being met and that marketing policies are being pursued in its international markets. Good liaison between corporate headquarters and local operations is essential, demanding effective internal reporting, and frequent visits between the two.

The Reasons for Marketing Overseas

In general, companies may be *pushed* into overseas marketing because of excess capacity, unfavourable conditions in the domestic market, etc; or they may be *pulled* by the prospect of making additional profitable sales. Among the more specific reasons for entering international markets are:

(a) a 'mature' domestic market;
(b) 'technological imperatives';
(c) a need to reduce dependence on the domestic market;
(d) to reap opportunities in overseas markets.

The Mature Domestic Market

For many products, the UK market may be in its mature or even decline stage with a deceleration or cessation of growth in demand. Competition from both domestic and foreign manufacturers is likely to be intense and prices will be low. Under such conditions, companies may seek sales in foreign markets.

Technological Imperatives

The nature of the product technology may be such that large sales are required in order to cover the high costs of research and development and/or the technology may have large production economies of scale. The domestic market may not be sufficient to enable manufacturers to recover costs and operate at an optimum level of production. They may thus be compelled to seek sales overseas. Examples of such industries are aviation and main-frame computers.

Reduce Dependence on Domestic Market

The company may seek to go overseas in order to spread its risks, and not have 'all its eggs in one basket'. In this way, a downturn in sales in one market may be more than offset by sales in another.

Seek Opportunities

Companies may, of course, be attracted by the opportunities raised by overseas markets. For example, many construction firms have identified Middle Eastern markets, with their large oil revenues and their tremendous need for development, as targets; they saw possibilities for hospitals, schools, roads, and so on.

There are, of course, other explanations; companies may as a result of historical accident − for example, by taking over a company that had a subsidiary trading overseas − find themselves carrying out exporting; or they may be emulating companies that are successfully trading overseas.

Market Selection

The selection of the target foreign markets should, of course, rest on a detailed analysis of the potential for the product, the likely realisable demand, and the company's market share. Although, for developed countries, market data are generally easily accessible, the information on 'third-world' countries is often sparse and inaccurate. In such cases, nothing can surpass having good personal contact with people 'on the spot'. The company will need to have an understanding of the climate, institutions, distribution channels and culture of the country − it may, for example, need to revise its existing marketing strategy in the light of any differences. In its selection decision, it may consider whether or not it intends to use its target markets as a springboard for entering other markets and it is important, in general, that the decision is made with regard to its intended long-term strategy. A further factor that needs to be taken into account is the risk arising from political instability. This becomes particularly important where investment in the country is being considered. In general, it has been suggested that successful exporters, for instance, tend to focus on specific markets in which they develop efficient marketing operations, rather than dissipating their marketing effort by indiscriminantly exporting to several markets.

Entering Foreign Markets

Companies have a number of alternative means of entering overseas markets, from exporting from a domestic manufacturing base to investment in a manufacturing and marketing operation situated in the foreign country. It is generally assumed that a company will develop an overseas 'presence' gradually, starting with the export of small quantities of its products − perhaps in response to a direct request from a foreign customer − that are generally marketed through an agent or other representative in that market. Exporting in this way is a relatively risk-free means of testing the demand for the market

Table 11.1 *Alternative Means of Entering Overseas Markets*

I	Exporting: (a) indirect exporting (b) direct exporting
II	Licensing
III	Contract manufacture
IV	Direct investment: (a) joint ventures (b) wholly-owned manufacturing/assembly plant
V	Multinational marketing

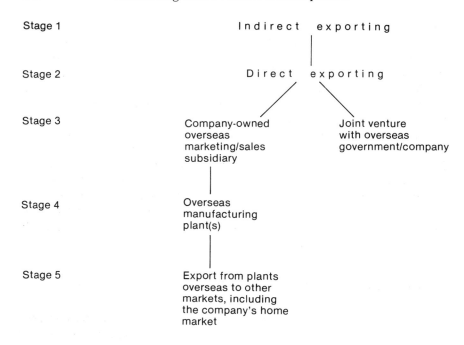

Figure 11.1   *Possible Stages in the Development of a Company's International Marketing Capability*

since it involves little investment by the company. Assuming that there is a favourable demand, the company may decide to invest in its own sales and marketing operation there, in order to develop the market further. Eventually, the demand may reach a level such as to justify the investment in production facilities specifically for that market. Of course, there may be factors that encourage direct investment earlier: for example, tariff barriers may be so high as to make manufacturing overseas necessary if the product is to be sold at an economic price. In this case, though, the company may be initially tempted to license or contract domestic companies to manufacture the product. Figure 11.1 suggests a possible sequence of stages for the development of a company's overseas marketing capability. The alternative means of entering foreign markets are presented in Table 11.1, and discussed separately below.

Indirect Exporting

Indirect exporting involves selling the product to a domestically-based

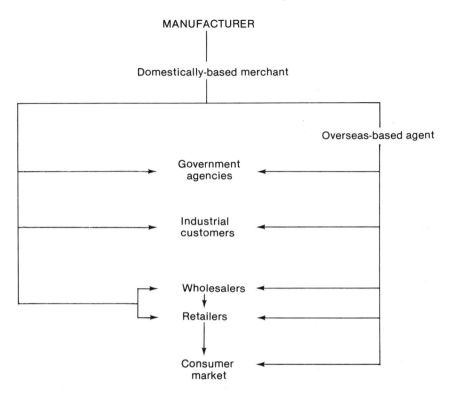

MANUFACTURER

Domestically-based merchant

Overseas-based agent

Government
agencies

Industrial
customers

Wholesalers

Retailers

Consumer
market

Figure 11.2 *Indirect Exporting Channels*

middleman (e.g. merchant) who then assumes responsibility for selling it overseas. It may sell directly, or through an overseas-based agent (see Figure 11.2). Often, the manufacturer is merely getting rid of surplus production and may not be fully committed to exporting. The manufacturer obviously loses control over all aspects of the marketing of the product, and will only sell the amount determined by the merchant.

As in all cases where middlemen are employed, the product may not be given the support necessary to achieve optimum sales: middlemen, after all, will generally be selling a range of products from different manufacturers, and they will be mainly concerned with those that offer the highest profits, often for the minimum of effort. This approach can suffer from another disadvantage too: for as in all cases of exporting, the product may be subject to tariffs, or quota restrictions.

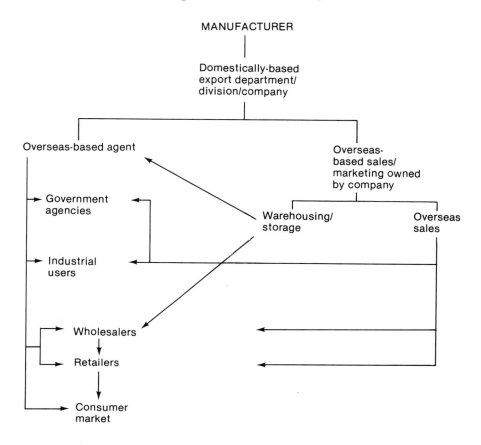

Figure 11.3 *Direct Exporting Channels*

Direct Exporting

In this case, the company exports its products to middlemen actually based in the overseas markets, or to its own overseas-based sales branch, although even in this case distribution may be delegated to agents or a subsidiary (see Figure 11.3). The company may even have a domestically-based export department concerned with central administration and export sales planning. Obviously, the product will generally have to surmount tariff and other barriers, as well as incurring transport costs. Where commitment is fullest, the company may well have invested in marketing and sales-planning facilities stationed in the foreign market, and thus will have a high degree of control over the marketing of the exported product.

Sykes Pickavant (SP) is a small, privately-owned company that markets a comprehensive range of approximately 500 product items aimed at satisfying most of the requirements for automotive and general engineering maintenance and repair work. Most of its manufacturing is subcontracted, the firm's major activities focusing on design of the product range, packaging and promotion. Approximately 42 per cent of its turnover is from exports, and main overseas markets are Australasia, South Africa, the Middle East, and Europe. Because of its size, it has been virtually compelled to employ agents and distributors in its overseas markets. In selecting its intermediaries, SP searches for aggressive, growth-conscious agents, preferably those with a complementary product range that could, of course, have a favourable impact on the sales of SP products. SP believes that it is essential that the intermediary does not have a large number of other product ranges which might reduce the marketing effort applied to its own product range. SP personnel visit their intermediaries frequently, and supply them with promotional literature.

Licensing

A low-risk means of overcoming the tariff, transport costs and similar disadvantages of exporting is to license the technology of manufacture to a company in the foreign market for a fee, some part of which is usually related to the quantity sold. This implies that the technology is not widely known and available. The licensing company may, for example, have some highly specialised process which is patented. Such an approach requires little expenditure, but it involves lower profitability, some (if not a major) loss of control over marketing of the product, and the possibility that the company is developing a competitor in its own technology.

Pilkington of St. Helens is a major manufacturer of glass. In 1959, it introduced its radical float glass process by which high quality flat glass is manufactured by floating the glass, as it emerges from the oven, onto molten tin in an inert atmosphere of nitrogen — it replaced the traditional and expensive process which involved drawing the molten glass from the oven through rollers. Not only did the drawing operation produce distorted glass, but the rollers marred the glass surface, and in order to produce high quality flat glass of the type needed for shop windows and mirrors, the surface had to be ground and polished by large machines that absorbed large amounts of energy. Vast quantities of waste glass were produced. Pilkington lacked the large finance necessary to invest in capacity sufficient to satisfy the world demand for float glass; yet, on the other hand, it wanted to prevent competitors undermining its position by developing rival processes. Pilkington therefore licensed selected glass manufacturers throughout the world. Provisions were built into agreements – for example, the licensing firm had to inform Pilkington of any technological developments it made to the process. The strategy has been highly profitable: in 1980, Pilkington's revenue from licensing was £35.03 million.

Franchising is a form of licensing whereby companies offer a business idea and relevant management advice, usually for a fixed fee and a percentage of sales. Usually, a franchise operates in the following way: the franchise owner (franchisor) enters into an agreement with the purchaser of the franchise, who pays a fixed amount for the franchise. The purchaser will usually have to invest in hardware, fittings, etc. according to the specifications of the franchisor. In addition, he will have to pay a percentage of his sales to the franchisor, and he may also have to purchase some or all of his supplies from the franchisor. The franchisor may periodically send inspectors to ensure its standards (of, for example, service, cleanliness) are being satisfied.

Contract Manufacture

A company may contract local manufacturers to produce the product, whilst retaining responsibility for its marketing. Apart from being comparatively low risk, it also permits speedy, large-scale entry into the market. Obviously, such a strategy results in lower profits.

Direct Investment

Although some of the options listed above will have involved a degree of direct investment, this will have been on a relatively minor scale. The alternative of 'direct investment' can involve investment in service operations, assembly operations, full manufacturing and other facilities. Companies involved in raw-materials mining overseas will, naturally, have had to invest in exploration and extraction; but other companies will generally wait until the market has developed sufficiently to justify the risks involved. There are, of course, a number of advantages from direct investment: first, it is a means of circumventing tariff barriers and obtaining entry to other countries in free-trade areas. Secondly, the company will be able to use indigenous raw materials and labour, which may be cheaper. Thirdly, the company will obviously save on transport costs, a particularly important consideration where the product is bulky. Finally, the company will have greater control over the manufacture and/or marketing of the product.

Direct investment may merely consist of expenditure on a salesforce and on facilities to supply marketing support (e.g. marketing research, promotion, etc). Alternatively, a company may invest in an assembly plant which uses components made in the company's home country, or it may invest in a full production plant to supply the overseas market in which it is situated, and perhaps neighbouring countries as well.

When considering direct investment overseas, a company may attempt to lower its risks by entering into a joint venture, that is, a partnership with some other company or with the host government. Joint ventures involve a sharing of management responsibilities, but they need not necessarily involve equity sharing. They are particularly appropriate where the company wishes to enter the market quickly on a large scale, and where the company finds it difficult to research the local market. On the other hand, it may take an equity stake in a firm already operating in that market; in this way, it easily gains access to experience and knowledge of the market it is striving to enter.

Such moves to invest may not necessarily be a direct response to a build-up in demand for the company's products; it may have been prompted by, say, restrictions imposed by foreign governments on imports, or in response to direct investments in that country by competitors which have thereby secured some economic advantage.

Multinational Marketing

Multinational companies will have investments in several countries, and a high proportion of their total sales will be generated in overseas markets (from, say, 20 per cent to perhaps as high as 50 per cent of total company turnover). They will not feel particularly obligated to their country of origin: investment decisions will be taken from a global perspective, with manufacturing and assembly plants being located so as to obtain an optimum return for the company as a whole.

> Ford markets its range of automobiles in many countries and has manufacturing and assembly plants in several countries. In Europe, for instance, Ford's Bridgend plant supplies engines for cars produced not only in the UK but also in Spain and Germany. UK automobile manufacture concentrates on Escorts with some Fiestas being produced as well; the Escorts are exported to other markets, including Spain and Germany. However, Ford's product range in the UK is completed by importing Fiestas from Spain, and Capris and Granadas from Germany. Each uses components that may be manufactured in other countries.

Other international marketers may operate on a more decentralised basis, with almost independent companies responsible for each overseas market.

The International Marketing Mix

Given that the company is marketing its product range in several countries, should it have several marketing mixes, each specifically tailored for a particular market? Alternatively, should it have a completely standardised approach involving the same marketing mix for each country? Or should it adopt some intermediate approach? At least four alternatives have been suggested:

(1) localised strategy;
(2) sub-global strategy;
(3) adaptation strategy;
(4) completely standardised strategy.

The localised strategy involves the development of individual marketing mixes for each market. Such a strategy may be formulated in two stages: in the first stage, the company defines a broad marketing strategy for the whole organisation worldwide, involving a definition of turnover, market share, profit and product range. Within this framework, in the second stage, marketing programmes may be devised for each area of the world, often by local staff. Such autonomy in devising the marketing mix generally implies that there would be little, if any, commonality between the marketing mixes for different countries. This approach to international marketing demands considerable corporate resources: more corporate personnel would be required to make decisions on the pricing, distribution, advertising and products appropriate for each market. Moreover, 'it would be logical to suppose that the task of organising a collection of totally diverse marketing programmes would also confront the international marketing staff at corporate headquarters with complex organisational, co-ordination and communication problems' (Hovell and Walters (1972) pp.69–79). The proliferation of individual marketing mixes can be said to maximise the costs of international marketing; but the approach can be justified for selected markets, given certain conditions – for example, where end-user requirements are fundamentally different from those in other markets, or where patriotism is high and there is an intense dislike of alien cultural influences.

The sub-global strategy entails grouping markets together according to common features, such as the state of economic development, common culture, and so on. Marketing mixes are developed for each of these subgroups. The adaptation strategy involves taking a strategy that was developed for the domestic market, or developed for regions (as suggested in the sub-global strategy), and modifying it in some way to take account of the individual preferences and features of the specific overseas market.

The completely standardised strategy, at its most extreme, employs the strategy developed for the domestic market for every country in which the company markets its products. An alternative to this direct extension approach is a strategy based on the search for common denominators that link markets, using these as a basis for the standardised approach. This, of course, may lead to a marketing mix that is too bland and does not appeal to anyone in particular. There are obvious advantages to the standardised approach: it generates substantial savings in design and production costs since it permits large-scale, continuous output with the consequent economies of scale. There are, in addition, savings in management time.

An alternative perspective on the approach to developing a policy for international marketing mix is presented in Table 11.2. The important influences are assumed to be the need for which the product is bought and the conditions under which it is used, whilst the changeable marketing variables are the product and the communications, both or either of which can be adjusted.

In general, it is assumed that there is a greater homogenisation of culture through the impact of mass communications and travel, leading to a tendency towards an environment facilitating greater standardisation. Nevertheless, there are barriers that cannot be

Table 11.2 *International Marketing Mix Policy*

Market conditions		Adjustment response
Reason product purchased	*Way product used*	*Change required*
Same	Same	None
Different	Same	Change advertising, promotion, etc.
Same	Different	Change Product
Different	Different	Change both product and advertising, promotion, etc.

ignored, some of which have already been mentioned. Amongst those that can be considered more important are:

(a) the differences in regulations regarding advertising, permitted ingredients, performance, safety;
(b) climatic conditions;
(c) the nature of the communications channels;
(d) language differences that impede the translation of slogans;
(e) differences in culture, even between countries close in terms of geography and industrial development.

In general, it is most likely that companies will select the adaptation strategy: companies are unlikely to devise completely distinct marketing programmes for every market in which they sell their products; yet it is also extremely unlikely that companies will be able to effectively market their products using an approach involving the complete replication of their marketing programmes from one country to another.

Summary

International marketing involves marketing between countries that may have significant differences in, among other things, culture, environment, and regulations with which the marketer must become familiar. A company may be pushed or pulled into marketing overseas, and may enter foreign markets using several alternatives, from indirect exporting to direct investment in manufacturing plant. When considering developing its marketing strategy, a company may decide on a standardised marketing approach, or it may adapt a general marketing strategy in some way, to suit the particular features of a foreign market.

Further Reading

Engel, J.F., Blackwell, R.D. and Kollat, D.T. (1978) *Consumer Behaviour*, Holt-Saunders.
Hovell, P.J. and Walters, P.G.P. (1972) 'International marketing presentations: some options', *European Journal of Marketing*, Vol. 6, No. 2.
Littler, D.A. and Hovell, P.J. (1977) *Export Marketing*, BOTB.

Review Questions

(1) Why is international marketing important?

(2) Contrast the means of entering foreign markets open to a large manufacturer with those suitable for a small manufacturer.

(3) What factors are likely to differentiate a 'successful' exporter from an 'unsuccessful' exporter?

(4) Select a multinational marketing company. Find out its country of origin, its main markets, and the location of its principal manufacturing/assembly plants.

(5) What special problems do you consider international marketing raises? How can these be minimised?

Glossary

Advertising: impersonal communications, promoting goods and services, that appear in the mass media (newspapers, television, etc.) and are paid for.

Agent: a distribution intermediary which negotiates purchase or sales, but does not own the goods in which it deals. It is usually paid by a commission or fee.

Apportionable Costs: a product's variable and fixed costs that are incurred as a direct result of producing and marketing that product, as opposed to overhead (or nonapportionable) costs which cannot be said to be totally directly incurred by particular products.

Brand: the name and other features of the product that are employed by manufacturers to differentiate their product from competitors' products.

Broker: a distribution intermediary (agent) who does not have physical control of the goods in which he deals and who represents either buyer or seller in negotiating purchases or sales.

Consumer Goods: those products and services which are bought for final consumption without undergoing further processing or transactions.

Contribution: the surplus remaining after the apportionable costs of a product have been subtracted from the product's revenue. The contribution covers nonapportionable costs and profits.

Corporate Plan: a written document which specifies corporate objectives, the assumptions about the future environment in which the company will be operating, and the means (i.e. the products and ways of marketing these) the company will adopt in order to meet these objectives.

Corporate Strategy: the 'overall direction' for the company. It

251

252   *Marketing and Product Development*

embraces decisions on the businesses the company is in, its objectives over a specified time period, the products it aims to sell, and the markets where it plans to sell them.

Customer Service Level: a term used to denote the availability of the product in terms of number of outlets in which it is stocked, and the time period between ordering by the stockist and delivery by the manufacturer.

Demand Philosophy: the identification of customer requirements and the formulation of products and services to meet those requirements.

Derived Demand: the demand for a product that is generated as a result of the demand for other goods and services of which the product is an ingredient. The demand for industrial goods is derived.

Discretionary Income: the income remaining after paying income tax and national insurance, and after satisfying 'basic necessities'.

Durable Goods: often high-unit-value goods which are purchased infrequently, and which tend to have a life span of years.

Fast-Moving Consumer Goods: usually low-value products that are purchased frequently (often with little pre-purchase consideration), and that have a short life span, often weeks or months as opposed to years.

Industrial Goods: goods or services which are bought by other firms (or organisations) and which are then used in the production of other goods or services.

Invention: a new idea or technique that is often not developed further, and is not offered for sale or adopted.

Market Demand: the amount of product that could be purchased per time period for a specified environment and a specified marketing effort.

Market Potential: the maximum sales of a product that could be achieved per time period for a specified environment and a specified marketing effort.

Market Segmentation: the division of the total market into smaller groups or segments which have similar wants.

Market Share: a company's share of the total sales of a particular product class.

Marketing: involves the implementation of the 'demand philosophy', that is, the selling of goods and services that meet target-customer requirements. But this is undertaken whilst, at the same time, satisfying organisational objectives.

Marketing Mix: a collection of marketing variables including price, sales promotion, advertising, personal selling, distribution, and product features such as packaging, branding, design, and so on.

Marketing Plan: a written document that contains details of the objectives, past performance, future marketing policies, and the marketing budget for each product.

Marketing Research: those activities concerned with gathering and analysing information to enable marketers to make decisions on target markets, products, pricing, promotion, distribution, and so on.

Penetration Pricing: low-pricing strategy aimed at securing high volume and market share.

Primary Data: information which is collected from the original source(s).

Product Differentiation: means of distinguishing one manufacturer's products from those of its competitors.

Product Innovation: a new product that is offered for sale (as distinct from an invention, which is not).

Product Life Cycle: an ideal representation of the sales of a 'product' (class, type or brand) over time. There are four stages: introduction; growth; maturity; and decline.

Product Line: a group of closely related products aimed at satisfying the same need.

Product Mix: the range of products the company offers for sale. The mix may consist of a number of product lines.

Product Planning: the process of monitoring the performance of the company's product mix, planning modifications to, and (where appropriate) deletions of existing products, and the development of new products.

Sales Promotions: non-personal communications that do not appear in the media. They embrace point-of-sale promotions, short-term offers (money off, coupons, gifts).

Sample Frame: the list of units (individuals, firms) and contact addresses of all the members of a target population to be interviewed in a market research survey.

Secondary Data: information obtained from sources other than the original source. They are usually published data (for example, government and trade statistics).

Skimming Pricing: setting a high price initially, with a gradual reduction in price over time.

Speciality Goods: usually high-unit-value items that are infrequently purchased and are not stocked widely. Certain customers will actively seek these for their special features.

Test Marketing: the testing of the marketing strategy (product, price, advertising, etc.) of a product, in a small area representative of the target market.

Index